THE BLINDING TORCH

Modern British

Fiction and

the Discourse

of Civilization

THE

BLINDING

TORCH

Brian W. Shaffer

The University of Massachusetts Press   *Amherst*

Copyright © 1993 by
The University of Massachusetts Press
All rights reserved
Published in the United States of America
LC 92-36623   ISBN 0-87023-831-0
Designed by Mary Mendell
Set in Janson Text by Keystone Typesetting, Inc.
Printed and bound by Thomson-Shore, Inc.
Library of Congress Cataloging-in-Publication Data
Shaffer, Brian W., 1960–
    The blinding torch : modern British fiction and the discourse of
civilization / by Brian W. Shaffer.
        p.   cm.
    Includes bibliographical references (p.   ) and index.
    ISBN 0-87023-831-0 (alk. paper)
    1. English fiction — 20th century — History and criticism.
2. Modernism (Literature) — Great Britain.   3. Literature and
history — Great Britain — History — 20th century.   4. Literature and
society — Great Britain — History — 20th century.   5. Civilization,
Modern, in literature.   I. Title.
    PR888.M63S3   1993
    823'.912091 — dc 20   92–36623 CIP
British Library Cataloguing in Publication data are available.

TO RACHEL AND HANNAH

Civilization has done its little best by our sensibilities for whose growth it is responsible. It has managed to remove the sights and sounds of battlefields away from our doorsteps. But it cannot be expected to achieve the feat always and under every variety of circumstance. Some day it must fail, and we shall have then a wealth of apallingly unpleasant sensations brought home to us with painful intimacy. — Joseph Conrad, *"Autocracy and War" (1905)*

Since from August 1914 to November 1918 Great Britain and her Allies were fighting for civilization it cannot, I suppose, be impertinent to enquire what precisely civilization may be. "Liberty" and "Justice" have always been reckoned expensive words, but that "Civilization" could cost as much as I forget how many millions a day came as a surprise to many thoughtful taxpayers. The story of this word's rise to the highest place amongst British war aims is so curious that . . . I should be tempted to tell it. — Clive Bell, CIVILIZATION *(1928)*

Civilization is not *always with us. It is not self-sustaining. Civilization is artificial and requires an artist or an artisan. If you want the fruits of civilization but do not care to cultivate and nuture it—you are fooling yourself. In a trice, you can be left without civilization. A moment of carelessness, and when you next look around you will find everything vanished into thin air! Just as if the tapestries you had hung to cover nature had suddenly been removed, and the primitive jungle had reappeared.* —José Ortega y Gasset, THE REVOLT OF THE MASSES *(1929)*

Civilisation is . . . brought
Under a rule, under the semblance of peace
By manifold illusion. . . .
—W. B. Yeats, *"Meru" (1935)*

Contents

Acknowledgments   xi

1. Introduction: Literature and the Discourse of Civilization   1
The Blinding Torch: Civilization in Literature   2
Coming to Terms with "Civilization"   14
The Law of Civilization: Progress Enthroned or Disease Unleashed?   18
The Will to Civilization: Nation-State or State of Mind?   25
The Rhetoric of Civilization: Preservation or Propaganda?   28
Modernist Fiction and Cultural Discourse   35

**2. "Rebarbarizing Civilization": Conrad's African Fiction
and Spencerian Sociology**   45
Conrad and Spencer at the Fin de Siècle   46
Spencer's "Militant/Industrial" Distinction in *Heart of Darkness*   47
Spencer's "Rebarbarized" Civilization in *Heart of Darkness*   53
Beyond Spencer: The Suggestion of a Military-Industrial Complex in
Heart of Darkness   55
From Progress to Parody: Spencer's "Law" and Conrad's "Outpost"   57

3. The London Fog: Civilization as Rhetoric and Game in Conrad 63

The Rhetoric of Civilization in *Heart of Darkness*   65
The Game of Civilization in *The Secret Agent*   70

4. Civilization in Post–Great War Bloomsbury: Woolf's "Twenties" Novels and Bell's *Civilization* and *On British Freedom*   79

Woolf and Bell in the 1920s   80
Censorship as a Threat to Civilization in *Mrs. Dalloway* and *On British Freedom*   84
Women and Civilization in *To the Lighthouse* and *Civilization*   89
Class in *Mrs. Dalloway* and *Civilization*   93
Bell Ringers: Images of the Man in Woolf's Novels   97

5. Discontent and Its Civilization: Rereading Joyce's "Paralyzed" Dubliner   101

The Illusion of a Future: Gerty MacDowell and Little Chandler   103
The Myth of Enlightenment: The Experience of Leopold Bloom   112

6. The Sense of an Ending: Spenglerian *Decline* and the Mexican Novels of Lawrence and Lowry   121

The Literary Fate of *The Decline* between the Wars   121
The Spenglerian Shape of Civilization in *The Plumed Serpent* and *Under the Volcano*   125
Spengler Dialogized: The Resistance to Civilization and the Aesthetics of Decline in *The Plumed Serpent* and *Under the Volcano*   133

7. The Subject of Civilization: Narcissism as Disease in Lowry's Early Fiction   143

Narcissus under the Volcano   143
Self as Civilization: Psychoanalytic Matrices of Narcissism in *Under the Volcano*   146
Narcissistic Civilization in *Under the Volcano* and *Ultramarine*   152

Notes   163

Works Cited   189

Index   205

Acknowledgments

Writing a book may be a lonely experience at times, but it is a single-handed one never. My debts are as great as they are numerous. I am deeply appreciative of a number of scholars who read one or more chapters of this study over the past years and provided helpful suggestions for improvement: Keith Carabine, Keith Cushman, Mary Ellis Gibson, Gerald Graff, Hunt Hawkins, Eloise Knapp Hay, Katherine Hayles, Rudolf Kuenzli, Brooks Landon, Henry Levinson, Paul Lorenz, Margot Norris, Sherman Paul, and Daniel Schwarz. Without their guidance this study could not have progressed beyond its earliest stages. In particular, I wish to thank Professor Cheryl Herr of the University of Iowa. Not only did she see this project through from inception to completion, but she also offered sound advice and warm encouragement at each point. I would also like to thank Professors Gerald Bruns and R. B. Kershner, who read the manuscript for the University of Massachusetts Press. They provided me with more helpful ideas in their ten pages of criticism than most would be lucky to receive in a hundred. This project could not have been undertaken without the feedback of a number of friends at Washington University, the University of Iowa, and elsewhere, who provided models of intellectual seriousness and personal integrity: Jo Ellyn Clarey, Joseph Greenberg, Robert Franciosi, Bruce Krajewski, and Eric Parens. Nor would it have been undertaken without the inspiration I received from a number of scholars with whom I worked in earlier years, whose passion for literature and ideas helped fuel my own: William H. Gass, Egon Schwarz, Craig Werner, and Burton Wheeler. I would also like to thank a number of institutions and endowments for supporting me (and, by extension, the present study) at various stages: the University of Iowa, for a teaching-research fellowship (1984–88); the University of North Carolina at Greensboro, for a postdoctoral fellowship in its Center for Critical Inquiry in the Liberal Arts (1989–90); the National Endowment for the Humanities, for including me in its 1990 Summer Seminar for College Teachers at Cornell University, "Critical Perspectives on the High Modernist Tradition"; and Rhodes College, for a summer 1991 Faculty Development Endowment Grant and for funds to pay for indexing and proofreading. I am also appreciative of so many colleagues at Rhodes College, within and outside the English department, for being supportive coworkers and valued friends. Clark Dougan, senior editor of the University of Massachusetts Press, provided indispensable help in seeing this study (and its author) through the often intimidating publication process. I cannot overestimate the gratitude I feel toward him. Finally, I wish to thank family members: my sister for keeping me young, my mother for boundless love and encouragement, and my father for reading and editing every single page of this book. My only regret is that he did not live to see it emerge in print. Whatever merits this study may possess I owe to him and to the other individuals named above. My greatest debt of all, however, I owe to my wife, Rachel, and daughter, Hannah. Rachel was generous both with substantive critical advice and with her patience. Hannah has been a constant source of joy and inspiration. Above all, Rachel and Hannah endured the writing of this book, and so it is dedicated, with love, to them.

I am grateful to the presses, journals, and editors who generously gave permission to use material that has previously appeared. Chapter 2 appeared in slightly altered form in *PMLA*, and is reprinted by permission of the copyright owner, the Modern Language Association of America. A portion of Chapter 5 appeared in *Joyce in Context*, edited by Vincent Cheng and Timothy Martin, and is reprinted by permission of Cambridge University Press. A portion of Chapter 4 appeared in *Journal of Modern Literature*, and is reprinted by permission of Morton Levitt and Temple University. A very small portion of Chapters 1 and 3 first appeared in *Conradiana*, and is reprinted by permission of David Leon Higdon and Texas Tech University Press.

THE BLINDING TORCH

1

Introduction: Literature and the Discourse of Civilization

*The question . . . which now arises is whether literature —
in relation to history or society — reflects something special
that neither philosophies of history nor sociological theories
are able to capture. . . .*

*As the product of a particular culture, literature draws
life from tensions with and impacts on the cultural context
from which it has emerged. It intervenes in its real environment and establishes its uniqueness not least by high-
lighting its otherness in relation to the situations that have
conditioned it. In this manner it adumbrates new regions
that it inscribes into the already charted topography of
culture. — Iser, "Toward a Literary Anthropology"*

*Art will live on only as long as it has the power to resist
society. . . . What it contributes to society is not some directly
communicable content but something more mediate, i.e.
resistance. Resistance reproduces social development in aesthetic terms without directly imitating it. Radical modernism preserves the immanence of art by letting society into*

its precincts but only in dimmed form, as though it were a dream. If it refused to do so, it would dig its own grave. . . .

A critical concept of society is inherent in all authentic art works and incompatible with how society conceives of itself. —*Adorno,* AESTHETIC THEORY

To be hopeful in an artistic sense it is not necessary to think that the world is good. It is enough to believe that there is no impossibility of its being made so. — *Conrad, "Books"*

✳ The Blinding Torch: Civilization in Literature

In the midst of Conrad's *Heart of Darkness* Marlow encounters a painting by Kurtz described as "a small sketch in oils . . . representing a woman, draped and blindfolded carrying a lighted torch. The background was somber — almost black. The movement of the woman was stately, and the effect of the torchlight on the face was sinister" (27–28). Many readers of Conrad's novella have grasped the ironic significance of this image: instead of enlightening the world this "stately," civilized woman is in fact "blinded" despite the torchlight, oblivious to what actually transpires in the jungle.[1] Within the context of Conrad's entire tale this painting — this image of a torch that fails to enlighten Europe as to its true actions and motivations — suggests a "sinister" yet alluring side to the "stately," civilized West. This is made clear early in the story when the torch is symbolically related to civilization. There, the narrator evokes images of past English explorers, of "Hunters for gold or pursuers of fame [who] all had gone out on that stream, bearing the sword, and often the torch, messengers of the might within the land, bearers of a spark from the sacred fire" (8). The trope of blindness is then explicitly linked with the activities of civilization when Marlow remarks that "robbery," "violence," and "murder" — "men going at it blind" — are "very proper for those who tackle a darkness" (10).

This moment in *Heart of Darkness* (1899), a text poised on the eve of the twentieth century, is for me emblematic of British modernism's representation of civilization. Indeed, I believe that the fictions of Conrad, D. H. Lawrence, James Joyce, Virginia Woolf, and Malcolm Lowry refigure this "blinding torch" — this trope of civilization's duplicity — in various shapes and guises, and to various ends. More specifically, I will argue that such works as *The Secret Agent, The Plumed Serpent, Dubliners, Ulysses, Mrs. Dalloway, To the Lighthouse,* and *Under the Volcano* also portray civilization in the paradoxical image of blindness and insight, obfuscation and enlightenment. Put yet another way, each of these fictions depicts civilization to be shedding light while obscuring vision, captivating the eye while deadening perception. In these works civilization is represented as duplicitous and paradoxical in that the price of allegiance demanded to civilization appears to necessitate thought and actions which diverge sharply from its purported tenets. In this sense these fictions exist in a double bind; they function as both civilization's crowning achievements and its severest critics. In *Art as Experience* (1934), John Dewey addresses this double bind. "Esthetic experience," he writes, "is a manifestation, a record and celebration of the life of a civilization, a means of promoting its development, *and is also the ultimate judgement upon the quality of a civilization*" (326; my emphasis). "As long as art is the beauty parlor of civilization," Dewey further argues, "neither art nor civilization is secure" (344). I hope to demonstrate that modernist British fiction, even for its fetishization of form and language, is anything but "the beauty parlor of civilization" and instead is deeply engaged with the "quality," and particularly the discourse, of its civilization.

This literature–civilization connection I belabor might seem to beg the question as to the importance of the concept of "civilization" between 1897 (Conrad's "Outpost of Progress") and 1947 (Lowry's *Under the Volcano*), the period I consider here. Indeed, in a recent reassessment of Oswald Spengler's *Decline of the West*, Northrop Frye concludes that "the question of whether Western Civilization will survive, decline or break down is out of date, for the world is trying to outgrow the conception of 'a' civilization, and reach a different kind of perspective" (13). Similarly, Lucy McDiarmid notes of the career of "civilization" in the present century "a greater self-consciousness and even embarrassment about the word with each generation; its value becomes dubious, and it seems less and less to be a standard of behavior or sophistication" (10). And in the preface to a recent collection of essays devoted to exploring "anthropological perspective[s] on the discontents of civilization," the editors write that "civilization, once considered the pinnacle in art, science, and virtue, seems now . . . almost cancerous, a self-induced malignancy that threatens to blacken the human spirit" (Richardson and Webb ix). The idea of civilization, however, as these comments on its decline suggest, was not always viewed with such suspicion. Indeed, this concept, if we may judge from the plethora of popular, academic, theoretical, and "propaganda" books devoted to it, was intensely debated in British life and letters from the fin de siècle to the conclusion of the Second World War.[2] As John Katz observed in *The Will to Civilization* (1938), "civilization, from being a theme for academic study, has become a public interest and an international problem" (1).

It is against the background of what might be called this "discourse of civilization" — the various voices that constitute the debate over the nature and function of civilization — that I explore the fiction of Conrad, Lawrence, Joyce, Woolf, and Lowry. I will argue that these fictions represent and critique this discourse and hence that they enter the debate over civilization in ways that shed light on the fictions themselves and on the self-images of the age. An investigation of the literary appropriation and subversion of this discourse will also provide insights into then current "theories" (or systematic conceptualizations) of civilization and into the various ways civilization itself was represented — whether as ideal or reality, process or achievement. This study will explore not only a series of literary modernist representations and critiques of civilization, then, but the complex and ambiguous ways these fictions sought to redeem the civilization of their production and initial consumption. David Daiches noted long ago that the twentieth-century renaissance in the British novel was "the product of what might be called a crisis in civilization" (6), yet this insight has remained largely unexplored and untested.

To date, only one major study, Lucy McDiarmid's *Saving Civilization: Yeats, Eliot, and Auden between the Wars*, has examined literary modernism's interest in the idea of civilization. While McDiarmid's study succeeds brilliantly as an exploration of the differing ways in which three poets sought to "save civilization" *entre deux guerres*,[3] the present study explores the fiction, essays, and letters of five novelists who collectively, if variously, interpreted British (and Western) civilization between 1897 and 1947.[4] I will not claim that this period's obsession with civilization is unique, only that it takes distinctive directions during this age of imperialism and two world wars. Nor will I claim that the literature of these five novelists is unique for investigating the idea of civilization. There can be no question of choosing the "right" authors, for my argument is that the civilization question is pervasive in the British literature of this period. Indeed, this study could also have included works by Ford Madox Ford, E. M. Forster, Wyndham Lewis, and Evelyn Waugh, to name only the most obvious examples. Given that I could not possibly have presented all of the literary texts that in some way wrestle with the civilization question, I selected those which, with as little repetition as possible, show the complexity and range of literary responses to the culture's "civilization crisis."

Whereas my thesis that the works of Conrad, Lawrence, Joyce, Woolf, and Lowry represent and critique the idea of civilization is not likely to be contested, it is nevertheless the case that this fiction's radical experimentation with form and innovative representation of consciousness have led to readings disproportionately oriented toward formal and linguistic, intra-psychic and subjective, considerations, rather than toward broadly so-ciocultural ones. For this reason I believe it is useful to demonstrate the great degree to which these fictions reflect an explicit interest in civiliza-tion, and particularly the discourse of civilization — the various attempts to persuade the public of civilization's "true" nature and function. It is to this discourse that I will turn after introducing the five novelists' interventions in the civilization debate.

In *The Conventional Lies of Our Civilization* (1884), Max Nordau, an eventual correspondent of Joseph Conrad's, maintains that "In England the ground appears solid and the structure of State firm, to a superficial ob-server. But if he lay his ear to the ground . . . and if he examine the walls closer, he will see that underneath the varnish and gold plating, dangerous cracks extend from top to bottom" (4). This passage aptly characterizes Conrad's representation of European (and particularly English) civiliza-tion. On the one hand, Conrad's fiction celebrates Western civilization; on the other, it peels away civilization's "varnish and gold plating" to reveal the "cracks" in its foundation, the contradictions in its logic and language. Indeed, the case can be made that each of Conrad's works is deeply engaged with the discourse of civilization. With this in mind, it is no coincidence that, in the Author's Note to his first publication, *Almayer's Folly* (1895), Conrad defends himself against the charge that his works, because set in "far off countries . . . amongst honest cannibals and the more sophisticated pioneers of our own glorious virtues," must therefore be "decivilized" (Wright 159). Nor is it merely coincidental that the majority of his novels place "Western civilization" in tension with the "non-West" (the Congo of *Heart of Darkness*, the Patusan of *Lord Jim*, the Costaguana of *Nostromo*, the Russia of *Under Western Eyes*, and the Samburan of *Victory*), thereby high-lighting, yet at the same time resolutely questioning, the boundaries be-tween them. To be sure, civilization in these works is depicted more as a set of problems than a realm that can be delineated or a quality that can be defined.

Dating from the earliest critical comments on Conrad's works there have arisen charges that his fiction, as E. M. Forster puts it, "is misty in the middle as well as at the edges," that "the secret casket of his genius contains a vapour rather than a jewel" (*Abinger Harvest* 138). Similarly, F. R. Leavis argues that *Nostromo* possesses a "certain emptiness" and that its "rever-beration" has "something hollow about it" (*Great Tradition* 200). Even as great an admirer of Conrad as Edward Garnett likens *Youth*'s style to a "dream-like illusion of an unforgettable reality" (quoted in Sherry, *Critical*

Heritage 133). This latter judgment prompts a letter from Conrad in response: "your brave attempt to grapple with the foggishness of H of D," he writes Garnett, "to explain what I myself tried to shape blindfold, as it were, has touched me profoundly" (*Letters* II, 467–68). Yet this "foggishness," I will argue — a foggishness or mistiness apparent in the writing itself *and* in the descriptions of various landscapes — far from being a "defect" in Conrad's style, is meant to suggest civilization's now intriguing, now mystifying power: its ability both to impress its subjects with its magnificence and to blind them to its true motivations, interests, and activities. The clearest example of this is in his short story "An Outpost of Progress," where the "heavy mist" (European civilization invading the African jungle) is depicted as descending "upon the land: the mist penetrating, enveloping, and silent; . . . the mist that clings and kills; the mist white and deadly, immaculate and poisonous" (115). "White" yet "deadly," "immaculate" yet "poisonous," civilization is depicted throughout Conrad's writings in such paradoxical and nefarious terms.

A neglected memoir and essay of Conrad's provide further insights into his fictional representation of civilization as a duplicitous force — as a "blinding torch." In Conrad's memoir, *The Mirror of the Sea* (1906), the role of this "haze" is made explicit. Although Morton Dauwen Zabel is correct to assert that *Mirror* is "a valuable document on [Conrad's] thought" and "a study which, of its kind, has no exact rival in English literature" (xxvii), the work remains generally neglected and misconstrued. Zabel himself, for example, likens Conrad's "haze of words" in *Mirror* and elsewhere to "an overelaboration of his material, a weakening of his sensory and dramatic instinct, a tendency to allegorize or metaphorize" (xxv). And Robert Foulke speaks of certain sections of Conrad's memoir as "overblown" and even exasperating for their "unrestrained personification" (154). However, it is precisely for these reasons that *Mirror* stands as a brilliant if quirky piece of self-fashioning and culture criticism, a meditation on artistic production and on the discourse of civilization — on the rewards, demands, and obfuscations of civilization. Sometimes allegorical and sometimes symbolic, this text repeatedly invokes the sailor and his craft (ship) as a means by which to comment on the artist and his craft (artwork). A highly fictive recreation and interpretation of Conrad's own initiation into the life of sailing and artistry, *The Mirror of the Sea* is more a veiled *Künstlerroman* than the autobiographical memoir it at first appears to be.

It is the dead center of this enigmatic text that most interests me. There, in a section entitled "Rulers of East and West," Conrad turns from considerations of self-understanding to those of world-understanding. In this section the "West Wind" confronted by the sailor on board his ship becomes a trope for the blinding power of civilization's discourse over its subjects. For example, we read that "The West Wind hangs heavy grey curtains of mist and spray before your gaze" (87). Further, the West Wind's "kingly melancholy" is capable of "blowing great guns, and unrolling thick streamers of fog in wanton sport at the cost of his own poor, miserable subjects" (83). Indeed, "the West Wind rules his realm on which the sun never sets" (83) and is repeatedly associated with "duplicity" (it possesses a "double-edged sword"), suggesting that it intimidates not only its sworn enemies but its own "poor, miserable subjects." The West Wind's ability both to intrigue and to blind, impress and oppress, is touched on at numerous points.

> The end of the day is the time to gaze at the kingly face of the Westerly Weather, who is the arbiter of ships' destinies. Benignant and splendid, or splendid and sinister, the western sky reflects the hidden purposes of the royal mind. . . . Some of his sunsets are like pageants devised for the delight of the multitude, when all the gems of the royal treasure-house are displayed above the sea. (72–73)

At other times,

> Denser and denser grows [his] dome of vapours, descending lower and lower upon the sea, narrowing the horizon around the ship. And the characteristic aspect of Westerly Weather, the thick, grey, smoky, and sinister tone sets in, circumscribing the view of the men, drenching their bodies, oppressing their souls, taking their breath away with booming gusts, deafening, blinding. (73–74)

Conrad's persona himself remarks of the West Wind, "I have been too much moulded to his sway to nurse now any idea of rebellion in my heart." "Moreover," he reasons, "what [good] is a rebellion within the four walls of a room against the tempestuous rule of the West Wind?" (88).

In this memoir sight is likened to freedom, blindness to enslavement. "[E]ach mean starved sunset," Conrad's persona explains, leaves us "calling with imprecations upon the West Wind even in its most veiled misty mood to wake up and give us our liberty" (86). After all, "to see!" is "the craving of the sailor, as of the rest of blind humanity" (78). Replete with references to a "lighted torch" (77) and to a "blindfold" (79) — to the West Wind's ability both to illuminate and to obfuscate in "the dismal secrecy of thick, very thick, weather" (79) — *The Mirror of the Sea* depicts civilization as fundamentally duplicitous.

Conrad's sense of his own ambivalent feelings for the West, and of civilization's duplicity, is also evident in his later essay, "Poland Revisited" (1915). There, Conrad writes of arriving in England on the eve of the Great War, in July of 1914. "But, truth to say, on this July day I reflected but little on the condition of the civilised world. Whatever sinister passions were heaving under its splendid and complex surface, I was too agitated by a simple and innocent desire of my own, to notice the signs or interpret them correctly. The most innocent of passions will take the edge off one's judgement" (144). I take the "sinister passions . . . heaving under [civilization's] splendid and complex surface" here to be the blinding torch of *Heart of Darkness* refigured — the subjects of civilization in both cases too enamored of the splendid and complex appearance, or discourse, of civilization to grasp, or even to wish to grasp, the more "sinister passions" beneath it.[5]

D. H. Lawrence's fiction, like Conrad's, harbors deep suspicions toward, yet is deeply intrigued with, the idea of civilization. As K. K. Ruthven puts it, "Lawrence shares with Conrad a fascination for what civilization excludes, and also a conviction that the act of exclusion has severed us from sources of great vitality" (50). Of the five British modernists to be considered here, however, D. H. Lawrence stands out as a special case in one respect. The sole genuine nostalgist of the group, Lawrence, like Oswald Spengler in *The Decline of the West*, views "civilization" to be encroaching upon "culture" and modernity to be ushering in not the West's spiritual liberation but its physical death.

In each of his most acclaimed early novels — *Sons and Lovers*, *The Rainbow*, and *Women in Love* — an organic socioeconomic order is supplanted by an alienated, materialistic, and mechanistic one, as gemeinschaft gives way to gesellschaft. This is symbolized most clearly in *Women in Love*, in the great changes that come about in the Midlands mines when Gerald Crich takes over from his father. Gerald's treatment of his workers as "mere mechanical instruments" in order to maximize profits and speed modernization — like the Hands of Dickens's *Hard Times* — is shown to lead to an alienated, disaffected labor force. Although psychology is a central focus of these novels, particularly as manifest in Lawrence's gender-obsessed explorations of human interaction, the issue of civilization's present worth and future course is also pointedly raised in each of them. As E. M. Forster put it of Lawrence shortly after this "reactionary's" death, "his dislike of civilization was not a pose, as it is with many writers. He hated it fundamentally, because it has made human beings conscious, and society mechanical" (quoted in Draper 345). In Lawrence's most acclaimed later novels, *The Plumed Serpent* and *Lady Chatterley's Lover*, civilization is once again depicted as a force that crushes vital human instincts.

However, Lawrence betrays his hand most clearly in an essay, "Enslaved by Civilization" (1930), where natural instinct is pitted against the constraining powers of civilization. "The one thing men have not learned to do," Lawrence begins, "is to stick up for their own instinctive feelings, against the things they are taught" (137). For Lawrence, civilization is perpetuated by state education, which leads to the enslavement of the populace: "Little boys are trundled off to school at the age of five, and immediately the game begins, the game of enslaving the small chap" (137). Not surprisingly, he lays much of the blame for this system at the doorstep of women. For Lawrence, these enslaving teachers "are all maids: young maids, middling maids, or old maids. . . . none of them know anything about men" (138). "Nothing," he continues, "is more insidiously clever than an old maid's fingers at picking off the little shoots of manhood as they sprout out from a growing boy, and turning him into that neutral object, a good little boy" (141). "But to be a good little boy like all the other good little boys is to be a slave, or at least an automaton, running on wheels" (141). For Lawrence, the educational system in England is thus little more than "a very elaborate railway system where good little boys are taught to run upon good lines till they are shunted off into life" (140); this system is civilization's attempt to quell individual feeling in the service of national order and good citizenship.

Lawrence's quasi-Freudian understanding of civilization, as harnessing nature for the ends of culture while maintaining order by dividing available wealth — all at the expense of the id, of instinctual feeling, of "individuality" — is nowhere more evident than here. At one point in "Enslaved by Civilization," after asserting that state education ends in the formation of the "good" boy, Lawrence defines what "goodness," in this context, means. "It means, in the end, being like everybody else, and not having a soul to call your own. Certainly you mustn't have a feeling to call your own. You must be good, and feel exactly what is expected of you, which is just what other people feel. Which means in the end you feel nothing at all" (142). Thus, for Lawrence, civilization is virtually synonymous with social conformity, with milk-toast morality, with the enslavement of the spirit. Unless one is a "freethinker" like Birkin in *Women in Love* or, presumably, Lawrence himself, civilization, via state education, enslaves rather than liberates the civilized. As Lawrence puts it in his essay "Education of the People" (1920), "you can obtain one kind of perfect citizen by suppressing individuality and cultivating the public virtues" (113), even if real individuals have a spark of danger in them. "Quench this spark and you quench the individuality, you obtain a social unit, not an integral man. All modern progress has tended, and still tends, to the production of quenched social units: dangerless beings, ideal creatures!" (114). "We, the educators," Lawrence warns, "have got to decide for the children: decide the steps of their young fates, seriously and reverently," if they are ever to be able to negotiate the "whirling industrial machine and the warren of back streets" they will encounter (106).

Lawrence's attempt to "decide" on their behalf was not long in coming. In an endeavor to remake education and hence, for him, civilization itself, Lawrence wrote a history textbook for adolescents, *Movements in European History* (1921), initially published under the pseudonym of Lawrence H. Davison. In this history of civilization from "Rome" to "The Unification of Germany" Lawrence seeks to "introduce the deep, philosophic note into education: deep, philosophic reverence" (Salgado 246). "Whoever misses his education in history," he continues, "misses his fulfillment in the past" (*Movements* xiii). For Lawrence, this textbook is no less than "an attempt to give some impression of the great, surging movements which rose in the hearts of men in Europe, sweeping human beings together into one great concerted action, or sweeping them apart for ever on the tides of opposition" (xi). In the end, according to Lawrence, here sounding like Spengler,

> the cycle of European history completes itself, phase by phase, from imperial Rome, through the medieval empire and the papacy to the kings of the Renaissance period, on to the great commercial nations, the government by the industrial and commercial middle classes, and so to that last rule, that last oneness of the labouring people. So Europe moves from oneness to oneness, from the imperial unity to the unity of the labouring classes, from the beginning to the end. (344)[6]

Like "Enslaved by Civilization," this textbook on European history reveals Lawrence's sense of civilization's duplicity — his feeling of suspicion and pride, hostility and intoxication, toward the "stream of civilization."[7]

The fictions of the precise contemporaries James Joyce and Virginia Woolf also stand as provocative dialogues with and interpretations of "civilization." In their works most of all, a fascination with the inner workings of the mind, with the "streaming" of consciousness, and with structural and linguistic experimentation has spurred psychological and formal criticism that has usually seen its subject as "apolitical." However, such fictions as *Dubliners* and *Ulysses, Mrs. Dalloway* and *To the Lighthouse* also clearly exhibit a fascination with the discourse of English and Irish civilization.

That Joyce's fiction — all of it set exclusively in Dublin — is concerned with Anglo-Irish civilization is clear not only when we consider its roots in literary naturalism, by definition political, but when we consider Joyce's hyperbolic statement that he wishes *Ulysses* "to give a picture of Dublin so complete that if the city one day suddenly disappeared from the earth it could be reconstructed out of my book" (Budgen 67–68). Or when he asserts, speaking of the mimetic accuracy of *Dubliners*, "I seriously believe that you will retard the course of civilisation in Ireland by preventing the Irish people from having one good look at themselves in my nicely polished looking-glass" (*Letters* I, 64). In each case Joyce insists that his work is to be both a historically accurate and a therapeutically beneficial portrait of his civilization.

A look at one of Joyce's most substantial essays, "Ireland, Island of Saints and Sages" (1907), reveals an important aspect of his complex posture toward Irish civilization. Originally delivered as a lecture in Trieste, this essay begins by explaining that the reference to Ireland as an island of saints and sages "was not invented yesterday or the day before. It goes back to the most ancient times, when the island was a true focus of sanctity and intellect, spreading throughout the continent a culture and a vitalizing energy. It would be easy to make a list of the Irishmen who carried the torch of knowledge from country to country as pilgrims and hermits, as scholars and wisemen" (154). Reminiscent of Conrad in *Heart of Darkness*, Joyce here deploys the symbol of a torch to illustrate his nation's glory as an outpost of civilization in Europe, as a light unto the world. Joyce portrays Ireland as pursuing "its own culture" not so much as "the demand of a young nation that wants to make good in the European concert as the demand of a very old nation to renew under new forms the glories of a past civilization" (157). For Joyce this explains why Ireland is always backward-looking, seeking to recapture a past more treasured than its present can ever be. For him the Irish nation is also a mongrel breed, linguistically and racially "impure." Sounding like Mikhail Bakhtin, Joyce celebrates the fact that civilization is "a vast fabric, in which the most diverse elements are mingled." "In such a fabric," he continues, "it is useless to look for a thread that may have remained pure and virgin without having undergone the influence of a neighboring thread. What race, or what language . . . can boast of being pure today? And no race has less right to utter such a boast than the race now living in Ireland" (165–66).

That Joyce is hard on the discourse of Irish civilization does not mean that he is soft on the discourse of English civilization.[8] This fact is reflected in Joyce's fiction at numerous points, from Gabriel Conroy's ambiguous relationship with Irish civilization in "The Dead," in which he is depicted as more attached to Irish history and culture than he believes, to the

Citizen's ambiguous relationship with it in *Ulysses*, in which he is depicted as far less in touch with Irish history and culture than he believes. Although Joyce deems it "naive to heap insults on England for her misdeeds in Ireland" ("Ireland" 166), and although he does not "see the purpose of the bitter invectives against the English despoiler, the disdain for the vast Anglo-Saxon civilization, even though it is almost entirely a materialistic civilization" (173), he nevertheless blames many of Ireland's problems on England's policy of dividing and conquering it. "A conqueror cannot be casual," Joyce maintains, again reminiscent of Conrad, "and for so many centuries the Englishman has done in Ireland only what the Belgian is doing today in the Congo Free State" (166). Ruminating on the Irish revival, Joyce writes that it would be interesting "to see what might be the effects on our civilization of a revival" of the Celtic race (173): "the economic effects of the appearance of a rival island near England, a bilingual, republican, self-centred, and enterprising island with its own commercial fleet, and its own consuls in every port of the world." He also imagines the beneficent "moral effects" that would follow "the appearance in old Europe of the Irish artist and thinker" (173) — someone like Joyce, perhaps.

If Joyce's sense of civilization's duplicity hinges on Anglo-Irish tensions, Virginia Woolf's sense of it hinges on male–female tensions. At one point in *A Room of One's Own*, for example, Woolf writes, "if one is a woman one is often surprised by a sudden splitting off of consciousness, say in walking down Whitehall, when from being the natural inheritor of that civilisation, she becomes, on the contrary, outside of it, alien and critical" (101). As opposed to Marlow's portrayal of women in *Heart of Darkness* as blindfolded and in the dark, as "out of touch with truth" and as properly belonging in "that beautiful world of their own" (16, 49), Woolf's sense of womankind's standing in civilization as sometimes central, sometimes marginal, pervades her novels and essays. This is particularly true for Mrs. Dalloway in the novel of that name and for Mrs. Ramsay in *To the Lighthouse*, both of whom are "housewives" depicted as simultaneously the standard-bearers of civilization and ostracized within it, as the lesser men (Tennyson's phrase in "Locksley Hall") who nevertheless comprise civilization's normative voices in principle as well as its marginal ones in fact. While each of these characters has a husband socially more prominent than she — Richard Dalloway is a member of Parliament, Mr. Ramsay a professor of philosophy — both women are depicted as capable of advancing civilization against the overwhelming forces of social chaos and psychological fragmentation. Indeed, Woolf's writings stand as highly charged debates on the nature and function of civilization, particularly as it affects the women who are in such a tenuous relation with it.

This issue resurfaces in *A Room of One's Own* where Woolf declaims of women, "You have never made a discovery of any sort of importance. You have never shaken an empire or led an army into battle . . . and you have never introduced a barbarous race to the blessings of civilisation. What is your excuse?" (116). Woolf's bitter irony here is clear: if civilization involves war and imperialism — in short, violence and coercion — then it is just as well that women do not play a leading role in it. On the other hand, if civilization is something else — a realm in which art and ideas are freely expressed, for example — then womankind's exclusion from it derives from long-standing material inequalities. Like her friend Clive Bell in *Civilization*, Woolf in *A Room of One's Own* argues that "Intellectual freedom depends upon material things" and that "Poetry depends upon intellectual freedom." "And women have always been poor," she continues, "not for two hundred years merely, but from the beginning of time": women "have not had a dog's chance of writing poetry" (112). In any case, for Woolf, it is important to recognize that truly civilized beings are neither "male" nor "female" — if such pure forms can be said to exist at all — but androgynous, a salutary combination of both genders.[9]

Malcolm Lowry's fiction also engages the triumphs and discontents of civilization. In many ways Lowry's *Under the Volcano* (1947) is the last child of British fictional modernism, a work which can claim parentage in the novels of Conrad, Lawrence, Joyce, and Woolf, yet which precedes — conceptually and chronologically — the advent of postmodernism. Like Lawrence, Lowry in his novel finds Mexico to be "an analogue to the world itself" (*Selected Letters* 92) and finds Spengler to be the most compelling theorist of civilization; like Joyce and Woolf, Lowry is fascinated with the inner workings of the mind and with the compression of the novel's spatiotemporal coordinates (*Under the Volcano* is a novel composed of internal monologues and situated largely in one place during one day); and like Conrad, Lowry worries the distinction (or lack thereof) between "civilized" and "uncivilized" domains.

For example, like *Heart of Darkness, Under the Volcano* sets up and then subverts numerous cliché distinctions between civilization and jungle. As early as the first page of *Under the Volcano* we read that "a fine American-style highway leads in [to Cuernavaca] from the north but is lost in its narrow streets and comes out a goat track" (3). Lowry's town may thus be said to exist between "civilized" (the American-style highway) and "uncivilized" (the goat track) realms, the two becoming blurred in the maze that is the town. Indeed, our entire introduction to Cuernavaca is shot through with such a "blurring of realms." Not only does Maximilian's palatial chapel appear "overgrown with weeds," its crumbling walls "splashed with urine, on which scorpions lurked" (14), but "two ragged Indians" approaching "through the dust" are described as arguing "with the profound concentration of university professors wandering in summer twilight through the Sorbonne" — "the gestures of their refined grimy hands . . . unbelievably courtly, delicate" (11). Further, the description of the terrain around Cuernavaca approximates Conrad's blurring of "jungle" and "civilization": "Elsewhere, to the left, were scattered huts of dark thatch, merging into the jungle which on all sides surrounded the town, glowing now in the unnatural livid light of approaching storm" (340). And like Marlow's encounter with Kurtz's portrait of the blindfolded torchbearer in *Heart of Darkness*, the Consul and Jacques Laruelle encounter Diego Rivera's frescoes on Cortez's palace in *Under the Volcano*, prompting Laruelle to muse that "the slow darkening of the murals as you look from right to left . . . seems somehow to symbolize the gradual imposition of the Spaniard's conquering will upon the Indians" (212). Explicit here rather than implicit, the frescoes paint an unflattering picture of Europe's colonization of Mexico.[10]

In a letter written from his British Columbia retreat, Lowry himself comes to sound like the Consul: "Our house is still here but civilization, so called, is closing in on us a little too much for our liking" (*Selected Letters* 90). This telling comment — and the numerous other allusions to the "civilization" crisis in the works of Conrad, Lawrence, Joyce, Woolf, and Lowry — cannot adequately be understood without a detailed look at this discourse of civilization itself. What did the discourse of civilization look like, and how did these novels engage it? What voices made up the civilization debate, and how did modernist British fiction access it? First I will address the term and concept of "civilization" itself.

✳ Coming to Terms with "Civilization"

Like other terms of its magnitude and weight, "civilization" means so much, and so diversely, that it can seem to mean nothing at all. Although it is perhaps true that "a hundred years ago no one would have had much difficulty with the meaning of civilization" (Bierstedt 273), the proliferation of numerous (and contradictory) definitions of the word between the turn of the century and the close of World War II cannot now be disputed. In *Civilisation: Its Cause and Cure* (1889), for example, Edward Carpenter writes that, in suggesting "the part which Civilisation has played in history, I am aware that the word itself is difficult to define — is at best only one of those phantom-generalizations which the mind is forced to employ" (47).

Similarly, Joseph McCabe, writing in *The Evolution of Civilization* (1922), maintains that we ought "to begin such a study as this with a precise definition of civilization. But a moment's reflection will show the reader that this is impossible." For "civilization is not a fixed standard of institutions, or of mental and moral cultivation," he continues; "it is a relative term" (1–2).

Nevertheless, the vast majority of commentators during this period were less tentative than Carpenter and McCabe, assuming, with the *Oxford English Dictionary* (1933), that such a term as civilization could be defined without much difficulty:

> 1. Law. A law, act of justice, or judgement, which renders a criminal process civil; which is performed by turning an information into an inquest, or the contrary. . . . 2. The action or process of civilizing or of being civilized. . . . 3. (More usually) Civilized condition or state; a developed or advanced state of human society; a particular stage or a particular type of this. (448)

In this spirit John Storck, in *Man and Civilization: An Inquiry into the Bases of Contemporary Life* (1927), concludes that "civilization is a form of culture characterized by a sedentary population grouped around the state as the central institution, and having a symbolic form of writing and an economic structure which makes fairly extensive use of the divisions of labor" (54). If there is any definition that has more or less held sway, it is this one.

Yet the history of the usage of the word "civilization" belies such bland assurance.[11] Not gaining wide currency until the late eighteenth century ("Dr. Johnson declined to include it in his dictionary of 1772, even though Boswell urged him to do so" [Bierstedt 264]), civilization is initially associated with post-Enlightenment thinking, with its "emphasis on secular and progressive human self development" (Williams, *Keywords* 49). For Edmund Burke, civilization is nearly synonymous with the refinement of manners. Writing in *Reflections on the French Revolution* (1790), for example, Burke speaks of "our manners, our civilization, and all the good things which are connected with manners, and with civilization" (*Keywords* 49). For John Stuart Mill, in "Civilization" (1836), "the word civilization" is "a word of double meaning. It sometimes stands for *human improvement* in general, and sometimes for *certain kinds* of improvement in particular" (70). For Mill it is in any case clearly "the direct converse or contrary of rudeness or barbarism" (71). As Raymond Williams has noted, civilization thus comes to express "two senses which were historically linked: an achieved state, which could be contrasted with 'barbarism' " ("in practice the metropolitan civilization of England and France"), and "an achieved state of *development*, which implied historical process or progress." "This was the new historical rationality of the Enlightenment," Williams continues, "combined with a self-referring celebration of an achieved condition of refinement and order" (*Marxism and Literature* 13–14).

On the other hand, romantic judgments of civilization, following the Rousseau of *Two Discourses*, were less sympathetic, distinguishing genuine "culture" from civilization, the mere "cultivation" of manners and sensibility.[12] Writing in *On the Constitution of Church and State* (1830), for example, Coleridge deems civilization to be "but a mixed good, if not far more a corrupting influence, the hectic of disease, not the bloom of health," a nation "more fitly to be called a varnished than a polished people" (quoted in Gunn 10). As if invoking these very tropes, John H. Wilkins, in his abysmal and deservedly forgotten play, *Civilization* (1852), has his hero Hercule liken civilization to "gilt-chased bells" which, when scrutinized closely, shed their "lacker" to reveal "the baser metal underneath" (47). Concluding ironically that he is "wiser now; / more civilized," Hercule insists that he therefore knows "the way to lie, / to cheat, deceive, and be a zealous Christian!" (58):

> I am overwhelmed with Civilization. . . . Here are tale-tellers that bring the blush into the listener's cheek. Intriguantes that ape modesty, and libel it. Courtiers, the painted dolls of the great puppet-show fashion, recounting before admiring auditors the adventures of last night. . . . On this side gambling, profligacy — on the other, debauchery and riot! Everywhere shame, folly, hypocrisy — the golden husks of the fruit of vice, with bitterness and death within. And this — heaven save us! — this is Civilization! (45)

Unlike culture, civilization in this romantic drama stands for everything pretentious and affected, the sophisticated vices of the city. In romantic thought generally, civilization increasingly is associated with the alienating "external properties," structures, mechanics, and customs of society, culture with the "inner" or "spiritual" needs and impulses of humanity: "religion, art, the family and personal life" (Williams, *Marxism and Literature* 14).

Given the term's complex legacy as it enters the twentieth century, then, it is necessary to distinguish it from three other terms often used synonymously — culture, society, and history — to the extent that civilization alone retains a normative status as an expression of value throughout the period under consideration. Whereas "culture," during this time, undergoes a nearly complete transformation from its Arnoldean sense as an achieved state of sensibility to its anthropological one as the collective social forms and expressions of a given group, "civilization," during this same period — construed as a particular stage in the social history of a culture — cannot shake its value-laden connotations. Hence, whereas bees may be said to have a society, volcanoes a history, and "primitives" a culture, civilization always carries a value judgment; it is always an expression of the boon or bane, the weal or woe, of a people. Civilization, it might be said, is a *particular kind* of culture. All groups possess a history, constitute a society, and maintain a culture, but "civilization" necessitates the idea of "uncivilization," an external, threatening, barbarian realm lacking civilized forms of life.[13] By definition, then, the term is divisive; to invoke it seriously is to distinguish a morally superior and technologically advanced group from a morally inferior and technologically backward one. As John Katz recognized in *The Will to Civilization* (1938), "etymologically, civilization is the way of life peculiar to city-dwellers. And as city-dwellers are inclined to approve of themselves," he continues, "they have given to the term 'civilization' a eulogistic connotation" (1–2). For Raymond Williams this is why the concept becomes ambiguous: "denoting on the one hand enlightened and progressive development and on the other hand an achieved and threatened state," civilization becomes "increasingly retrospective and often in practice identified with the received glories of the past" (*Marxism and Literature* 15).

As should already be clear, I will not advance the claim that "civilization" is ultimately definable or, still less, that it is a stable concept over time. Rather, I will demonstrate how various definitions of the term and treatments of the concept — the discourse of civilization — informed the kinds of questions posed and problems unmasked in representative works of modern British fiction. Moreover, what is at issue is precisely how Conrad, Lawrence, Joyce, Woolf, and Lowry represented and critiqued this discourse of civilization in its numerous manifestations. More significant to me than metaphysical questions about civilization, then, is the heuristic one of what it meant to those embroiled in the debate. What did "civilization" look like, what did it mean, and how did it function from the perspectives of 1899, 1914, 1947?

In order to begin to answer such questions I identify three recurrent nodal points through which the culture articulated its debate over civilization and hence articulated a self-image: civilization as progressive or retrogressive entity, nation-state or state of mind, and sacred domain to be preserved or propaganda tool to be exploited. Although British materials will be central to my reconstruction of these three matrices of understanding, French, German, and American ones will also be consulted for two reasons. First, translations made intellectual crosscurrents among various languages and nations possible, and war alliances made them necessary (Spengler's and Schweitzer's works on civilization were available in English soon after their publication in German, for example). Second, each of the five writers under consideration was as conversant in his or her adopted as in his or her native languages and cultures: Conrad was as familiar with French as with English writing; Lawrence with German as much as British; Joyce with German as much as Anglo-Irish;[14] Woolf with French as much as English; Lowry with American as much as British, and so forth. By resurrecting these three nodal points through which the culture articulated its debate over civilization — this discourse of civilization — I hope to reveal an unacknowledged context for a number of representative novels of British modernism.

✳ The Law of Civilization: Progress Enthroned or Disease Unleashed?

At a number of points in Wilkins's drama, *Civilization* (1852), discussion ensues as to whether civilization

> ... is a key
> Which opens upon Nature the high gates
> Of learning, taste, refinement, — lacking which
> Life drags a ponderous chain and bar along,
> Clogging its heels with its own manacles! (20)

or whether, in fact,

> This Civilization is a mighty maze
> Where he who steps, confounds himself and strangles
> The little common sense he had about him. (30)

This formulation of the debate over civilization's merit — whether it is the straight path to the liberation of sensibility or the mazelike one to its corruption — suggests how quickly its key issues had shifted by the fin de siècle. In 1892, for example, John B. Crozier maintains that "the first great question that must be scientifically determined — the question into which all others merge — is, what is the goal of civilization?" (134). Indeed, Crozier's point here is telling precisely for its insistence that civilization has a "goal." Between 1897 and 1947 teleological notions of progress and retrogression, and biological ones of evolution and devolution, health and disease, arose virtually whenever "civilization" was invoked, and were taken to characterize "those great Laws of civilization which previous thinkers had left undetermined" (Crozier viii). "Once the cause of social progress is discovered," Hector MacPherson writes in 1900, "we have within our grasp the key to civilization" (125), an understanding of "the great laws of civilization and progress" from "barbarism up to the present time" (1). Whether one viewed civilization as the triumph of rationality and individual freedom or the downfall of community and autonomy, such teleological and biological tropes were everywhere to be found in the discourse of civilization.[15]

In the use of organic and teleological metaphors to expound the "laws" of civilization, two figures from this period stand out as particularly influential and as master synthesizers of what came before: Herbert Spencer (1820–1903) and Oswald Spengler (1880–1936). Indeed, each figure provides the most encyclopedic formulation of his respective position, with Spencer positing the inevitable progress and perfection of Western civilization and Spengler prophesying its inevitable decline and death.

In many respects an intellectual ally of Charles Darwin, Spencer is the leading Victorian and Edwardian philosopher of civilization and prophet of progress.[16] For Spencer, the law of the inevitable progress of civilization — that "the course of civilization could not have been other than it has been" (*Social Statics* 233) — is predicated upon his theory that the simple, repressive, corporate organization of militant society evolves into the complex, democratic, and individualistic one of industrial society. In "Progress: Its Law and Cause," for example, Spencer argues that progress is universal, affecting everything "from the earliest traceable cosmical changes down to the latest results of civilization" (10), and, moreover, that progress is neither "an accident" nor "a thing within human control, but a beneficent necessity" (60). Militant societies are further distinguished from the industrial ones into which they evolve to the extent that the former are "static" and war-oriented whereas the latter are "dynamic" and work-oriented. Further, Spencer relates the "free-trade" and "individual freedom" of the industrial type of civilization with the multiplicity of "associations, political, religious, commercial, professional, philanthropic and social" that encourage the "free-play of the sympathies" and "the growth of altruistic sentiments" (Wiltshire 250).

Social Spencerians such as Hector MacPherson, writing in 1900, went as far as to predict "universal felicity" for "the future of civilization" (186): "if the Spencerian theory is true, there is no escape from the conclusion that morality is a natural product of social evolution. It is the consequence rather than the cause of progress" (187). Even those not directly under the spell of Spencer seemed incapable of resisting similar progressivist representations of civilization. Writing in 1917, for example, Stanton Coit insists that "civilization is still advancing by leaps and bounds" (126); and six years later, writing in his two-volume *Philosophy of Civilization*, Albert Schweitzer refers to "the stream of civilization" as "the sum total of all progress made by men and the individual man in every sphere of action and from every point of view, in so far as this progress helps toward the spiritual perfecting of individuals" (*Ethics* 7–8). Writing in 1926, Sigmund Mendelsohn argues that civilization is "saturated," that the spirit of "modern social progress" is almost completely triumphant, having "reached the boundary line of political possibility in establishing freedom, universal suffrage in all civilized lands," and having "imbued the human family with higher ideals regarding its earthly existence and its duties toward fellow men" (179).

Two years later Clive Bell, in *Civilization*, writes on the same theme: "So soon as savages begin to apply reason to instinct, so soon as they acquire a rudimentary sense of values — so soon, that is, as they begin to distinguish between ends and means, or between direct means to good and remote — they have taken the first step upward" (119). Yet this Bloomsburyite offers a historical justification, beyond Spencer's, for the inevitability of progress: "it seems that the most highly civilized people in any century at all should be more highly civilized than their counterparts in the preceeding one, always provided that they have easy access to, and the means of enjoying, the legacies of the past" (87). In 1929 Raoul Allier argues, "between the starting-point of uncivilized man and his present situation, incalculable ages have intervened" (252), and, mustering as much generosity as he can, reasons, "it would be useless to imagine that, in a single day . . . men can be in a position to rush through all the stages, the very ones that our most civilized races have taken centuries to traverse. *The problem is to turn all these [primitives] into true men, fully developed and capable, of all that progress which will be theirs eventually*" (271; my emphasis). Even as late as 1950 the editor of *War and Civilization* (selections from Toynbee's *Study of History*) presumes a "chaotic past out of which civilized man has struggled" (vi).

If there was one major phenomenon that tempered such progressivism (before it was entirely delegitimized by the wholesale genocide of World War II), it was the Great War of 1914–18. Writing soon after this conflict began, F. S. Marvin, in *The Unity of Western Civilization* (1915), used medical metaphors to trivialize the war's significance. For him, although the West is fraught with "great convulsions," the European system is nevertheless "the necessary nucleus of any civilized order embracing the whole world":

> We strive and hope for a more lasting state of general health, and do not despair of the patient even in this grave attack. He has survived even more serious illness. For though the present war is the most gigantic that the world has ever seen, its very greatness is the result of some of those modern developments — scientific skill, improved communications, national cohesion — on which ultimately the better organization of the whole commonwealth of nations will be built. (18–19)

In *The Evolution of Civilization* (1922), Joseph McCabe also seeks to have his cake and eat it too. Maintaining, with Tennysonian echo, that "when the war drums beat no longer and the strong have ceased to exploit the weak, the fundamental condition of progress" will "be provided on a higher plane," McCabe seeks to make a virtue of necessity by viewing the war as a minor setback. Defining civilization as "the slow and gradual development of the higher and more complex institutions" (2), McCabe argues that, in fact, civilization "has not yet had a fair trial," that "it has barely begun." "We must, in view of the facts which we now know," he continues, "regard it as a thin film of idealism which has developed on top of a million years of human savagery" (4).

However, Sholto Douglas in *A Theory of Civilisation* (1914) overtly admits into his calculus of civilization's development the "opposite movement" of progress — retrogression. Seeking to "elucidate" the "causation of civilisation and decivilisation" (23), "climax" and "decadence" (242), Douglas argues that, "as other periods of civilisation have grown, have reached a climax, and have then declined, so too our present civilisation must surely decline when it has lost the driving force that has raised it to its greatest possible height. There seems to be no sufficient reason to suppose that our present civilisation is different in kind from earlier civilisations" (239). And Stanley Casson in *Progress and Catastrophe* (1937) concurs: "That progress does in fact occur on occasions nobody except a fool would deny," he writes; "that it is cumulative and inevitable no one but an idiot would accept" (5). Concluding that "contemporary conditions suggest the reappearance of retrogressive forces," Casson dedicates his book to arresting these forces and reversing "the direction of [the] disruptive tendencies" (x). "Consciousness" of this threat of retrogression alone, he hopes in closing, "may contribute to stopping the downward trend of modern civilization" (231). Surprisingly, it is Spencer himself who early on notes this "retrogression," this "disruptive tendency" of civilization on its otherwise progressive path.

As early as 1902, for example, Spencer warns of the "re-barbarization" of Britain (*Facts and Comments* 196): the "re-development of armed forces and [the] revival of the predatory spirit," the "return towards the militant type in our institutions generally" (*Principles* I, 570). As R. B. Kershner suggests in his masterful essay "Degeneration," Spencer's about-face may itself be the result of Huxley's famous Romanes lecture of 1893 in which this evolutionist argues that "civilization is waging a losing struggle against the 'State of Nature' which will continue until 'the evolution of our globe shall have entered so far upon its downward course that the cosmic process resumes its sway; and, once more, the State of Nature prevails over the surface of our planet.'" "Less abstractly put," Kershner adds, "savagery would triumph over civilization" (429).

This sense that civilization has reached its apex and is now in decline — that civilization, in Ezra Pound's words in "Hugh Selwyn Mauberley," is "botched," an "old bitch gone in the teeth" (64) — receives its fullest expression in Oswald Spengler's *Decline of the West* (1918, 1922). Spengler employs the same teleological and biological tropes as Spencer to characterize the course of the West. Yet for him, far from representing the triumph of progress, reason, health, and democracy, civilization coincides with the triumph of retrogression, disease, and repression — the devolution of a once vital culture.

It should be noted that although Spengler is the great encyclopedist of the anti-linear-progress camp, he is by no means its progenitor. As early as 1889, for example, Edward Carpenter, in *Civilisation: Its Cause and Cure*, complains that the word "civilisation" "is sometimes used in a kind of ideal sense . . . to indicate a state of future culture towards which we are tending — the implied assumption being that a sufficiently long course of top hats and telephones will in the end bring us to this ideal condition; while any little drawbacks in the process . . . are explained as being merely accidental and temporary" (3). Similarly, in *The Salvaging of Civilization* (1921), H. G. Wells argues that we can no longer count on "the *certainty* of progress" (99), just as D. Elton Trueblood, in "The Sickness of Civilization" (1944), insists that we must reject those twin habitual beliefs: "the essential goodness of man" and "automatic progress" (8).[17]

To the extent that the conception of civilization as increasingly rational, healthy, and democratic is a legacy of Enlightenment thinking, the conception of it as increasingly more corrupt, diseased, and decadent is a legacy of post-Rousseauian romantic thinking. As early as 1830, for example, Coleridge speaks of civilization in terms of "disease" not "health" (quoted in Gunn 10). This equation of civilization and disease persists well into the period under consideration. For example, in Max Nordau's *Conventional Lies of Our Civilization* (1884) and *Degeneration* (1892), and in Brooks Adams's *Law of Civilization and Decay* (1896), this same metaphor of pathology creeps in. "[T]he world of civilization," Nordau writes in the former book, "is an immense hospital-ward, the air is filled with groans and lamentations" (1). Further, in *Civilisation: Its Cause and Cure*, Edward Carpenter maintains, "We find ourselves to-day in the midst of a somewhat peculiar state of society, which we call Civilisation, but which even to the most optimistic among us does not seem altogether desirable. Some of us, indeed, are inclined to think that it is a kind of disease which the various races of man have to pass through" (1). In *Is Civilization a Disease?* (1917), Stanton Coit argues that "Carpenter's indictment of civilization" is "incontrovertible" (55) and judges civilization to be "nearing its close" (46).

One year later, however, the first volume of Spengler's massive synthesis saw the light of day. Immensely popular, appropriately gloomy to fit increasing disillusionment on all sides, *The Decline of the West* codified what earlier theorists of civilization only hinted at: that civilization is categorically the "organic-logical sequel, fulfillment and finale of a culture" (31). Deploying the biological and teleological metaphors also prevalent in Spencer, Spengler, in true postromantic style, pits culture *against* civilization, arguing that the two exist in "*organic* succession," with civilization no more than "the inevitable *destiny*" of culture (31). Indeed, far from being the flowering of a culture, civilizations, for Spengler, are "a conclusion . . . death following life, rigidity following expansion, intellectual age . . . following mother earth." "They are an end," Spengler continues, "irrevocable, yet by inward necessity reached again and again" (31).

For many *entre deux guerres* Spengler's sense of impending Western decline (and cyclical rebirth) was infectious. Consider, for example, Albert Schweitzer's comment of 1923 that "it is clear now to everyone that the suicide of civilization is in progress" (*Decay* 3). Or consider Sigmund Mendelsohn's determination of three years later: "Retrogression implies also inherent forces of progression, and though civilizations and nations become extinct, the human forces eventually find new outlets and move forward to the formation of a new civilization" (xviii–xix). In 1951, E. M. Forster, also deploying Spenglerian rhetoric, writes of the imminent "signs of the progress of science and the retrogression of man" (*Two Cheers for Democracy* 304). "Civilisation has its mysterious regressions," Forster maintains, "and it seems to me that we are fated now to be in one of them, and must recognize this and behave accordingly" (46). Similarly, T. S. Eliot, writing after the close of World War II, assumes a Spenglerian position:

> We can assert with some confidence that our own period is one of
> decline; that the standards of culture are lower than they were fifty
> years ago; and that the evidences of this decline are visible in every
> department of human activity. I see no reason why the decay of culture
> should not proceed much further, and why we may not even anticipate
> a period, of some duration, of which it is possible to say that it will
> have *no* culture. Then culture will have to grow again from the soil.
> (*Notes* 17)

It is the American D. Elton Trueblood, however, who puts in no uncertain
terms precisely what many others felt but did not say: "we [now] know that
the disease of Western civilization was much further advanced than it
appeared to be" and that "it took a prophet to know that the First World
War was a revelation instead of a mere war" (11).

Trueblood's reference to Spengler's "prophecy" of the rise of "Caesarism" in the West — the rise of tyrannical dictators like Hitler, Stalin, Mussolini, and Franco — as an indication of his civilization's decline suggests
another aspect of Spenglerism embraced by those in the "retrogression"
camp: that civilization coincides not with the rise of individual freedoms, as
for Spencer, but with the rise of repression, external and internal; that
civilization, as Stanley Diamond has recently asserted, "originates in conquest abroad and repression at home" (1). As early as 1917, for example,
Stanton Coit cites Lord Cromer maintaining that "civilization begins with
the crack of the whip" (35) and argues that "civilization was the organization of man's mastery over Nature on a basis of self-interest; it was the giving only so much of wealth and power to the many as was compatible with
the retention of one's own ascendancy." "Indeed," he continues, "civilization is the incarnation of self-interest" (86–87). And Albert Schweitzer
furthers this line of reasoning: civilization is for him "twofold in its nature"
as it realizes "itself in the supremacy of reason, first, over the forces of
nature, and, secondly, over the dispositions of men" (*Decay* 36). Of course,
this equation of civilization with the renunciation of individual "instinct" or
"id" gains its fullest expression in Freud's late writings, particularly in *The
Future of an Illusion* (1927) and *Civilization and Its Discontents* (1930). In
these works, and in the works of Theodor Adorno and Christopher Lasch
discussed in later chapters, civilization is depicted as playing upon the
weaknesses of its inhabitants to maintain social order. Civilization is also
seen in these works to force its subjects into irresolvable contradictions and
to affect detrimental symptoms — particularly narcissism — of which these
subjects may not even be aware.[18]

Despite the great extent to which the Spencerians and the Spenglerians are opposed, their sharing of biological and teleological tropes to address the direction of civilization masks a common hope: that civilization, like any organism, has a life and a history which, once known and understood, can be prolonged, altered, even redeemed. Indeed, for all of this talk about the inevitability of Western development, one cannot help but wonder whether it was felt that, if the "meaning" of civilization could be ascertained, then its course, whether evolutionary or devolutionary, could be controlled. For even though both Spencer and Spengler insist that the knowledge they uncover about the "laws" of civilization cannot alter it, their caveats, precisely because formulated in the guise of biological and teleological metaphors, suggest otherwise.[19]

❊ The Will to Civilization: Nation-State or State of Mind?

To the extent that both sides of the foregoing debate view civilization to be a material, collective, technological phenomenon, another view is obscured: that civilization may be a mental, attitudinal, and individual phenomenon. As Herbert von Beckerath puts it in 1942, "civilization is not only a complex and disciplined social intercourse, but it is also individual refinement." "This relationship between society and the individual," he continues, "is one of the most important and, at this juncture, one of the most controversial problems of civilization" (8). To be sure, this "controversial" problem — the question of who or what constitutes civilization — is hotly argued throughout the period under consideration.

The majority of evolutionist and devolutionist theorists of civilization regard the object of their scrutiny to be a material and corporate structure. In *The Evolution of Civilization*, for example, Joseph McCabe argues that "since we live in social groups, and a man's actions depend upon and influence his neighbors, [civilization] is what we choose to make [life] *collectively*" (137); and John Katz, in *The Will to Civilization*, agrees. "Civilization is the greatest of all human creations," he writes. "Civilization is the unity in which all human beings are one" (340). Moreover, for many of these writers civilization aspires to universal global unity. Hector MacPherson, for example, notes that the nineteenth century saw "the greatest share in the work of nation-creation." "Out of the chaos of conflicting interests," he continues, "have been evolved the various harmonies which give to the respective nationalities a common unity" (184). And Leonard Woolf, although adhering to a vastly different world view than MacPherson, closes his *Imperialism and Civilization* (1928) with a call for "the end of imperialism, the end of conflict, and the beginning of a synthesis of civilizations" (135).

A plan for such a "synthesis of civilizations" was mapped out most painstakingly seven years earlier by H. G. Wells in *The Salvaging of Civilization: The Probable Future of Mankind*. There, in what is clearly a post–Great War effort, and in what must now strike us trite and evasive, Wells calls for "the utopia of a World State" (44) — one world nation-state with representation similar to that of the League of Nations. Speaking of "the spectacular catastrophe of the great war," Wells warns that the "easy general forward movement of human affairs which for several generations had seemed to justify the persuasion of a necessary and invincible progress towards greater powers, greater happiness, and a continual enlargement of life, has been checked violently and perhaps arrested altogether" (1). Insisting that "only one alternative" to "retrogression seems possible, and that is the conscious, systematic reconstruction of human society to avert it" (10), Wells argues for the need to produce and distribute a "Bible of civilization" in order to "re-cement our increasingly unstable civilization" (104). Recognizing the pervasive sense of a lost *religio* or "binding up" — we need to "recover again some or all of the steadfastness and dignity of the old religious life" (137) — Wells advocates the dissemination of a secular Bible urging salvation in *this* world. "It seems to me that such a Book made universally accessible, made a basis of teaching everywhere, could set the key of the whole world's thought" (133).

However, while many viewed civilization to be a corporate and material phenomenon, others believed it also to be individual and mental. Albert Schweitzer, for example, states that "the development of civilization comes about by individual men thinking out ideals which aim at the progress of the whole" and that "*civilization is progress, material and spiritual progress, on the part of individuals as of the mass*" (*Decay* 15, 35). Similarly, Leonard Woolf, writing in his provocative *Barbarians Within and Without* (1939), conceives of civilization as residing "partly in social structure and partly in individual psychology" (30): "civilization is the social order secreted by men who are civilized." "The reason," he continues, "is that civilization is a quality of societies or of individuals in their social relations" (31–32). For Woolf, therefore, "looked at from one angle" civilization "is a particular type of social organization; looked at from the other it is standards of value in social organization, judgements as to what ought to be the relation between the individual and the community" (56).

Yet there were those who felt civilization to be primarily, even exclusively, mental and individual. For example, Crozier views "the goal of civilization" to be "the *elevation and expansion of the individual*" (137), and E. M. Forster holds that "the only sound foundation for a civilisation is a sound state of mind" (*Two Cheers for Democracy* 44). In *A Theory of Civilisation* (1914), Sholto Douglas maintains that the "variant" that distinguishes the civilized from the uncivilized "is mental, rather than physical," for "brains are subject to the same evolutionary laws as the rest of our animal nature" (244). In *The New Leviathan; or, Man, Society, Civilization, and Barbarism* (1942), R. G. Collingwood goes even farther: "the will to civilization is just will," he asserts. "Civilization is the process in a community by which the various members assert themselves as will" (307). Moreover, for Collingwood, civilization is a "thing of the mind" (280), a "mental process" (299); being civilized for him means constantly striving "to convert every occasion of non-agreement into an occasion of agreement" (326).

Undoubtedly as a response to angst generated in the period between the wars — anxiety that true civilization might never be realized in the material world — the belief that civilization is a state of mind must have provided some comfort. Writing from America in 1926, for example, Hendrik Van Loon introduces an essay collection, *What Is Civilization?*, with his determination that "civilization is essentially a question of the inner spirit" and not "an accumulation of material things," not "wealth," not "military glory or the possession of vast colonial domains." "In short," he holds, "all these many things which to the average citizen spell c-i-v-i-l-i-z-a-t-i-o-n mean just about as much as an old derby on the head of a Congo savage or a phonograph in a Greenland igloo" (6–7). As Van Loon's rhetoric makes clear, critiques of imperialism and materialism do not necessarily preclude racism and national chauvinism. As late as 1942, Herbert von Beckerath argues that "civilized society and the higher forms of individual and social existence are made possible by the spiritual nature of man." "Civilization," he continues, "is not only a complex and disciplined social intercourse, but it is also individual refinement" (8).

In *Civilization* (1928), Clive Bell (1881–1964) provides the most systematic and extended conception yet of civilization as a state of mind, as an "artificial" construction of sensibility. For Bell, civilization requires more than government acquiescence: "there must be the will." "This will to civilization," he continues, "may be nothing more than the desire for pleasure refined and intellectualized" (175). True to his Bloomsbury roots in Matthew Arnold's, Walter Pater's, and G. E. Moore's writings,[20] and to his Bloomsburyite fetishizing of individuality, Bell here speaks of civilization as "a means to good states of mind" (17) and as "an attitude toward life"

(121). Civilization, Bell continues, "must be the product of civilized individuals," and "any attempt to understand the nature of the thing or account for its existence leads inevitably and directly to human beings who create and maintain it" (19). "It is in the mind of man," he asserts, "that we must seek the cause and origin of civilization" (122). This is because civilization, for Bell, "is the flavour given to the self-expression of an age or society by a mental attitude: it is the colour given to social manifestations by a peculiar and prevailing point of view" (121). Moreover, "the state cannot be an end in itself: it can be no more than a means to those good states of mind which alone are good as ends, and are to be found only in individuals" (79).

Bell takes this notion of civilization as "individual" and "mental" phenomenon one step farther. Adumbrating Ortega's statement of a year later in *The Revolt of the Masses* that "[c]ivilization is artificial and requires an artist or an artisan" (76), Bell maintains that "civilization is artificial" (53) and that "civilized man is made not born: he is artificial; he is unnatural. Consciously and deliberately he forms himself with a view to possessing and enjoying the best and subtlest; and yet in another sense, all sophisticated though he be, he is the least distorted of human beings" (134). Bell's sense that the will to civilization ultimately involves a state of mind, and not a state of the state, raises the question of whether or not the discourse of civilization — the popular invocation of the need to "protect" and "preserve" civilization[21] — is in fact a legitimate call to arms or instead a propaganda ploy in the service of maintaining war, imperialism, and a system of class stratification.

❋ The Rhetoric of Civilization: Preservation or Propaganda?

In *Civilization* Clive Bell formulates the question around which a third matrix of the discourse of civilization may be constructed: the question of whether civilization needs defending or whether, to borrow from Leonard Woolf, the "delusions of the civilized" are in fact "propaganda" tools by which to mobilize a fighting force, justify colonization, and maintain present class structures. In other words, to what extent is the cry to defend the civilization of this period a marketing ploy on the part of those seeking to maintain the status quo? Bell's articulation of this problem with respect to nationalism and war clearly shows where he stands.

> Since from August 1914 to November 1918 Great Britain and her Allies were fighting for Civilization it cannot, I suppose, be impertinent to enquire what precisely civilization may be. "Liberty" and

"Justice" have always been reckoned expensive words, but that "Civilization" could cost as much as I forget how many millions a day came as
a surprise to many thoughtful taxpayers. The story of this word's rise
to the highest place amongst British war aims is so curious that, even
were it less relevant, I should be tempted to tell it. (13)

Given that "civilization" was also a leading rationale for colonization and
socioeconomic stratification, it is worth exploring both sides of the debate,
from John Dewey's sense that "civilization" is used divisively — "civilization
is uncivil because human beings are divided into non-communicating sects,
races, nations, classes and cliques" (*Art as Experience* 336) — to von Beckerath's sense that it is a legitimate means by which to manipulate the masses:

> It is the function of the masses to carry on the humdrum routine of
> social human life according to tradition and habit or according to the
> example and command of the leading groups, and to give to civiliza-
> tion their weight and their defensive power. In this, their unreflective
> emotional identification with the fundamental tenets and institutions
> of their respective culture is indispensable. (22)

By exploring the discourse of civilization with respect to war, imperialism,
and wealth, a further dimension of this term's currency will be revealed.

Of those who believe that "the enterprise of Civilization" justifies war,
Albert V. Fowler and R. G. Collingwood are most unequivocal. Fowler
writes that "Mr. Toynbee realizes that if our society is unable to spiritualize
its aggressive tendencies, it is better for it to practice the arts of war in the
flesh rather than leave its house swept and empty for the invasion of even
worse devils" (vi). And Collingwood, after making a careful philosophic
distinction between "Civilization" and "Barbarism," deems the Germans of
the Nazi era to be barbarians (*New Leviathan* 375–87) and wonders "why
barbarists have always in the end been beaten." "The only valid reason," he
concludes, "would be that you saw through the fallacy they involve" (386–
87).

Equally pervasive, however, were those voices which, as Terry Eagleton
puts it, called English civilization "into radical question" (*Exiles and Emigrés*
15). For while many viewed the Great War to be "a struggle of civilization
against its successor" (Coit 97), many others viewed the effort to protect
civilization via war to be a perverted and perverting ploy. H. G. Wells, for
example, complains of the educational system, "the British learn nothing
but the glories of Britain and the British Empire." "Every country in
Europe is its own *Sinn Fein*," he continues, "cultivating that ugly and silly
obsession of 'ourselves alone.'" This policy, Wells concludes, "is the sure

guide to conflict and disaster, to want, misery, violence, degradation and death" (74). Similarly, Trueblood argues that, since "we are not free from the basic trouble ourselves," the fact that we are in a war should not allow us to pretend that the world can be divided "neatly into two camps, ourselves and our enemies" (12). And Leonard Woolf, in *Barbarians Within and Without*, deems war itself to be the "supreme barbarism" (10) and warns that "at almost every stage of European history many people have always and usually quite wrongly thought that the world — their world — was just on the point of coming to an end, that barbarism was breaking in and that civilization was on the point of being destroyed" (25).

Woolf's lament over this "myth of catastrophe" is precisely what Schweitzer addresses when he seeks to dissociate the "severe crisis" of "our civilization" from the war. For the war, he writes, "with everything connected with it, is only a phenomenon of the condition of uncivilization in which we find ourselves" (*Ethics* 1). Holding that "during the war the control of thought was made complete" and that "propaganda definitely took the place of truth" (*Decay* 32), Schweitzer, like Wells, decries the fact that "nationality was raised to the level of a valuable ideal of civilization" (*Decay* 49). Deeming the concept of a "national civilization" to be "an unhealthy phenomenon," Schweitzer argues that "modern nations *seek markets for their civilization, as they do for their manufactures*" and that "national civilization, therefore, *is matter for propaganda and for export*" (*Decay* 53, 55; my emphasis). In *Civilization* Clive Bell too maintains that civilization is "marketed":

> "You are fighting for civilization," cried the wisest and best of those leaders who led us into war, and the very soldiers took up the cry, "Join up, for civilization's sake." Startled by this sudden enthusiasm for an abstraction in which till then politicians and recruiting sergeants had manifested little or no interest, I, in my turn, began to cry: "And what is civilization?" I did not cry aloud, be sure: at that time, for crying things of that sort aloud, one was sent to prison. But now that it's no longer criminal, not unpatriotic even, to ask questions, I intend to enquire what this thing is for which we fought and for which we pay. I propose to investigate the nature of our leading war-aim. (13)

Calling nationalism a "disease" and an "enemy to civility" (84), Bell insists that "a highly civilized person can never unquestioningly accept the ethics of patriotism" (84, 83).

Imperialism was also a rallying point for preserving and, moreover, "spreading" civilization. "The scramble in China, the race for territory in

South Africa, the expansion of Britain in Egypt," Hector MacPherson asks in 1900, "what are all these but evidence of the fact that civilization is beginning to overflow its old boundaries, and is becoming world-wide in its aspirations?" (185). And Raoul Allier warns of the "propaganda" within Europe itself which might dissuade the "savages" in colonized lands from believing that good turns are being done them by the colonizers. The duty of the colonizer (Allier quotes Colonial Minister Albert Sarrout in a talk of 1923) "is at the same time to take in hand the incapable native and make him useful, to train him physically and morally, to protect him from himself and the miseries that assail him, in short to educate him and above all to teach him to become our ally in the management, the working and the profits of the common property" (266). Likewise, as late as 1948 Eric Fischer asserts that "history teaches us" that "there is a way out for civilizations to avoid the final catastrophe": "their transplantation to new, to colonial soil" (197).

Of course, the use of civilization to justify imperialism also had its opponents. If the torch blinded most people, it was held high enough by a few to enable sight. Writing in 1889, for example, Edward Carpenter insists that civilization today "is no longer isolated, as in the ancient worlds in surrounding floods of savagery and barbarism, but it practically covers the globe, and the outlying savagery is so feeble as not possibly to be a menace to it" (48). And Leonard Woolf, in *Imperialism and Civilization* (1928), holds that "the most important aspect of imperialism is the conflict of civilizations" (28). More recently, Stanley Diamond advances the claim that civilization "has always had to be imposed, not as a psychodynamic necessity or a repressive condition of evolved social life, as Freud supposed, and not only in terms of the State's power securing itself against its own subjects, but also with reference to the barbarian or primitive peoples who moved on the frontiers" (8). Reminiscent of Orwell's *1984*, Diamond argues that, "as civilization spreads and deepens, it is ultimately man's self, his species being, which is imperialized" (10), and that, "as civilization evolves, the central authority permits less, commands more; and states grow more, not less, totalitarian" (17). For Diamond, the will to imperialize has little to do with civilization and everything to do with power: "given the opportunity and driven by certain needs," he writes, "some men will compound their profit and seek an illusory freedom, based on the exercise of power, at the expense of others" (18).

Yet the efforts to maintain civilization were directed not only against "external barbarians" with whom Britain fought and whom it colonized but against those *within* civilization impatient with the reigning social order.

Indeed, both Bell's *Civilization* (1928) and T. S. Eliot's *Notes towards the Definition of Culture* (1948) possess the secret agenda of justifying why, in order to make a true civilization, some people must have considerably more wealth and power than others.

In *Civilization*, Bell's argument takes on a syllogistic ring. Writing that "to be completely civilized, to experience the most intense and exquisite states of mind, manifestly a man must have security and leisure" and that, "unluckily, material security, leisure, and liberty all cost money; and ultimately money is to be obtained only by productive labor" (147), Bell reasons that

> Civilization requires the existence of a leisured class, and a leisured class requires the existence of slaves — of people, I mean, who give some part of their surplus time and energy to the support of others. If you feel that such inequality is intolerable, have the courage to admit that you can dispense with civilization and that equality, not good, is what you want. Complete human equality is compatible only with complete savagery. (146)

Believing, moreover, that "on inequality all civilizations have stood" (149), Bell defends his position with the disclaimer that "I have no love of despotism" but "I am surprised at the frivolity of those earnest people who, without a moment's reflection, assume that it cannot be good as a means." "If despotism and its correlative slavery" are "the means to the . . . maximum of good states of mind," he continues, "I should suppose only bad men would be averse from employing them" (160–61).

Likewise, in *Notes towards the Definition of Culture*, T. S. Eliot maintains that "one important condition for culture" (synonymous for him with "civilization") is "the persistence of social classes" (13). In a chapter entitled "The Class and the Elite," Eliot defines his belief in the need for the "hereditary transmission of culture" (13) based on the maintenance of an elite class. "What is important is a structure of society in which there will be, from 'top' to 'bottom,' a continuous graduation of cultural levels: it is important to remember that we should not consider the upper levels as possessing *more* culture than the lower, but as representing a more conscious culture and a greater specialisation of culture." "I incline to believe," Eliot continues, differing from Bell, "that no true democracy can maintain itself unless it contains these different levels of culture" (47).

On the other hand, many insisted that true civilization would be diminished if it maintained an inegalitarian class structure. In *The New Leviathan* (1942), for example, Collingwood devotes a chapter, "Civilization and

Wealth," to arguing that "the only motive for which men accumulate wealth [should be] in order to pursue civilization": "to accumulate wealth in order to create by its means a contrast between rich and poor is to use it for the destruction of civilization, or the pursuit of barbarism" (325). Because, for Collingwood, "civilization implies a set of rules so determining the conduct of members of a given community that each refrains to some extent" from "the use of force primarily in his dealings with other members of that community," therefore "the existence of the contrast between rich and poor is an offense against the ideal of civility, for it involves the constant use of one kind of force by the rich in all their dealings with the poor" (324). Here Collingwood's argument against a grossly inegalitarian civilization scarcely masks his quiet sanctioning of a mildly inegalitarian one.

More strongly, and from a socialist position, Leonard Woolf, in *Barbarians Within and Without* (1939), deems the class structure of Western civilization itself to be "barbarian" (9). In a chapter entitled "Anatomy of Civilization," Woolf explores the "conflict and dilemma at the very heart of civilization": that it has always "begun in a class society and has at first been a privilege of a small upper class" (67). "Hence Civilization," for Woolf, "always starts with this conflict between the class structure of society and its own fundamental principles and ideals; it is always faced with the dilemma of either destroying the class privileges and class structure or of destroying itself by abandoning its aims and standards of value" (68). Writing on the eve of the Second World War, Woolf considers not only the contradictory beginnings and development of civilization but its uncertain future as well.

A final issue deserving brief treatment is suggested by the three nodal points in the discourse of civilization I have been exploring: that conceptions of "uncivilization" are every bit as divided and self-contradictory as those of "civilization" during this period. Indeed, at least two extremely different notions of uncivilization gained wide currency around 1939: a sense of it as threateningly "barbarian" and a sense of it as inspiringly "primitive." To my knowledge this savagery/barbarism distinction was first articulated by R. G. Collingwood: "I distinguish two ways of being uncivilized. I call them savagery and barbarism, and distinguish them as follows. Savagery is a negative idea. It means not being civilized, and that is all. . . . By barbarism I mean hostility towards civilization; the effort, conscious or unconscious, to become less civilized than you are" (*New Leviathan* 342). Although Collingwood reserves the appellation "barbarian" for such "undesirables" as the Saracens, the Albigenses, the Turks, and the Nazi Germans, all of whom have "from time to time pitted themselves against European civilization" (350), he uses "savage" nonpejoratively to characterize any group that has yet to develop to the point of civilization.

Others, however, following the romantic conception of the Noble Savage, were to invest the terms "primitive" and "savage" with distinctly positive connotations. In Wilkins's play *Civilization*, for example, Hercule remembers, with irony, his "barbarian days" when he used to speak "the truth," when he

> Wrong'd not my neighbor . . .
> . . . held a friend to be a gift,
> Precious as stars dropt down from heaven: bowed
> Before the works of God: beheld in them
> His presence, palpable, as at an altar:
> And worshipp'd heaven at the mountain's foot. (58)

And Edward Carpenter, in *Civilisation: Its Cause and Cure*, maintains that "we must allow [the barbarian] superiority in some directions" (6) and that "if Civilisation be not renovated by the influx of external savagery its own inherent flaws will destroy society all the sooner" (48). Raoul Allier, in *The Mind of the Savage*, does not go as far as Carpenter, who believes that primitives provide the civilized with a means of connecting up once again with nature; yet he does "feel justified in asserting [like Conrad's Marlow] that, between uncivilized man and ourselves there exists, not an irreducible difference but a fundamental identity" (211). Although there is little consensus, then, as to precisely what uncivilization is, it is clear that it is primarily used for purposes of Western self-identification and self-justification: whatever uncivilization may be, it is certainly "other" and "lesser" than what we are. As one writer, missing his own irony, insists in 1927, "nothing is clearer . . . than that we are civilized" (Storck 49). And another, writing eleven years later, insists that "England, with her Protestant, empiricist, and revolutionary traditions is the ideal leader of the West," that "English culture and the English outlook still dominate the world," and that "Englishmen have won their great position in the world because they have been imbued with the spirit of the pioneer" (Katz 338–39).[22]

Given the pervasiveness, importance, and variety of this discourse of civilization between the turn of the century and the close of World War II — regardless of how banal or trite it may appear to us now — it comes as little surprise that the norm-challenging literature of Conrad, Lawrence, Joyce, Woolf, and Lowry would have engaged, represented, and questioned it. Before exploring this fiction's appropriation of the discourse of civilization, however, the issue of how literature engages, represents, and questions this cultural discourse is in need of scrutiny. How might we characterize the interrelation of literary text and cultural context? How might we describe the dialogic interaction of modernist fiction and the discourse of civilization? How might we legitimately view the modern novel as a critique of civilization?

✴ Modernist Fiction and Cultural Discourse

In a 1925 essay, "Britain's Place in Western Civilisation," F. S. Marvin writes: "reviewing historically the growth of Great Britain and her place in Western civilisation, we can and ought to maintain, without national arrogance, that the principles on which our own country and her sister nations have risen to peaceful power are those on which the world community . . . must proceed, if the same security, political freedom, and peaceful alliance are to be maintained" (183). What was, in 1925, a credible comment must now strike us, one world war later and the British Empire having disintegrated, as ironic at best — less an accurate measure of circumstances than an example of the discourse of civilization, an expression of how Britain viewed itself and its destiny. To be sure, Marvin's views, and the many others presented above, today are of interest less for their credibility than for reflecting the ongoing conversation about civilization, for contributing to a sense of what civilization meant and how it functioned, and for exposing various conflicting interests manifested in this discourse of civilization. Yet by what means might we simultaneously represent this discourse of civilization — display its meaning in its own time while not abandoning its connection to our own — and reveal the extent to which the literature of Conrad, Lawrence, Joyce, Woolf, and Lowry engages it in a dialogue? In what way might we explore the fictional appropriation of this cultural discourse, by which these attempts to persuade an audience are exposed to be value-laden rather than "scientifically neutral," self-interested rather than "selflessly humane"? And how, given the presumably "disengaged" posture of modernist literature, might we demonstrate this literature's dialogic interaction with this frequently banal discourse of civilization?

Indeed, for years it has been a truism that high literary modernism is properly viewed as eschewing the language of the world for the language of art; that instead of *representing* the world this art *competes* with it, seeking to "replace" a debased external world with an autotelic literary one, a self-enclosed, self-referential linguistic universe that can realize a perfection and order unavailable outside of it.[23] According to this scenario, high modernist poetics views literary language as not only different in *degree* from cultural rhetoric (more ordered and more beautiful, for example) but different in *kind* as well: unlike the interested and ephemeral language of the "real world," literary language is uninterested and permanent (because existing "for the art," because nonreferential).

In *Modern Poetry and the Idea of Language*, Gerald Bruns articulates the two preeminent postromantic conceptions of literary language as "Orphic" ("the speech of the world") and "hermetic" ("the speech of language"). Named for Orpheus — "the primordial singer whose sphere of activity is governed by a mythical or ideal unity of word and being, and whose power extends therefore beyond the formation of a work toward the creation of the world" — the Orphic conception views literary language "as the ground of all signification — as an expressive movement which 'objectifies' a world for man." By contrast, the hermetic conception views literary language as "pure expressiveness" in which "a writer's use of language deviates sufficiently from the structures of ordinary experience to displace or arrest the function of signification." In this second instance,

> the direction of the poet's activity is toward the literary work as such, that is, the work as a self-contained linguistic structure (the ideal or absolute form of which would be Flaubert's imaginary "book about nothing, a book dependent on nothing external, which would be held together by the strength of its style, just as the earth, suspended in the void, depends on nothing external for its support; a book which would have almost no subject, or at least in which the subject would be almost invisible"). (1)[24]

As Bruns admits, however, both conceptions of literary language place "a value upon the act of speech precisely to the extent that it frees itself from the discourse of everyday life," both "oppose language to the formation of 'mere' meaning" (232). In both cases, then, we are encouraged to view literary and cultural discourse as worlds apart, as ontologically distinct, as language systems that can have little to do with one another. Moreover, such a "schism" between text and context has been all the more encouraged by mainstream trends in literary analysis — from Russian formalism to American new criticism, from structuralism to certain forms of deconstruction — which have been fascinated with intratextual patterns of meaning and symbolic architectures (or breakdowns thereof).

In demonstrating the dialogic interaction of literary and cultural discourse, the theories of Mikhail Bakhtin, Terry Eagleton, and Clifford

Geertz are particularly useful. Collectively, these theories may be seen as constituting a "tradition" in thinking about the relationship of text and context which evades the limitations of aesthetic formalism, and which enables us to see how the extraliterary discourse of civilization informs the fictional texts produced and consumed in its midst. Moreover, all three theorists posit a theory of "reference," maintaining that all literature represents, appropriates, and transforms — as well as is transformed by — the larger social languages and interests at play. Finally, all of them eschew "textualism" in favor of "materialism," insisting that operative within language is a nonlinguistic cultural process, a nexus of meanings and material power relationships by which people live and die.[25] However, rather than rehearse their already influential ideas, or simply invoke them as authorities, I wish instead to weave a course through particular aspects of their thought which, in the relations I reveal — hermeneutic, dialogic, and ideological — collectively comprise the theoretical assumptions of this project and demonstrate the relevance of the discourse of civilization to modern British fiction.

The approach to literature and culture that I advocate here comports in some respects with recent trends in the new historicism and the sociology of literature (both legacies of Marxist criticism) but eschews identification with either one.[26] However, like these trends, my study concerns itself with the relationship of sociocultural self-reflections and literary texts, with the "negotiation" or "circulation" of meaning between text and informing context. Like these trends, too, this study is "interdisciplinary" in thrust, promoting a "blurring of genres," as Geertz calls it, an erosion of the rigid and limiting boundaries that for years have stood between literary text and extraliterary context.[27] Because I view literary texts to be not only aesthetic artifacts that conform to and/or revolutionize earlier conventions of literary form but social artifacts as well — artifacts of culture that are written (whether the author wills it or not) in dialogue with numerous other (not necessarily literary) contexts of the period — I am more comfortable with the less prescriptive appellation "cultural criticism" to characterize the present work, as a rubric that allows for more investigative openness and theoretical eclecticism.

The work of Mikhail Bakhtin is of particular relevance here. In 1979 one critic lamented that with few exceptions Bakhtin's "works have been treated simply as exercises in 'practical criticism,' little or no attempt having been made to quarry them for their theoretical yield" (Tony Bennett 97). Bakhtin's standing has risen sharply since then, and Tzvetan Todorov's estimation that he is "the greatest theoretician of literature in the twentieth century" (ix), for example, today is taken for granted by many. A quirky mixture of Russian formalism and Marxism that challenges the conclusions and usefulness of Saussure's structural linguistics (viewed by Bakhtin as the most baleful influence in textual criticism), Bakhtin's theory undermines the separation of "autotelic literary" from "worldly practical" language, indicating the great degree to which reality, as E. H. Gombrich has maintained, can only be perceived generically, through preconceived conventions. Rather than drawing on Bakhtin's two cardinal and well-known notions of "Carnivalization" (from the Rabelais book) and "Polyphony" (from the Dostoyevsky book), however, I will draw on his less discussed notion of the dialogic interaction of text and culture, particularly between the novel and other genres of discourse. "After all," Bakhtin writes, "the boundaries between fiction and nonfiction, between literature and non-literature and so forth are not laid up in heaven." "Every specific situation," he continues, "is historical" ("Epic and Novel" 33).

One middle and one late essay of Bakhtin's are of particular interest in this connection. In "Discourse in the Novel" (1934–35) Bakhtin argues that, because "discourse lives, as it were, beyond itself, in a living impulse toward the object [it represents]," each "word tastes of the context and contexts in which it has lived its socially charged life; all words and forms are populated by intentions" such that "contextual overtones" are "inevitable in the word" (292–93). Given this anti-Saussurean (and undeconstructive) understanding of language,[28] Bakhtin goes on to argue that the novel "permits the incorporation of various genres, both artistic" and "extra-artistic (everyday, rhetorical, scholarly, religious genres and others)." "In principle," he continues, "any genre could be included in the construction of the novel" (320–21). And hence, for him, prose fiction presumes "a deliberate feeling for the historical and social concreteness of living discourse, as well as its relativity, a feeling for its participation in historical becoming and in social struggle; it deals with discourse that is still warm from that struggle and hostility, as yet unresolved and still fraught with hostile intentions and accents" (331). In short, for Bakhtin, novelistic language de facto absorbs, partakes of, questions, and parodies cultural discourse.

In his late essay "Response to a Question from the *Novy Mir* Editorial Staff" (1970), Bakhtin succinctly articulates what might be called a cultural hermeneutics. Calling for a "deeper study of the inseparable link between the literature and culture of the epoch" (3), Bakhtin maintains that

> literary scholarship should establish closer links with the history of culture. Literature is an inseparable part of culture and it cannot be

understood outside the total context of the entire culture of a given epoch. . . . In our enthusiasm for [scholarly] specification we have ignored questions of the interconnection and interdependence of various areas of culture; we have frequently forgotten that the boundaries of these areas are not absolute, that in various epochs they have been drawn in various ways; and we have not taken into account that the most intense and productive life of culture takes place on the boundaries of its individual areas and not in places where these areas have become enclosed in their own specificity. (2)

It is precisely on this "boundary" between the "discourse of civilization" and its literary portrayal and evaluation that my inquiry is located. Bakhtin closes his essay by stating, "It is only in the eyes of *another* culture that foreign culture reveals itself fully and profoundly." "A meaning only reveals its depths once it has encountered and come into contact with another, foreign meaning: they engage in a kind of dialogue which surmounts the closedness and one-sidedness of these particular meanings, these cultures" (7). It is this hermeneutic and dialogic impulse which is at the heart of the present study: to indulge contemporary concerns in past debates as well as to put prose fiction and cultural discourse in dialogue — indeed, to demonstrate the fiction's appropriation and transformation of such discourse — in order to reveal aspects of the literature that we have often overlooked.[29]

Whereas this "philosophical anthropologist" suggests a cultural poetics for this project, a means of linking literary discourse with the discourse of civilization without succumbing to the naive realism of a reflector model of literary representation, Terry Eagleton suggests for it a conception of ideology and power, of "the ways in which what we say and believe connects with the power-structure and power-relations of the society we live in" (*Literary Theory* 14). Unlike Bakhtin, who views ideology as little more than an "idea system" (similar to a Weltanschauung), Eagleton views ideology as a "practical means of discriminating between antagonisms which we judge for the present of more than purely local or causal significance, and those which for the present we do not" ("Ideology and Scholarship" 115). Moreover, Eagleton defines ideology as "a set of discourses which wrestle over interests which are in some way relevant to the maintenance and interrogation of power structures central to a whole form of social and historical life" ("Ideology and Scholarship" 116). Like Bakhtin's *Novy Mir* essay, Eagleton's "Ideology and Scholarship" is no less than a call to arms for literary scholars: "it surely remains the case that until literary scholarship once again becomes 'ideological,' in the nonpejorative sense of the word, it will remain shuttled between ineffectual humanism and an indefensible hermeticism. Unless the literary institution discovers a need for 'society,' it might quickly discover that society has little need for it" (125).[30]

Clifford Geertz provides a concrete way of bringing "society" back into play within the "literary institution" and provides a means of talking about literature in terms that avoid the abstract formalism — for Eagleton the "hermeticism" — of the past years. If Eagleton offers us a critical theory, Geertz offers us a critical practice.

In "Art as a Cultural System" Geertz complains of our obsession with talking about art in "craft terms" — the belief "that technical talk about art, however developed, is sufficient to a complete understanding of it" (96). "[T]he modern move toward aesthetic formalism," Geertz writes, "best represented right now by structuralism, and by those varieties of semiotics which seek to follow its lead, is but an attempt to generalize this approach into a comprehensive one, to create a technical language capable of representing the internal relations of myths, poems, dances, or melodies in abstract" terms (95). Maintaining, with Bakhtin, that "one can no more understand aesthetic objects as concatenations of pure form than one can understand speech as a parade of syntactic variations, or myth as a set of structural transformations" (98), Geertz seeks to talk about art in terms and concepts that "derive from cultural concerns art may serve, or reflect, or challenge, or describe, but does not itself create" (96).

Yet, how can we construct a representation of the discourse of civilization that the fictions of Conrad, Lawrence, Joyce, Woolf, and Lowry may be seen to serve, reflect, challenge, and describe? In "Thick Description: Toward an Interpretive Theory of Culture," Geertz provides an answer and defines his approach as ethnographic, as one of "sorting out the structures of signification" under consideration and "determining their social ground and import" (9). For Geertz, thick description is therefore an understanding of interpretation: the attempt to grasp and render a culture's "multiplicity of complex conceptual structures, many of them superimposed upon or knotted into one another, which are at once strange, irregular, and inexplicit" (10). "Cultural analysis," he writes, is "guessing at meanings, assessing the guesses, and drawing explanatory conclusions from the better guesses, not discovering the Continent of Meaning and mapping out its bodiless landscape" (20). Moreover, "culture is not a power, something to which social events, behaviors, institutions, or processes can be causally attributed; it is a context, something within which they can be intelligibly — that is, thickly — described" (14).[31]

It is in this sense that I have attempted to interpret the discourse of civilization as a context within which the texts of Conrad, Lawrence, Joyce,

Woolf, and Lowry mean and function and with which they engage in a dialogue.[32] As Geertz writes, "a good interpretation of anything" takes us "into the heart of that of which it is the interpretation." "When it does not do that," he continues, "but leads us instead somewhere else — into an admiration of its own elegance, of its author's cleverness . . . — it may have its intrinsic charms; but it is something else than what the task at hand" calls for ("Thick Description" 18). My present task is to explore the ways in which representative works of British fictional modernism absorb the discourse of civilization even as they assault it, appropriate this cultural discourse even as they transform it.

To this end, this book explores literary responses to various theories (or systematic conceptualizations) and practices (or material activities) of civilization. The first aspect is founded on the view expressed in Gerald Graff's summary of the lessons of recent criticism: "that no text is an island, that every work of literature is a rejoinder in a conversation or dialogue that it presupposes but may or may not mention explicitly" (10). One such implicit dialogue these modernist novels engage in is with works — by Herbert Spencer, Clive Bell, and Oswald Spengler — in the "theory of civilization." In *A Theory of Civilisation* (1914), Sholto Douglas outlines his rationale for attempting systematically to conceptualize civilization's "laws." "It seems," he writes, "most essential to find out upon what general principle civilisation has been evolved." "Such a principle must exist," he continues, "if only we can detect it, because all Nature works under definite laws which cannot be broken," and civilization "will continue to be evolved upon the same principle as long as humanity possesses any kind of culture that can be called civilisation" (238). It is this belief that reason can apprehend "civilization's laws" that motivates the works of Spencer, Bell, and Spengler, and it is precisely this belief that the fictions to be considered here throw into question.

In Chapter 2, " 'Rebarbarizing Civilization': Conrad's African Fiction and Spencerian Sociology," for example, I examine the appropriation and subversion of Herbert Spencer's influential "typology of Civilization" in Conrad's "Outpost of Progress" and *Heart of Darkness*. I argue that these fictions invoke Spencer's crucial opposition of "militant" and "industrial" society, yet that they ultimately undermine Spencer's progressivist theory by expunging the difference between these oppositions. This is accomplished by showing how, in Europe's colonization of Africa, militancy and industrialism are mutually reinforcing tendencies rather than mutually exclusive ones, and that Spencer's celebration of civilization and progress ultimately works to justify imperialism as it obscures the existence of a "military-industrial complex." *Lord Jim* is also examined briefly as it provides interesting alternatives to and modified examples of Conrad's intersection with Spencerian ideas.

Similarly, Chapter 4, "Civilization in Post–Great War Bloomsbury: Woolf's 'Twenties' Novels and Bell's *Civilization* and *On British Freedom*," explores the ways in which Woolf's *Mrs. Dalloway* and *To the Lighthouse* invoke and parody Clive Bell's theory of civilization. While *Mrs. Dalloway* represents approvingly Bell's notion in *On British Freedom* that censorship poses a grave threat to civilization, *To the Lighthouse* and *Mrs. Dalloway* subvert Bell's notions, in *Civilization*, of the appropriate roles of women and class divisions in civilization. That Woolf and Bell were friends (and relatives by marriage) who shared the Bloomsbury tendency to view civilization as individual and mental rather than collective and material, and that Bell dedicates his *Civilization* to Woolf herself, makes this textual dialogue even more provocative than it might otherwise be.

And Chapter 6, "The Sense of an Ending: Spenglerian *Decline* and the Mexican Novels of Lawrence and Lowry," examines the shaping influence of Spengler's popular theory of the inevitable decline of civilizations on Lawrence's *Plumed Serpent* and Lowry's *Under the Volcano*. While Spengler's, Lawrence's, and Lowry's texts all depict Western civilization as "Faustian" for its decadence and corruption, *The Plumed Serpent* envisions an escape from civilized sterility in the guise of mythic rebirth, and *Under the Volcano* succumbs to Spenglerian pessimism and can only "aestheticize" Western decline, turn it into poetry.

In his engaging study of propaganda and fiction between 1914 and 1933, *The Great War of Words*, Peter Buitenhuis concludes, "it is probably significant that those [writers] who have survived the test of time" are "those who subscribed least to the propaganda myth of the Great War" (180). By analogy, I would argue that Conrad, Lawrence, Joyce, Woolf, and Lowry are among the novelists who subscribed to least, and showed up most, the "propaganda myth" of civilization. Along these lines, the remaining three chapters of this book explore modernist British fiction less for its intersections with popular theories of civilization than for the means by which it depicts and challenges various practices of civilization. Whether in the case of Conrad's *Heart of Darkness* which represents civilization as built upon self-contradictory and self-deceiving rhetoric, *The Secret Agent* which depicts it as a deadly game, Joyce's *Dubliners* and *Ulysses* which represent civilization as paralyzed and discontented, or Lowry's *Under the Volcano* and *Ultramarine* which depict it as thoroughly narcissistic, the great extent to which such "objective portraits" of civilization are in fact "subjective interpretations" of it cannot be overemphasized.

In Chapter 3, "The London Fog: Civilization as Rhetoric and Game in Conrad," for example, I argue that *Heart of Darkness* and *The Secret Agent* together reveal a major tension in Conrad's representation of civilization. While *Heart of Darkness* deconstructs the very language by which the West claims moral and intellectual superiority over the non-West, *The Secret Agent* reconstructs civilization as a game one either masters or loses, thrives or perishes by, but which in any case cannot be escaped. Moreover, both works focus on London — *The Secret Agent* at its very center and *Heart of Darkness* at its periphery (in the novella London is the "gloom to the west" in view of all aboard the *Nellie*).

Similarly, Chapter 5, "Discontent and Its Civilization: Rereading Joyce's 'Paralyzed' Dubliner," explores the psychosocial condition of Joyce's Dubliners within the context of late-Freudian and Frankfurt School ideas linking narcissism, civilization, and the social determination of subjectivity. I argue that these ideas provide the seeds for a new understanding of Joyce's characters in *Dubliners* and *Ulysses* in terms of culturally encouraged narcissism and anti-Semitism — both of which keep a people without hope from comprehending, much less altering, the inequalities they face with respect to wealth, power, and social opportunity. Joyce's characters mentally rewrite their lives — thanks to forms of thinking afforded them by the popular culture industry — to obscure a reality otherwise unbearable. Civilization takes its toll on Joyce's subjects to the extent that even narcotics as potent as narcissism and anti-Semitism cannot alleviate their feelings of discontent. It can only induce a paralysis of thought and action that renders them "Dubliners."

And Chapter 7, "The Subject of Civilization: Narcissism as Disease in Lowry's Early Fiction," uses concepts from psychoanalysis and cultural criticism to reveal the great extent to which civilization is represented in *Ultramarine* and *Under the Volcano* as narcissistically diseased — as helplessly, even fatally, enamored of its own distorted reflection.[33] Further, the chapter implicitly makes the case for including *Under the Volcano* in the literary canon on the grounds that this novel enacts those most sophisticated forms of sociopsychological criticism that we rightly laud in works by the canonical figures considered here.

The balance of this study, then, is devoted to readings of modern British fiction's engagement with the civilization debate.[34] If this study at times appears to be more a collection of interrelated essays than one sustained thesis, it is because I have resisted the temptation to force a unity in the fictional responses to the civilization debate, just as I have resisted the temptation to impose a single method by which to explore all of the fiction in question. Although it is clear that these fictions do not uniformly refer to the same "civilization" — just as the discourse of civilization discussed above comes to no single consensus as to what this phenomenon is or should be — the critiques enacted by these fictions do speak to one another, attesting to the coherence of the debate if not to its "resolutions." What is clear is that the various perspectives reflected in this fiction amount to a representation of civilization which is less a realm that can be delineated or defined than a set of collective problems and contradictions, memories and desires. It is to the literary articulations of these various problems and contradictions, memories and desires, that I now turn.

2

"Rebarbarizing Civilization": Conrad's African Fiction and Spencerian Sociology

Evidently, therefore, the conquest of one people over another has been, in the main, the conquest of the social man over the anti-social man; or, strictly speaking, of the more adapted over the less adapted. — Spencer, SOCIAL STATICS

The conquest of the earth, which mostly means the taking it away from those who have a different complexion or slightly flatter noses than ourselves, is not a pretty thing when you look at it too much. — Marlow, in Conrad, HEART OF DARKNESS

The text lives only by coming into contact with another text (with context). Only at the point of this contact between texts does a light flash, illuminating both the posterior and anterior, joining a given text to a dialogue. — Bakhtin, "Toward a Methodology for the Human Sciences"

✳ Conrad and Spencer at the Fin de Siècle

One would have difficulty imagining a writer more important to his own day, yet more out of currency in our own, than Herbert Spencer (1820–1903). Although Charles Darwin is typically viewed as the revolutionary scientist of late-Victorian thought, it is nevertheless Spencer who first posits a process of cosmic evolution involving the "survival of the fittest"; and it is Spencer who provides, in Leo J. Henkin's words, "the ablest and most influential development of the argument from evolution to progress" (198). In *History of the Idea of Progress* Robert Nisbet maintains that, "without question, Herbert Spencer is the supreme embodiment in the late nineteenth century of both liberal individualism and the idea of progress." "It is impossible," he continues, "to think of any single name more deeply respected . . . and more influential, in a score of spheres, than . . . Herbert Spencer" (229, 235). Indeed, from Alfred Russel Wallace's assessment of Spencer as "the greatest all-round thinker and most illuminating reasoner of the Nineteenth Century" to Darwin's own, that Spencer is "about a dozen times my superior" and "by far the greatest living philosopher in England; perhaps equal to any that have lived" (quoted in Carneiro ix),[1] confirmations of Henkin's and Nisbet's later judgments are frequently encountered in British writing during the forty years spanning the turn of the century.[2]

Immensely popular, available in inexpensive editions,[3] and concerned with subjects ranging from social and cultural evolution to the function of art and trade, Spencer's works were at the height of their influence during the years in which Conrad's early fiction was taking shape. The hypothesis that this fiction represents and challenges Spencerian ideas is therefore unlikely to be contested. Nevertheless, although it is a critical commonplace to acknowledge Conrad's debt to Darwinian and Huxleyan perspectives,[4] the relevance of the Spencerian canon to the Conradian one has been virtually overlooked.[5] In the only detailed explorations of this impact, John E. Saveson notes the novelist's "use of Spencerian terms and concepts" and maintains that "Conrad's earliest assumptions are 'scientific' in the sense that they are Spencerian" (22, 18); and Allan Hunter argues that "Spencer explains his own approach to sociology in . . . terms that are similar to Conrad's," holding that the novelist demonstrates "a certain familiarity with particular works" of Spencer (104, 86).[6] But whereas Saveson focuses on Spencerian anthropology and psychology, contending that Conrad's moral treatment of character derives from a Spencerian standard of measurement, and Hunter concerns himself with Spencer's "evolutionary ethics" in Conrad's work, I seek to illuminate the ways in which the fiction appropriates and tests Spencer's influential "typology of civilization."

More specifically, I am interested in the positive and negative ways this typology informs Conrad's African fictions — *Heart of Darkness* (1899) and the short story that is in many ways its Ur-text, "An Outpost of Progress" (1897).[7] Positively, these fictions invoke Spencer's crucial distinction between "militant" and "industrial" societies and echo his perception that late-nineteenth-century British civilization is on a "course of re-barbarization." Negatively, they ultimately undermine Spencerian resolutions: *Heart of Darkness* by expunging the difference between militant and industrial societies and by showing that, in Europe's expansion into the Congo, the two proclivities are mutually reinforcing rather than mutually exclusive; and "An Outpost of Progress" by parodying the Spencerian faith in the "beneficent necessity" of progress. *Lord Jim* (1899, 1900) also merits brief discussion here not only because Conrad repeatedly pleaded that this novel be considered together with *Heart of Darkness* but because it provides many interesting alternatives to and modified examples of Conrad's intersection with Spencerian ideas.[8] Thus, beyond Ian Watt's observation that "several aspects of evolutionary thought are present in *Heart of Darkness*" (153) and Cedric Watts's contention that the novella embodies "a critical summary of some important nineteenth-century preoccupations" (1), I seek to portray the complex "dialogic" posture — at once receptive and critical, reinforcing and subversive — that Conrad's Congo fictions assume toward the story of civilization embodied in Spencerian sociology.

✳ Spencer's "Militant/Industrial" Distinction in *Heart of Darkness*

Spencer's militant/industrial distinction, on which his typology of civilization rests, must be situated within his broader theory of universal progress. This theory holds that all phenomena — whether inorganic, organic, or "superorganic" (cultural) — necessarily evolve from indefinite, incoherent, and homogeneous states to definite, coherent, and heterogeneous ones (*First Principles* 380). Within this context Spencer's theory of the inevitable progress of civilization ("which could not have been other than it has been" [*Social Statics* 233]) takes shape: the simple, repressive, corporate organization of militant society evolving into the complex, democratic, individualistic organization of industrial society. Spencer's fullest formulation of the militant/industrial distinction appears in his three-volume *Principles of Sociology* (1876, 1882, 1896; hereafter cited as *PS* I, II, or III), completed only three years before the publication of *Heart of Darkness* and considered the culmination of his "synthetic philosophy." This dichotomy pervades Spencer's entire corpus.

In *Principles of Sociology* the difference between these types of social organization centers on the difference between the society that lives by work in order to benefit individuals and the society that lives by war in order to benefit the state (I, 620). Although this distinction between politically motivated "static-military" and economically motivated "dynamic-civil" societies dates back at least to Machiavelli (Rapoport 178), Spencer is the leading Victorian exponent of it, makes it the cornerstone of a teleological theory of social evolution, and posits its centrality to the rise of individualism. Further, he characterizes militant society as centralized and totalitarian, industrial society as democratic and civil libertarian (*PS* I, 584). Although Spencer fluctuates in *Principles of Sociology* between the positions that these two forms of society are necessarily "mingled" and that they are necessarily "antagonistic" in a given civilization, he consistently exemplifies them, as one critic notes, "in a series of paired opposites: status vs. contract . . . subordination vs. equality, guilds and the command economy vs. the free market . . . and so forth" (Peel 207).

Before I explore the extent to which *Heart of Darkness* represents and criticizes these distinctions, I would like to glance briefly at an essay of Conrad's that illustrates how pertinent this use of Spencer becomes. For if there is one thing that might have attracted a person of Conrad's political disposition to the Spencerian story of civilization, it would have been Spencer's consignment of modern Russia to the militant camp rather than to the industrial one.[9] "Modern Dahomey [Africa] and Russia," Spencer writes, exemplify "that owning of the individual by the state in life, liberty, and goods, which is proper to a social system adapted for war" (*PS* II, 602). Moreover, he maintains that, "of modern illustrations [of militant society], that furnished by Russia will suffice. Here again, with the wars which effected conquests and consolidations, came the development of the absolute ruler, who, if not divine by alleged origin, yet acquired something like divine *prestige*" (*PS* II, 584). How familiar this sounds, not only when we think of Kurtz's godlike standing within and his tyrannic rule of his African "tribe" but when we consider Conrad's vitriolic essay of 1905, "Autocracy and War." There, the Spencerian typology of civilization emerges as a means of distinguishing between a warlike and blindly absolutist Russia, which "lies outside the stream of progress," a "despotism [that] has been utterly un-European" (97), and a Europe wholly corrupt yet presumably aspiring to "the peaceful nature of industrial and commercial competition"

(106). Conrad further chastises Russia's militancy by referring to the country as a "bottomless abyss that has swallowed up . . . every aspiration
towards personal dignity, towards freedom" (100), "an autocracy whose
only shadow of a title to existence [is] the invincible power of military
conquest" (110–11). However, this is not to deny Conrad's earlier, fundamentally Polish anti-Russian sentiment.[10]

Likewise, although perhaps less obviously, the Spencerian distinction
between militant and industrial societies is embedded metaphorically in
Heart of Darkness (and invoked there for the benefit both of Marlow's
audience within the tale and of Conrad's initial audience without) to coun-
terpose Europe's self-image as a commercial and trading giant with Europe's image of Africa as the savage and warlike "dark continent." That this
distinction in the novella, as I demonstrate below, dissolves into thin air
when closely scrutinized does not invalidate the claim that *Heart of Darkness*
depends for a key register of meaning on the recognition of this Spencerian
distinction and on the view of civilized progress that underwrites it.

Focusing first on modern European industrial civilization, *Heart of
Darkness* opens with images of London as an economically dynamic
commercial and trading power, "the biggest, and the greatest, town on
earth" (7).[11] Barges, for the transport of goods and raw materials, appear on
the Thames,[12] just as steamboats, which Robert Kimbrough calls the
"nineteenth-century symbol of Western civilization" (413), carry European traders into and out of the African jungle.[13] The motif of an industrial
Europe is further emphasized when we learn, moments later, of the occupations of those aboard the *Nellie* — including an accountant, a lawyer,
and a merchant seaman — each of whom has a stake in the commercial
ventures of Europe and mirrors, as Hay notes (142), a European whom
Marlow encounters in Africa. The accountant of the outer station, for
example, tells Marlow that "when one has got to make correct entries one
comes to hate those savages — hate them to the death" (*Heart of Darkness*
22), a remark that suggests a Spencerian tension between the wealth orientation of industrial society and the presumed war orientation of "savagery,"
in which the bureaucratic keeping of business accounts has no place. Even
the doctor who earlier examines Marlow is depicted as having a hand in his
nation's industrial mission, even if he functions primarily as a means for
Conrad to ridicule the scientist emphasis of psychological experimentation. Insisting that he leaves "the mere wealth" to others, the doctor
glorifies "the Company's business" and accepts the "interests of science" as
his "share in the advantages [his] country shall reap" from its activity in the
Congo (14–15). Further, Spencer's notions that industrial societies depend

on trade and that trade is effected by free exchange resulting from a loss of economic autonomy (*PS* II, 614; *PS* I, 557) echoes in the novella's repeated allusions to Europe's "trading mission" in Africa: "custom-house," "trade secrets," "trading places," "trading post," "business," "commerce," and so on. As Marlow explains, the "Trading Society" was "a Continental concern" (*Heart of Darkness* 12). Like "An Outpost of Progress," which ironically assures us that "civilization follows trade" (116), *Heart of Darkness* clearly stresses the industrial basis of modern European social practice.

In *Principles of Sociology* Spencer also popularizes the assumption that the free trade and civil liberties of industrial civilization are organically related to the multiplicity "of associations, political, religious, commercial, professional, philanthropic and social" therein that encourage the "free-play of the sympathies" and that favor "the growth of altruistic sentiments and the resulting virtues" (quoted in Wiltshire 250). *Heart of Darkness* makes the same connection between free trade and philanthropy, however ironically. The manager of the central station, for example, tells Marlow that "each station should be like a beacon on the road towards better things, a centre for *trade* of course but also for *humanising, improving, instructing*" (34; my emphasis). And the "brickmaker" at that outpost sees Kurtz's European mission as comprising "pity, and science, and progress" and as deriving from "higher intelligence, wide sympathies, a singleness of purpose" (28). At other points, too, the novella informs us that the "noble cause" of Europe is executed with "philanthropic desire."

Just as *Heart of Darkness* appears to invoke Spencer's industrial trope to characterize the way Europe would like to view itself, so it may allude to his militant schema to characterize the way Europe views Africa. Within Spencer's militant society the civil and the military heads are one, all productive forces are devoted to maintaining a strong military posture, and a rigid social hierarchy prevails. For Spencer, whether the militant society is composed of "a horde of savages, [a] band of brigands, or a mass of soldiers" (*PS* I, 545), "chronic militancy tends to develop a despotism" and involves "a system of centralization" (*PS* II, 572). For this reason the militant type characteristically lacks commercial and philanthropic groups (*PS* II, 577).

All these phenomena are evident in the organization of Kurtz's tribe. Indeed, the natives of his circle, as well as the organization of the circle itself, are equated with "savage(s)" or "savagery" — by definition militant (the novella has twenty-five such references [Bender 269–70]). Further, Kurtz's society is associated with the "savage clamour" of "dances ending with unspeakable rites" (*Heart of Darkness* 43, 50), with "warlike yells" (47), with the "throb of drums" (65), and with the weaponry of battle — "spears, assegais, shields, knives" (27). Described "with spears in their hands, with bows, with shields, with wild glances and savage movements" (59), and as "a whirl of black limbs, a mass of hands clapping, of feet stamping, of bodies swaying, of eyes rolling" (37), Kurtz's men are depicted as implicitly trusting the authority of the civil and military leader who directs their raids on other tribes (56).[14] Even the "savage and superb, wild-eyed and magnificent" Congolese woman to whom Kurtz turns in the absence of his Intended is depicted as donning "barbarous ornaments," her hair done in the shape of a "helmet" (60). Hence, whether or not the "certain attempts at ornamentation," those "heads on stakes" around Kurtz's house (57), derive from Spencer's account of the "organized criminality" of African Dahomey society, in which "wars are made to get skulls with which to decorate the royal palace" (*PS* II, 236), the novella's appropriation of Spencer's militant/industrial opposition is suggested.

Lord Jim manifests a similar, if less ironic, appropriation of Spencer's typology of civilization. As Paul L. Wiley notes of the novel's Malaysian landscape, "[I]t is evident that the wilderness image has undergone changes relating it more closely to the almost surrealistic landscape of 'Heart of Darkness' than to the fecund jungle of *Almayer's Folly*." Indeed, no matter how tentative or superficial the presentation of Spencer's distinction may be in the novel, numerous images and allusions contribute to a sense, as Wiley puts it, that Jim's "civilized background" and Patusan's "barbaric surroundings" are opposed (49). References to European (and particularly to Stein's) "commercial" and "trading" interests abound in the novel (*Lord Jim* 134, 138–39, 151, 176, 181), as do suggestions that the "European mind" should possess "an unobscured vision, a tenacity of purpose, a touch of altruism" (160) toward the pursuit of an "orderly" social fabric, a "peaceful life" (227). Contrarily, groups indigenous to Patusan and environs are repeatedly associated with militancy: with "rifles" (179), "cannons" (161), "spears" (155, 184), and "armed men" (150). Doramin is called a "war comrade" (142), and the Rajah Allang is said to have "personal slaves" (202). If Jim possesses "racial prestige" (220) and the "power" and "virtues" of "races that never grow old, that have emerged from the gloom" (162), native Malaysians are associated with "a tumult of warcries, the vibrating clang of gongs, the deep snoring of drums, [and] yells of rage" (218–19).

Commenting on Spencerian social evolution, David Wiltshire writes that "there is no way to the more congenial industrial type, but through the regimentation and violence of the militant stage" (249); and *Heart of Darkness* speaks to this point as well. Although the evolutionary theory embedded in the novella is typically attributed to Darwin, one aspect points more in

Spencer's direction. This is the Spencerian notion — *by no means exclusive to but popularized by him* — that the relation between childhood and adulthood corresponds to that between savagery and civilization. Although this idea has ancient roots, Spencer's "Progress" essay popularized it for late-nineteenth-century audiences. There, Spencer likens the "progress in intelligence seen during the growth of the child into the man" to the development from "savage" to "philosopher" (8). Further, as Sarah L. Milbury-Steen observes, Spencer forges an "analogy between the African tribesmen and children," recognizing similarities in the intellectual traits of uncivilized adults and civilized children. For Spencer, "Children are ever dramatising the lives of adults; and savages, along with their other mimicries, similarly dramatise the actions of their civilized visitors. Want of power to discriminate between useless and useful facts, characterizes the juvenile mind, as it does the mind of primitive man" (quoted in Milbury-Steen 7). Instances of this trope are also rife in *Heart of Darkness*. Marlow, for example, notes that the African "settlements," while "some centuries old," are "still no bigger than pin-heads" (16) and that there is "something pathetically childish in the ruins of grass walls" (23). Moreover, Marlow compares African natives to children when he maintains that these "big powerful men" possess "courage" and "strength," yet lack the "capacity to weigh the consequences" of their potential to take action to free themselves. He also views them as still belonging "to the beginnings of time — [as having] no inherited experience to teach them" (42–43). Even Kurtz, who "forgets" himself among these "simple" natives, is characterized as "contemptibly childish" (67) and "not much heavier than a child" (66). But although readers have noted that the Africans of *Heart of Darkness* are represented as "stuck in time, prior to time, and outside it, in a 'perpetual childhood'" (Miller 179), to my knowledge no one has suggested that Conrad may be using Spencer's influential articulation of this all too common nineteenth-century European myth about Africans. When we consider this metaphor from the perspective of Conrad's diatribe against Russia in "Autocracy and War," his deployment of Spencer's association of militancy and inarticulate childhood is even more explicit:

> As [Russia's] boasted military force that, corrupt in its origin, has ever struck no other but faltering blows, so her soul, kept benumbed by her temporal and spiritual master with the poison of tyranny and superstition, will find itself on awakening possessed of no language, a monstrous full-grown child having first to learn the ways of living thought and articulate speech. (102)[15]

Just as *Heart of Darkness* associates "strings of amazing words that resembled no sounds of human language" (66) with the "monstrous passions"

(65) of African natives, "Autocracy and War" illustrates the Spencerian analogy between the "organic" metamorphosis from militancy into industrialism and from childhood into adulthood. Although Conrad seems not to have considered the ramifications of this use of Spencerian metaphors — and hence can be accused of bad anthropology here — these tropes, however deceptive their implications, undoubtedly struck him as awesome in their explanatory power.

✳ Spencer's "Rebarbarized" Civilization in *Heart of Darkness*

In *Civilization and Progress* (1898), John Beattie Crozier writes that whether Spencer's theory of evolution is "to be regarded as true or false, will depend not so much on how far it will explain the illusory phenomena of the past, as [on] how far it will explain the phenomena that lie amongst us in the present" (40). This observation also applies to the orientation of *Heart of Darkness* toward Spencerian thought. For *Heart of Darkness* suggests implicitly what Spencer states explicitly of the Europe, and more particularly the Britain, of his time: that it is undergoing a "process of re-barbarization" (*Facts and Comments* 173). In other words, while maintaining the legitimacy of the militant/industrial distinction, the man Hannah Arendt calls "the first philosopher of evolution" (178) is also perhaps the first philosopher of "devolution," to the extent that he sees industrial Europe, at the end of the century, as sliding back into militancy. Indeed, Spencer observes in the Britain of his day a renewed interest in arming, regimentation, and the predatory spirit generally (*PS* I, 570). Further, he envisions militancy, imperialism, and slavery as interrelated aspects of a general retrogression accompanying rebarbarization (*Facts and Comments* 159, 196). Sounding like Conrad, who insists in "Autocracy and War" that "the true peace of the world . . . will be built on less perishable foundations than those of material interests" (107), Spencer writes of his loathing for "that conception of social progress which presents as its aim, increase of population, growth of wealth, spread of commerce." "Increase in the swarms of people whose existence is subordinated to material development," he continues, "is rather to be lamented than to be rejoiced over" (*Facts and Comments* 7). My suggestion here is simply that, beyond Conrad's firsthand experience of Africa in 1890, when he was employed by the Société Anonyme Belge pour le Commerce du Haut Congo,[16] his insight into European decadence is deepened and qualified by Spencer's theory, anticipating Oswald Spengler's, of a "re-barbarized" civilization. Although culminating in the "Rebarbarization" chapter of *Facts and Comments* — a work not in currency until

1902 and hence postdating Conrad's African fictions — Spencer's observations on Europe's latent savagery nevertheless date from as early as his first book, *Social Statics* (1850; rev. 1892). There he writes, "while the mere propensity to thieve, commonly known under some grandiloquent alias, has been the real prompter of colonizing invasions, from those of Cortez and Pizarro downwards, the ostensible purpose of them has been either the spread of religion or the extension of commerce" (190). Maintaining that aggression has recently led colonists to perpetrate "atrocities that disgrace civilization" (198), Spencer argues that all profitable trade with colonies must be abandoned if it does not come naturally (193). In "The Morals of Trade" Spencer even asks how "in this civilized state of ours" there can be "so much that betrays the cunning selfishness of the savage" (143).

It is a truism of Conrad scholarship that *Heart of Darkness* attacks turn-of-the-century European imperialism and trading practices;[17] yet what has been overlooked is just how close this attack comes to Spencer's sense of a rebarbarized European civilization. Conrad's novella also uses the word "trade" as a euphemism for what is actually raiding and "grubbing" and emphasizes the connection among enslavement, imperialism, and militancy. Kurtz's possessiveness toward everything around him ("my ivory, my station, my river" [49]), for example, reflects the other Europeans' self-serving crimes in the name, as Spencer would have it, of the "spread of religion or the extension of commerce" (*Social Statics* 190). Marlow encounters a "chain-gang" (*Heart of Darkness* 19), disease and slow death, the apparent effects of "a massacre or a pestilence" (21), and the "glorious slaughter" of Africans (52), all on behalf of an "outraged" and "farcical law," a "fantastic invasion" of Europeans. "It was just robbery with violence," Marlow affirms, suggesting Spencer's complaint about forced trade, "aggravated murder on a great scale" (10). Moreover, instead of representing only native Africans as militant, *Heart of Darkness* also depicts weapon-toting European "pilgrims" as warlike, "bloodthirsty" savages. Carrying the "absurd long staves" of the Africans (26), gratuitously "squirting lead into [the] bush" (46), and resembling "mean and greedy phantoms" (67) who mercilessly scapegoat and beat innocent victims in an "imbecile rapacity" for ivory (26), these Europeans represent imperialism and slavery as two sides of the same coin — as indicative of industrial Europe's regression toward militancy.

It is in the metaphorical linking of "savagery" and animal life, however, that *Heart of Darkness* most forcefully refigures Spencer's caveat about "rebarbarization." Just as Spencer observes that "the forces at work exterminate such sections of mankind as stand in the way, with the same sternness that they exterminate beasts of prey and herds of useless ruminants" (*Social Statics* 238), so Kurtz in *Heart of Darkness* — after native Africans have been likened to "creatures," "brutes," hyenas, "bees," dogs, and "ants" — concludes his peroration for the International Society for the Suppression of Savage Customs with the postscriptum "Exterminate all the brutes!" (51). Even Marlow notes that the individual African native is of "no more account" to Europeans than is a "grain of sand in a black Sahara" (51),[18] a comparison that contradicts Europe's avowed religious mission, as articulated by Marlow's aunt, of "weaning those ignorant millions from their horrid ways" (16).

A look at *Lord Jim* is instructive too, for we are witness there to the suggestion that the "lies of our civilisation" (172) render non-Westerners brutes (206), "hyaenas" (146), and "cattle" (10, 245). And what better emblem of this rebarbarization than the exploits in Patusan of Gentleman Brown (who is every bit the "beetle" to Jim's "butterfly")? Like Kurtz (and Jim), Brown cannot succeed in Europe, and so he brings his "vulgar and greedy brutes" to Patusan (214). "Malicious," "lawless," "savage," and "revengeful," this "hollow sham" of a "buccaneer" and "ruffian," who ultimately proves to be Jim's nemesis, is little more than a "common robber" who brings "terror" to every situation in which he finds himself. One of the novel's most "civilized" characters, he is also, paradoxically, the most barbaric.

✳ Beyond Spencer: The Suggestion of a Military-Industrial Complex in *Heart of Darkness*

In his monumental study of Conrad, Ian Watt maintains that "the greatest authors are rarely representative of the ideology of their period; they tend rather to expose its internal contradictions or the very partial nature of its capacity for dealing with the facts of experience" (147). This comment on the nature and function of modern art aptly describes the representation of Spencerian ideology in *Heart of Darkness* as useful and suggestive but ultimately incapable of dealing with "the facts of experience." In this sense, as Cedric Watts writes of Conrad's relation to Darwinism, Conrad is both "Spencerian and anti-Spencerian," invoking Spencer's categories and absorbing his rubrics even if finally opposing his perceptions and undermining his conclusions. For while Spencer decries the West's loss of ground in its realization of the industrial ideal, he never doubts that the militant/industrial distinction is a legitimate means of characterizing the development of civilization. *Heart of Darkness*, in contrast, ultimately subverts this distinction altogether, for the novella represents not the mutual exclusivity of militant and industrial tendencies but their mutual reinforcement in what might be called a "military-industrial complex." Whereas this phrase, coined by Dwight D. Eisenhower sixty years after the publication of *Heart of Darkness*, has specific resonances not wholly germane to our discussion here,[19] its more general meaning—an informal alliance among a nation's political, military, and commercial interests—aptly characterizes what the novella glimpses of European activity in Africa. By suggesting that commercial and trading mastery depends on brute military force and that "foreign trade and modern war have always been one and the same thing" (John Seely, quoted in Coit 123),[20] *Heart of Darkness* disarms the rhetoric of "imperialist civilization." For such a discourse is predicated on the maintenance of oppositions like Spencer's, which *Heart of Darkness* undermines by highlighting the similarity between economically and politically motivated societal organizations. With the militant/industrial distinction, as with other dualities in the novella, meaning accrues through the invocation and then subversion of such dichotomies. As Eloise Knapp Hay points out, the novella accomplishes this feat "through repeated reversals or inversions of normal patterns of imagery" (137).[21]

Indeed, *Heart of Darkness* at many points conflates the two sides of Spencer's distinction, manifesting the "merry dance of death and trade" (17) in the image of a military-industrial complex. In "Autocracy and War," an essay in which Mark Conroy correctly observes a "wedding of arms and trade" (81), Conrad charges that "industrialism and commercialism . . . stand ready, almost eager, to appeal to the sword as soon as the globe of the earth has shrunk beneath our growing numbers by another ell or so" (107), and that "*Il n'y a plus d'Europe*—there is only an armed and trading continent, the home of slowly maturing economical contests for life and death, and of loudly proclaimed world-wide ambitions" (112). *Heart of Darkness* too depicts the militant "sword" and industrial "torch" as mutually reinforcing. For example, not only does Marlow liken the construction of a Congolese railway to the shelling of Africa by a French navy vessel ("Another report from the cliff made me think suddenly of that ship of war I had seen firing into a continent" [19]), but the French steamer that brings him to Africa visits ports for "the sole purpose of landing *soldiers* and *custom-house* officers" (16; my emphasis). Not only do European trading and military posts dot the land, but expeditions devoted to "exploring" the terrain in fact "tear treasure out of" its bowels "with no more moral purpose at the back of it than there is in burglars breaking into a safe" (32–33). Even the Thames and Congo rivers, one a waterway of "civilized commerce" and the other of "savage mystery" ("resembling an immense snake uncoiled" [12]), are conflated at the end of the novella, when the Thames itself seems to lead "to the uttermost ends of the earth . . . into the heart of an immense darkness" (76).

It is Kurtz's society, however, that most forcefully stands as a microcosm of the military-industrial complex. According to Ian Watt, "the romantic, anarchic, and psychopathic energies of Kurtz find their ultimate sanction in Western *industrial supremacy*, for Kurtz really asserts his claims to 'the rightness of God' through his *monopoly of firearms*" (165; my emphasis). Kurtz's wealth and power are linked symbiotically, both cut from the whole cloth of his "method" and "immense plans." Less a method of trading and barter, however, than one of raiding and murder, Kurtz's technique for bettering commercial interests tends to go beyond the militant (an "unsound method") to the genocidal ("Exterminate all the brutes!").[22] In commenting, after Kurtz's death, that "Kurtz's knowledge however extensive did not bear upon the problems of commerce or administration" (*Heart of Darkness* 70), Marlow is telling the truth to the extent that Kurtz's "trade secrets" were exclusively military: the annihilation of rival dealers in ivory. This conflation of Spencerian categories is further underscored when the steamer that removes Kurtz from the inner station is characterized as a "grimy fragment of another world, the forerunner of change, *of conquest, of trade, of massacres*" (67; my emphasis), and when Kurtz declares of the European administration, "You show them you have in you something that is really profitable, and then there will be no limits to the recognition of your ability" (67). In this sense *Heart of Darkness* stands as a riposte to the Spencerian claim that nineteenth-century Britain is a "compromise between militancy and industrialism," suggesting instead that the two "antagonistic" tendencies collectively constitute an unmistakably civilized form of activity — one that becomes "an instrument of pure brute force" (Tessitore 39).

❋ From Progress to Parody: Spencer's "Law" and Conrad's "Outpost"

In discussing the sources of Conrad's African fictions, Norman Sherry calls "An Outpost of Progress" "an interesting tail-piece to *Heart of Darkness*" (*Western World* 125); and this comment holds true as well for our consideration of both the debt and the antipathy these works show to the Spencerian story of civilization. For when we consider Spencer's place, in David Wiltshire's words, as "the last of the eighteenth-century Encyclopedists masquerading as a prophet of nineteenth-century scientific progress" (195), Sherry's claim that "the ironic treatment of the concept of 'progress'" pervades "An Outpost of Progress" takes on particular resonance (*Western World* 125). Indeed, the entire story can profitably be read as a parody of Spencer's best-known and most succinct presentation of this idea, his "Progress: Its Law and Cause" (1857).

There, Spencer posits a deterministic and teleological notion of progress as neither "an accident" nor "a thing within human control, but a beneficent necessity" (60). Whereas Spencer deems the "cause" of progress, in words that continually appear in Conrad's African fictions, "inscrutable" and "an impenetrable mystery" (61–62), he considers the "law" of progress organic, universal, and knowable:

> Whether it be in the development of the Earth, in the development of Life upon its surface, in the development of Society, of Government, of Manufacture, of Commerce, of Language, Literature, Science, Art, the same evolution of the simple into the complex, through successive differentiations, holds throughout. From the earliest traceable cosmical changes down to the latest results of civilization, we shall find that the transformation of the homogeneous, is that in which progress essentially consists. (10)

When we situate this essay in the context of Spencer's other thoughts linking civilization and progress, it becomes clear just how easily apologists for colonial expansion could appropriate his idea of progress. In *Social Statics*, for example, Spencer writes that "instead of civilization being artificial it is a part of nature," one that necessarily progresses to the point at which "evil and immorality disappear . . . and man become[s] perfect" (32). And in *Principles of Sociology* he writes, "[W]hat remains to be done, calls for no other agency than the quiet pressure of a spreading industrial civilization on a barbarism which slowly dwindles" (II, 664).

It is less Spencer himself, however, than a number of influential "social Spencerians" who use these arguments to justify imperialism and to whom "An Outpost of Progress" can be seen as a response.[23] In *Spencer and Spencerism* (1900), for example, Hector MacPherson suggests that "the scramble in China, the race for territory in South Africa, the expansion of Britain in Egypt . . . are all . . . evidence of the fact that civilization is beginning to overflow its old boundaries, and is becoming world-wide in its aspirations" (185). He then goes on to forecast a millennium:

> Human history, beginning with a sordid struggle for existence and an ethical code steeped in blood, ends with a harmonious civilization resting upon the all-embracing conception of human brotherhood.

Man and society, no longer at war, are destined to form one harmonious whole on the basis of reciprocity of service. With the magic wands of Reason, Science, and Industry, man on the basis of an egoism which is gradually being transfigured by sympathy, will yet lay the foundation of a new social order, in which peace, not strife, shall reign. Above the din of conflicting interests and warring passions may be heard, by those who listen in the spirit of evolutionary science, the inspiring tones of the humanitarian evangel — Peace on earth, and good will among men. (186–87)

MacPherson's comments typify a prevalent appropriation of Spencerian progress, as justifying the end for which the means is colonization.

Arthur Symons maintains that Conrad takes "his revenge upon science" by "borrowing its very terms, making them dance at the end of a string, derisively" (11); and in precisely this way the scathingly ironic "Outpost of Progress" takes its revenge on Spencerian scientific progress. Initially entitled "A Victim of Progress," Conrad's short story of a murder and suicide that result when two Europeans (of either French or Belgian extraction) are left alone at an African trading station, owing to a quarrel over a lump of sugar for afternoon coffee, incisively parodies Spencerian "progress and civilization and all the virtues" ("Outpost" 116). Hence, I disagree with Cedric Watts's claim that "Outpost" "has very little of the subversive impact of *Heart of Darkness*" (35). For it is reasonable to view this story and Conrad's essay "The Crime of Partition" (1919) as, among other things, trenchant critiques of Spencerian ideals. "Progress," Conrad writes in this essay, "leaves its dead by the way, for progress is only a great adventure[,] as its leaders and chiefs know very well in their hearts. It is a march into an undiscovered country; and in such an enterprise the victims do not count" (118). As in "Outpost," progress here is depicted as anything but a "beneficent necessity."

"An Outpost of Progress" takes us into the center of Africa, where Carlier and Kayerts, the Bouvard and Pécuchet of the jungle (Darras 53), earn profits by sitting still and gathering in "the ivory those savages . . . bring" ("Outpost" 90). Reduced to comic caricatures rather than raised to the level of psychologically dramatic characters, Carlier and Kayerts — respectively, a former commissioned officer of cavalry "in an army guaranteed from harm by several European powers" (88) and a former telegraph administrator — are depicted as blind, useless, and ineffectual "children" in the employ of the "ruthless and efficient" director of the "Great Trading Company" (88, 89, 87). For these two "Pioneers of Progress" "the river, the forest, all the great land throbbing with life, [are] like a great emptiness" and the natives of "this dog of a country" are little more than funny and "ungrateful brutes" who try their "civilized nerves" (92, 93, 103, 89).

This assault on Spencerian progress cuts in two directions: it challenges the belief that "industrial" Europe is more advanced than "militant" Africa, and it attacks the presumption that any "principle," as Conrad himself puts it in a letter, "can stand alone at the beginning of things and look confidently to the end" (*Letters* II, 348). Carlier and Kayerts, for example, capitalize on some Africans' misperception of them as gods, when all the while they enslave the natives whose lives they disrupt. In two uncharacteristically honest remarks Carlier admits to Kayerts that they are both slave dealers, because "there's nothing but slave-dealers in this cursed country" ("Outpost" 110), and, presaging Kurtz, that they face "the necessity of exterminating all the niggers before the country could be made habitable" (108). Further, the reality of their exploitative operations at the outpost clashes profoundly with the civilized rhetoric with which the European press surrounds their mission — "it spoke much of the rights and duties of civilization, of the sacredness of the civilizing work, and extolled the merits of those who went about bringing light, and faith and commerce to the dark places of the earth" (94–95) — while they themselves reduce "civilization" to a materialistic fetish: "the storehouse was in every station called the fetish, perhaps because of the spirit of civilization it contained" (93).[24]

More specifically, however, a parody of Spencerian progress is enacted in the sense that both the "law" of progress ("in a hundred years there will be perhaps a town here. . . . warehouses and barracks. . . . Civilization, my boy, and virtue" [95]) and the "cause of progress" (100) are invoked only to be devastated by the reality they know there. Even Spencer's notion of the "survival of the fittest" arises here,[25] when Carlier and Kayerts are deemed "unfitted for . . . a struggle" with even purely material problems. They are "unfitted," in fact, because they are the products of "the high organization" of "the crowd that believes blindly in the irresistible force of its own institutions and of its morals, in the power of its police and its opinion." Further, civilization is said to forbid Carlier and Kayerts "all independent thought, all initiative, all departure from routine," rendering them little more than "machines" (89–91). This attack on a fetishized notion of civilization, not to mention on Spencerian progress, may be the most blatant in all of Conrad's fiction, for it moves beyond the critical suggestion, in *Heart of Darkness*, that civilization depends for its perpetuation on the moral complacency and blindness of those who conduct its business (such as Marlow's "excellent aunt" and his audience aboard the *Nellie*).[26]

In his book on Conrad, Ford Madox Ford writes that he and Conrad "agreed that the novel is absolutely the only vehicle for the thought of our day." "With the novel," he continues, "you can do anything: you can inquire into any department of life, you can explore every department of the world of thought" (222). It is in this sense, I believe, that Conrad's African fictions inquire into Spencer's typology of civilization, both incorporating and criticizing it, both absorbing its rubrics and parodying its resolutions. As Bakhtin affirms, in reality "any utterance, in addition to its own theme, always responds (in the broad sense of the word) in one form or another to others' utterances which precede it." "The speaker," he continues, "is not Adam, and therefore the subject of his speech itself inevitably becomes the arena where his opinions meet those of . . . other viewpoints, world views, trends, theories, and so forth" ("Problem of Speech Genres" 94). It is in this sense too that Conrad's African fictions constitute an "arena" in which a dialogue with Spencerian sociology is enacted. Whereas Conrad's appropriation of Spencer might not equal Arnold Bennett's, for example (Bennett insists that "you can see [Spencer's] *First Principles* in nearly every line I write" [392]), it is clear that Spencer's typology, as a vital matrix of the discourse of civilization and progress during this period, seeped its way into Conrad's "transformative" African narratives. On the evidence suggested here, then, I would reject the claim that Conrad's work "transforms, subverts, and rescues the established norms, values, and myths of imperialist civilization" (Parry 7) and would suggest instead just the opposite: that the "subversive-conservative" novelist invokes only to destroy such norms, values, and myths — even those of one as "skeptical" of imperialist civilization as the philosopher/scientist Herbert Spencer.

3

The London Fog: Civilization as Rhetoric and Game in Conrad

I felt . . . that he thought of civilized and morally tolerable human life as a dangerous walk on a thin crust of barely cooled lava which at any moment might break and let the unwary sink into fiery depths. — Bertrand Russell, speaking of Conrad

Truth, work, ambition, love itself, may be only counters in the lamentable or despicable game of life, but when one takes a hand one must play the game. — Heyst, in Conrad, VICTORY

*I feel disenchanted — dreary. Our civilization is like the potted chicken of the USA — corrupt sir! Corrupt.
— Conrad, in a letter to John Galsworthy*

However influential Herbert Spencer's theory of civilization proved to be, it should be remembered that it was but one of the many voices to constitute the discourse of civilization at the turn of the century. Whereas Spencer would have claimed, with Aristotle, that humans are "rational" animals, Conrad's fiction instead suggests, with Freud, that humans are "rationalizing" ones — that individuals must play various games in order to abide the repressive pressures of civilization. In this connection, my discussion of Conrad's appropriation of Spencer glimpses, but does not explicitly address, a broader tension in this novelist's representation of civilization: his depiction of it as self-deceiving rhetoric, on the one hand, and as deceptive game, on the other. If Spencer's theory functions for Conrad as a blinding torch — specifically, by justifying and falsifying the "civilizing mission" of the English — it obscures the degree to which civilization is gamelike in practice. As early as "An Outpost of Progress" (1897), for example, Conrad links civilization with games when he has Carlier tell Kayerts: "[I]n a hundred years, there will be perhaps a town here. Quays, and warehouses, and barracks, and — and — billiard-rooms. Civilization, my boy, and virtue — and all" (95). And as late as his "Travel" essay (1915), Conrad deploys this same metaphor: "but even this is a game which is losing its interest, and in a very little time will have come to an end. Presently there will be no backyard left in the heart of Central Africa that has not been peeped into by some person more or less commissioned for the purpose" (89). While this tension between depicting civilization as rhetoric and game pervades Conrad's corpus — occasionally both sides of it even appear in the same work[1] — it is foregrounded most clearly in *Heart of Darkness* (1899, 1902) and *The Secret Agent* (1907), texts which, when viewed in juxtaposition, reveal Conrad's paradoxical proclivity to deconstruct the rhetoric of civilization and to reconstruct civilization as a game.

Despite the apparent incongruity of these two fictions, many readers have found it useful to juxtapose them. Cedric Watts, for example, argues that *The Secret Agent* "extends *Heart of Darkness*'s theme of 'the butcher and the policeman' with its analysis of the bases of moral and social order in an urban society" (153); and Anthony Winner holds that Conrad's irony in *The Secret Agent* "has much in common with the idea of work that Marlow advocates in *Heart of Darkness*." "The frequent foulness of London," he continues, "approximates in a sleazy secondhand way the horrors of the Congo" (70). For Jacques Darras, this textual relationship is chronological: "In *Heart of Darkness*, the sun was beginning to set on the Empire. In *The Secret Agent*, its final hour has come" (99); and for me these disparate texts together reveal a major tension in Conrad's representation of civilization. Specifically, whereas the former text deconstructs[2] the very language by which the West has claimed moral and intellectual superiority over the non-West, the latter reconstructs civilization as a game one either masters or loses, thrives or perishes by, but which in any case cannot be escaped. Moreover, both works center on London, the very center of European civilization at this time: *The Secret Agent* from within the thick of it and *Heart of Darkness* by its implicit presence. In this novella, it is worth remembering, London is "the gloom to the West" in view of all aboard the *Nellie*. Throughout Marlow's telling of the tale they never leave its view.[3]

✳ The Rhetoric of Civilization in *Heart of Darkness*

Contrary to what many have argued of *Heart of Darkness*, I believe that Conrad's novella is a critique of civilization far more than it is of the jungle.[4] Indeed, the text is as much concerned with the European cultures from which the major characters (and the author) derive as with the host culture, the Belgian Congo. Presented against the backdrop of an "unfamiliar" and "exotic" setting, the work — by juxtaposing "First" and "Third" Worlds — redefines and critically examines the civilization familiar to its original readers.

This emphasis on Europe over Africa is made clear when we learn that "[a]ll Europe contributed to the making of Kurtz" (*Heart of Darkness* 50).[5] Because Kurtz was born and bred in European circles (his "mother was half-English, his father half-French" [50]) and not in "the Jungle" (which we at no point view on its own terms), it is therefore principally *in Europe* that we must search for the elusive "darkness." This claim is substantiated by Marlow's comment to Kurtz: "Your success in Europe is assured in any case" (65). Clearly, the African perspective is insignificant here: success or failure, the entire meaning of Kurtz's and Marlow's presence on the "Dark Continent," is to be judged by European standards alone. Hence, when Benita Parry notes that "the blacks are not functional Protagonists but figures in a landscape who do not constitute a human presence" (33), she points to the fact that the novella's focus is not Africa per se at all but Europe and its presence there. Like Kenyan novelist Leonard Kibera, then, I take "*Heart of Darkness* as an examination of the West itself and not as a comment on Africa" (quoted in Sarvan 285) — as a "Eurocentric" critique. Analogously to historian H. Trevor-Roper's point that for years there was "no African history to teach" because there was "only the history of Europeans in Africa" (quoted in Diamond 2–3), Conrad's *Heart of Darkness* is more than anything else a novella about "Europeans in Africa." In short, Conrad's narrative is a descendant of Shakespeare's *Tempest*, Defoe's *Robinson Crusoe* and Swift's *Gulliver's Travels* to the extent that we ultimately learn more about the codes and contradictions of the worlds from which the protagonists and authors come than we do of the newly discovered lands and their peoples, the purported emphases of the books.

Two interrelated phenomena constitute the critique of the West enacted by *Heart of Darkness:* the text's deconstruction of the very language by which the West has claimed moral superiority over others, and its exposition of the exploitative and hypocritical activity that is colonization. The deconstructive side of Conrad's critique is carried out by reversing the metaphors used to distinguish civilization from jungle and by illustrating the ways in which the discourse of civilization is used to lie about and obfuscate reality, to obscure rather than illuminate that which it claims to describe. This reversal is accomplished by invoking a series of cliché dichotomies taken to represent the distinction between "civilization" and "jungle," only then to confuse and undermine such distinctions: godly/godforsaken, complex/simple, mind/body,[6] language/gesture, logic/illogic, rational/irrational, good/evil, efficient/inefficient, order/chaos, sane/insane, day/night, white/black, light/dark, historic/prehistoric, culture/nature, industrial/militant (pace Spencer's typology), and so forth.[7] As I have argued above, just as the "unfamiliar" is used to critique the "familiar," so also is the meaning of Marlow's yarn "not inside like a kernel but outside, enveloping the tale which [brings] it out only as a glow brings out a haze" (*Heart of Darkness* 9). In other words, to know something, as structuralism holds, one must know its opposite as well. Yet Conrad's fiction presages poststructuralism with even more precision, as the line dividing the above cliché oppositions dissolves before our very eyes, the farther into the narrative we read.

Heart of Darkness inverts and then destroys such distinctions at a number of points: when Marlow reports that he can see nothing for "the blind whiteness of the fog" (43), for "the blinding sunshine" (20), and for the white "smoke" of European guns (67); and when we read that "sunlight can be made to lie too" (71), that "white fog" is "more blinding than the night" (41), that Brussels, and not the Congo, is deadly white and reminiscent of a "whited sepulchre" (13), and that London, the "greatest" town in the world, was once "one of the dark places on earth" (9). Marlow also remarks that "What saves us is efficiency — the devotion to efficiency" (10), even when virtually every European we meet is not only *in*efficient and corrupted but a "hairdresser's dummy" (21), a "chattering idiot" (26), a "papier-mâché Mephistopheles" (29), or a "harlequin" (53).[8] Who, we are compelled to ask, are more barbarian, the enslaved blacks with "a bit of white worsted round" their necks (20) or the "imbecile crowd" of whites who gleefully and gratuitously enslave them? By this method, the text undermines the West's most cherished self-image; by forcing such questions upon us, the text exposes the veneerlike quality of civilization. Just as Conrad's memoir *The Mirror of the Sea* likens the riverfront of the Thames to "a village of Central African huts imitated in iron,"[9] so *Heart of Darkness* blurs the standard distinctions between civilization and jungle nearly beyond recognition.

Three further examples from the text extend this blurring of realms. The first is the example of the blinding torch itself, Kurtz's "small sketch in oils" depicting "a woman, draped and blindfolded, carrying a lighted torch. The background was somber — almost black. The movement of the woman was stately, and the effect of the torchlight on the face was sinister" (27–28). As I have argued in Chapter 1, instead of "enlightening" her "almost black" environment, this "stately" woman is only "blinded" despite the torchlight, oblivious to the "sinister" activities transpiring in her midst.

The second example of the text's blurring of the distinction between civilization and uncivilization is the phenomenon of Kurtz's "engagement" with two women, one representative of the "deadly sterility" that is the colonizing West (the Intended), the other representative of the "vitality and power" of a people the West does not understand (the native African woman). Clearly, Kurtz's Intended, herself ignorant and pretentious (Is it she Kurtz has painted?), pales next to Kurtz's "savage and superb, wild-eyed and magnificent" Congolese woman (60). Whereas there is a "terrible truth" to this native woman, there is a "lie" and an "illusion" about the Intended and her ghostly house (which, for Eloise Knapp Hay, serves as "a good image for the 'house' of all Europe" [151]). Indeed, Robert Kimbrough's estimation of her as "totally protected," "rhetorically programmed," "nunlike in her adoration," and living in "the wasteland of modern Europe" (410) seems not unfounded. Marlow is rightly convinced that the truth would be "too dark altogether" for her (72). It is also clear, however, that the Intended is more victim than villain of the civilized world that keeps her in the dark, for in the novella she is repeatedly defamed as "out of touch with truth" and as properly belonging in "that beautiful world of [her] own" (16, 49). She is thus, as Hay writes, "fully appropriate in character to the kind of world the West has made for her" (105).[10]

The third example of this blurring of "civilization" and "jungle" occurs when the text invokes, but then exposes as cliché, the notion that Africa corrupts even the most civilized beings, rendering them savages. In his *Civilization in Transition* C. G. Jung outlines, in baldly racist terms, this imagined phenomenon most clearly:

> Even today the European, however highly developed, cannot live with
> impunity among the Negroes in Africa; their psychology gets into him
> unnoticed and unconsciously he becomes a Negro. There is no fight-
> ing against it. In Africa there is a well-known expression for this:
> "going black." It is no mere snobbery that the English should consider
> anyone born in the colonies, even though the best blood may run in his
> veins, "slightly inferior." There are facts to support this view. (121)

This notion of "going black" is touched on at a number of points in the novella, most prominently when Marlow laments, after spending weeks in
Africa, that "I felt I was becoming scientifically interesting" (*Heart of Darkness* 24) and, because hungry and tired, that "I was getting savage" (25). He
also asks: "how many powers of darkness claimed [Kurtz] for their own"?
(49). In this sense, Marlow stands as a quasi–Herbert Spencer figure,
liberal-minded about race yet trapped in the Victorian mind-set that native
Africans are at a more "primitive" state of development than Europeans.[11]
Such racist judgments as Jung's and Marlow's have compelled a number of
readers to argue that Kurtz surrenders "to the atavistic temptations of a
corrupted primitive civilization" (Daiches 39), that he is "an anti-civiliza-
tion figure," and, moreover, that "there is something basically incompatible between the conventional trappings of European civilization and the
central Congo environment" (Tessitore 38, 32).

However, a closer look at *Heart of Darkness* militates against the validity
of such claims. For example, although Marlow's description of Kurtz's
"conversion" might at first seem to corroborate such notions, a more
careful look betrays a critique not of the jungle at all but of the "civilized"
themselves:

> the wilderness had found him out early, and had taken on him a terrible
> vengeance for the fantastic invasion. I think it had whispered to him
> things about himself which he did not know, things of which he had no
> conception till he took counsel with this great solitude — and the
> whisper had proved irresistibly fascinating. It echoed loudly within
> him because he was hollow at the core. (57–58)

As is typical of Conrad's prose here, subtle inversions crop up at every turn.
The African "wilderness" is invested with a significance that Kurtz, the
superman of civilization, can only marvel at but not understand. We read
that the jungle tells him things not about its own "primitive mystery" but
about his own civilized barbarity. Hence, adumbrating T. S. Eliot (and in a
very different sense Hannah Arendt), Conrad's text suggests that it is less

that the uncivilized are savage than that the civilized are banal and morally complacent — "hollow" to the core.

Another aspect of this deconstruction of the language through which the West secures its moral superiority is the repeated demonstration that this language "lies" — that there is a complete breakdown between words and their meanings.[12] A number of textual examples illustrate this point. To cite the most familiar one, Marlow points out that Kurtz, German for "short," is actually tall (59). Further, the enslaved natives, victims of aggression, are variously referred to as "enemies" (17), "criminals" (19), transgressors (28), and "rebels" (58). Moreover, language is used to distort what the Europeans actually do to the Africans. Instead of being "emissar[ies] of light" and "weaning those ignorant millions from their horrid ways" (16), of providing "a beacon on the road towards better things" for "humanizing, improving, instructing" (34), and being "the cause of progress" through "trading" (13, 12), the Europeans in Africa actually exploit the land and its people, the "philanthropic pretense of the whole concern" (27) exposed repeatedly. As Marlow notes of the Eldorado Exploring Expedition, who actually do everything but "explore," "To tear treasure out of the bowels of the land was their desire, with no more moral purpose at the back of it than there is in burglars breaking into a safe" (32–33). Even though Marlow himself insists that there is "a taint of death, a flavour of mortality in lies" (29), this does not deter him from lying both to Kurtz ("Oh, nonsense!" he tells the dying man who claims he is soon to expire [68]) and to Kurtz's Intended ("the last word he pronounced," he tells her, "was — your name" [75]). This linguistic "slippage" is partially explainable in terms of Conrad's own "indictment of the English language": that "no English word is a word." For Conrad, according to Ford Madox Ford, "the consequence is that no English word has clear edges: a reader is always, for a fraction of a second, uncertain as to which meaning of the word the writer intends." "Thus," Ford continues, "all English prose is blurred" (229). I would add to Ford's estimation that Conrad exploits this ambiguous quality of English in order to undermine the overconfidence with which the discourse of civilization is typically deployed.[13] Indeed, Conrad himself remarks that "half the words we use have no meaning whatever and of the other half each man understands each word after the fashion of his own folly and conceit" (quoted in Wasserman 107). Conrad is more pointed in a letter of 1898: "Words blow away like mist, and like mist they serve only to obscure, to make vague the real shape of one's feelings" (*Letters* II, 108). And in a letter to the *New York Times* in response to a review of *The Inheritors*, Conrad speaks of his collaborative novel with Ford as directed at "the self-seeking" and at "the falsehood that had been . . . 'hiding under the words that for ages had spurred men to [action]' " (II, 347). Thus, although Jerry Wasserman is correct to assert that language functions in *Heart of Darkness* "as an index and tool of civilization" and that "Conrad's ambivalence towards the powers of language is nowhere more evident than in 'Heart of Darkness'" — because Conrad shows how language "can cloak truth and feelings as well as reveal them" (102–4) — Wasserman is wrong to argue that for Marlow "the horror" is a recognition that "the basis of European man's life is an illusion, a lie; *yet one that must be maintained as the only viable alternative to the greater horror of the darkness*" (107; my emphasis). For it is clear that Marlow experiences a failure of nerve more than of the imagination and that there is little "viable" about Conrad's "sepulchral city," no matter how dark the jungle.[14]

In a 1900 letter to David Meldrum Conrad writes that *Heart of Darkness*, within the context of the *Youth* volume, "was meant in my mind as a foil" (*Letters* II, 271). Yet the novella, as I have been attempting to demonstrate, also serves as a foil to dominant assumptions about the nature and function of civilization. Conrad's agenda is known to have been to make his readers truly "see" ("Author's Note to *The Nigger of the 'Narcissus'*" 162); and in the case of *Heart of Darkness* one thing that may be *seen through* is the discourse of civilization by which Europe distinguishes itself from "savage" domains.[15]

✳ The Game of Civilization in *The Secret Agent*

To the extent that *Heart of Darkness* represents Western civilization from a distance, deconstructing the rhetoric by which it justifies its "improving" work in the jungle, *The Secret Agent* represents Western civilization from a vantage point at its center, reconstructing it as a game. Although Conrad's representation of civilization as a game is not unique to *The Secret Agent*, it is in this novel that the analogy receives its fullest treatment, characterizing no less than "the very centre of the Empire on which the sun never sets" (162).[16] It is here where game and play metaphors are deployed most pervasively to represent the nature and function of civilization.

Whereas readers from Albert J. Guerard on have noted in passing the prevalence of game imagery in *The Secret Agent*,[17] the relevance of this trope to the novel's representation of civilization remains in need of elaboration. The sole critic to address this issue thoroughly is Terry Eagleton, who argues that *The Secret Agent* mimes "the Wittgenstein of *Philosophical Inves-*

tigations in its consecration of that vast stalemated 'game' which is society."
"Stalemated games," he writes, "are in one way unachieved, in another way
complete; the world goes on, and this is at once the question, and the
answer, of the text" (*Criticism and Ideology* 140). In a later work Eagleton
extends this analysis, claiming that "indeed 'game' is a central metaphor of
The Secret Agent," that "the social game [therein] is arbitrary," and that
this stalemated game continues "even though neither side wins." "In this
sense," Eagleton continues, "incompletion is itself a solution — it is the
perpetuity of the social game which matters, to which the only threat is the
deathly spectatorial Professor" ("Form, Ideology, and *The Secret Agent*"
29). Apt though Eagleton is here in pointing out the importance of this
trope to the novel, I take issue with his claim that the Professor stands
outside the game, yet will use his ideas generally as a point of departure
from which to explore the complexities of the novel's depiction of Western
civilization as a game.

In setting out to examine *The Secret Agent* in terms of the game analogy,
one immediately faces the quandary of choosing among a number of
conflicting theoretical approaches to games — many of which "don't even
seem to be discussing the same subject" (Caillois 161). Thus, while Clifford
Geertz, in a brief discussion of the game analogy, and Daphne Patai, in an
application of it to fiction, cite such disparate figures as Wittgenstein,
Goffman, Huizinga, and Caillois, each of whom "mixes a strong sense of
the formal orderliness of things with an equally strong sense of the radical
arbitrariness of that order" (Geertz, "Blurred Genres" 24), Huizinga and
Caillois are of particular interest to me here for two reasons. First, these
two figures relate games and play to the makeup of civilizations. Second,
they are the closest in proximity to Conrad's conception of gaming and help
reveal the great extent to which the concept of "play" informs *The Secret
Agent*.

J. Huizinga's seminal *Homo Ludens* (1938) advances the argument that
"civilization arises and unfolds in and as play" (foreword), that "we might,
in a purely formal sense, call all society a game, if we bear in mind that this
game is the living principle of all civilization" (100–101). Refusing the
common misperception that play is by definition childish or trivial, Huizinga maintains that "all play means something" (1), that it is necessarily a
"social construction" (5), and that it "creates order, *is* order" (10). "Sum-
ming up the formal characteristics of play," Huizinga writes,

> we might call it a free activity standing quite consciously outside
> "ordinary" life as being "not serious," but at the same time absorbing

the player intensely and utterly. It is an activity connected with no material interest, and no profit can be gained by it. It proceeds within its own proper boundaries of time and space according to fixed rules and in an orderly manner. (13)[18]

In *Man, Play, and Games* (1958) Roger Caillois extends and qualifies Huizinga's conclusion that play is "a contest *for* something or a representation *of* something" (Huizinga 13) by increasing the variety of possible game categories. Aspiring to offer no less than a comprehensive typology of play, Caillois nevertheless extends Huizinga's program of exploring the interdependence of games and civilization. "Caillois has not hesitated to use play and games as a culture clue," the translator of *Man, Play, and Games* writes; "the patterns or basic themes of culture should be deducible from the study of play and games no less than from the study of economic, political, religious or familial institutions" (ix). Defining play similarly to Huizinga (Caillois 9–10), Caillois classifies games under four major rubrics, "depending upon whether . . . the role of competition, chance, simulation, or vertigo is dominant" (12). He calls these *agon, alea, mimicry,* and *ilinx,* respectively. Furthermore, games can also be situated on a continuum between two polar opposites: "*Paidia,* which is active, tumultuous, exuberant, and spontaneous," and "ludus, representing calculation, contrivance, and subordination to rules" (viii). In any case, for Caillois, the games we choose help "decide the future of civilization" (35).[19]

To be sure, major and obvious differences exist between Huizinga's and Caillois's conceptions of the game in civilization and the "game as civilization" trope in *The Secret Agent.* The most important of these is that for Huizinga and Caillois play is a positive force in the development of civilization, whereas in *The Secret Agent* it is a negative one to the extent that, as in Beckett's *Endgame* for Geertz, "individuals struggle . . . sometimes cleverly more often comically . . . to play enigmatical games whose structure is clear but whose point is not" ("Blurred Genres" 25). Nevertheless, these sociologists of play provide the conceptual apparatus for understanding social psychology and group behavior in Conrad's novel. Indeed, this behavior is represented as composed of and enacted through an intermeshing series of games, ruses, bluffs, disguises, gambits, ploys, and conspiracies that can be mastered or failed, by which people thrive or perish, but from which none can escape. Regardless of which of the novel's groups one scrutinizes— whether the diplomats, the police, the press, the anarchists, the rich, the poor, or even the Verloc family itself— each is represented as controlled by written and (more often) unwritten rules or conventions of play. Life, for each of this novel's inhabitants, as Geertz puts it in a different context, "is just a bowl of strategies" ("Blurred Genres" 25).[20] As the Professor muses, "The terrorist and the policeman both come from the same basket. Revolution, legality — counter moves in the same game; forms of idleness at bottom identical" (*Secret Agent* 58). As in *Heart of Darkness* where "civilization" is defined in relation to "the Jungle," in *The Secret Agent* the notions of "legality" and "criminality" are shown to be mutually interdependent, as two opposing sides of one game which honors the conventions of play, "the rules of the game" (96). Both burglars and the police "recognise the same conventions," Chief Inspector Heat reasons, "which is advantageous to both, and establishes a sort of amenity in their relations" (74). "Catching thieves," Heat further thinks, has "that quality of seriousness belonging to every form of open sport where the best man wins under perfectly comprehensive rules" (78). Sounding like philosopher/historian R. G. Collingwood, who in *The New Leviathan* confidently asserts that "the barbarist plays a losing game" because "the cards are stacked in favour of civilization, and he knows it" (347), Heat admonishes the Professor with the caveat, "You may be sure our side will win in the end. . . . Then that will be the game. But I'll be damned if I know what yours is. I don't believe you know yourselves" (76).

We need look no farther than the novel's title and subtitle — which invoke the genre of detective fiction with its spying, murder, and cat-and-mouse intrigues between criminals or foreign agents and the police[21] — and the subject of that title, Adolf Verloc, "agent provocateur," for clues that games figure prominently in the novel. Huizinga writes that play "promotes the formation of social groupings which tend to surround themselves with secrecy and to stress their difference from the common world by disguise or other means" (13) and, moreover, that "the exceptional and special position of play is most tellingly illustrated by the fact that it loves to surround itself with an air of secrecy" (12). This description accurately characterizes Verloc. Indeed, "the famous and trusty secret agent, so secret that he was never designated otherwise but by the symbol △" (*Secret Agent* 26), is Huizinga's *homo ludens* par excellence to the extent that, as a "double agent," he both plays roles (as well as both ends against the middle) and takes part in a three-way contest between the (probably) Russian embassy, the anarchists, and the English police. Moreover, Verloc's home is described as "kept up on the wages of a secret industry [spying] eked out by the sale of more or less secret wares [pornography]" (194). Similarly duplicitous is one possible meaning of Verloc's name — *ver*/true, *loc*/speech: "truth-speaker" — given that he is a double or, more likely, triple agent.

Ironically, he works finally not so much for one side or the other as for "the cause of social stability" (181)—for the maintenance of the game itself—"[a]narchists or diplomats" all being "one to him" (185). That Verloc is, in the final analysis, employed by the status quo "game of civilization" itself is emphasized at many points. The narrator informs us, for example, that Verloc's "mission in life" is "the protection of the social mechanism, not its perfectionment or even its criticism" (17). And, elsewhere, Verloc muses that the wealthy "had to be protected . . . and the source of their wealth had to be protected . . . the whole social order favourable to their hygienic idleness had to be protected against the shallow enviousness of unhygienic labour" (15–16). If Verloc is an accomplished player of the game (180), however, he nevertheless is defeated and perishes by it as well (as do Winnie Verloc and Stevie, all within a few hours of each other) because he wrongly assumes that the "game" cannot contaminate family relations. Indeed, the "seller of shady wares" and "protector of society" possesses a "single amiable weakness: the idealistic belief in being loved for himself" (215).[22] Yet it is repeatedly made clear that Winnie Verloc, far from marrying out of love, has done so in order to exercise a strategy of her own: to protect her "delicate" brother Stevie and her decrepit mother from a game outside the Verloc domicile they would undoubtedly lose. For this reason *The Secret Agent* stands as brilliant domestic and marital satire, a work that reveals nuptial relations to be a matter not of love but of socioeconomic and political expedience.[23]

As one might expect, of all of Huizinga's and Caillois's categories of play, that of "agon," or contest, is most useful for our purposes. Huizinga deems play to be inherently agonistic (76, 90); and Caillois's delineation of agon is similar. For him,

> the point of the game is for each player to have his superiority in a given area recognized. This is why the practice of *agon* presupposes sustained attention, appropriate training, assiduous application, and the desire to win. It implies discipline and perseverance. It leaves the champion to his own devices, to evoke the best possible game of which he is capable . . . so that in return the victor's superiority will be beyond dispute. (15)

This agonistic conception of play provides insights into the motivations of virtually everyone in *The Secret Agent*. Whether we consider the scientific, womanizing, and "robust anarchist" Alexander Ossipon (who helps drive Winnie Verloc to suicide), the unnamed and bomb-carrying Professor (who correctly realizes that "the game isn't good enough for any policeman" to get himself blown-up in arresting him [*Secret Agent* 55]), the archpessimist and "terrorist" Karl Yundt, the "ticket-of-leave apostle" and pseudo-Marxist Michaelis (who ironically becomes "annexed" to an older female member of the aristocracy), the sardonic Mr. Vladimir of the embassy (who insists that he is "a civilised man" who "would never dream of directing . . . a mere butchery, even if [he] expected the best results from it" [31]), the police (who for Winnie "are there so that them as have nothing shouldn't take anything away from them who have" [133]), or Chief Inspector Heat (who at a number of points appeals to "the rules of the game"), all pride themselves on the belief that they master the game more completely than their opponents. Here reminiscent of Kurtz, Karl Yundt expresses his sense of life's contest most clearly:

> I have always dreamed . . . of a band of men absolute in their resolve to discard all scruples in the choice of means, strong enough to give themselves frankly the name of destroyers, and free from the taint of that resigned pessimism which rots the world. No pity for anything on earth, including themselves — and death — enlisted for good and all in the service of humanity — that's what I would have liked to see. (38)

The Professor is also a latter-day Kurtz and perverted Nietzsche when it comes to his program for the "weak," the "faint of heart, and the slavish of mind": "Exterminate, exterminate! That is the only way of progress" (226).

Interestingly, Winnie Verloc's brother Stevie (whose name and violent death suggest Saint Stephen, the first Christian martyr) resembles the novel's various and sundry "anarchists" in numerous ways. Like them he is portrayed as "fanatical"[24] and "simplistic," his endless drawing of circles, like their colorful but ineffectual rhetoric, "suggesting chaos and eternity" (179). More precisely, Stevie is portrayed as an *inverse* revolutionist: he has an inverse response from theirs toward the "menaced social order." Whereas the revolutionists are depicted as possessing an ideological framework of understanding that lacks human compassion, Stevie is depicted as possessing a compassion that lacks an ideological framework. Whereas the revolutionists are depicted as disloyal and "indolent," Stevie is depicted as loyal and energetic, however incapable he is of focusing his thoughts and actions. Whereas the expressive revolutionists are depicted as oblivious to their own powerlessness, the inarticulate Stevie is depicted as "[s]upremely wise in knowing his own powerlessness" (130). Eloise Knapp Hay is right to conclude that Stevie offers "a genuine case of feeling to offset their sham sympathies" (252). "Simple" Stevie is genuinely concerned with social justice; yet his ability to judge the world around him, like his childish vocabulary, is strictly binary: everything and everyone is either "good" or "bad." At best he can muster, "Bad world for poor people" (132), yet he demonstrates little understanding of why this is so. This is evident when Winnie and Stevie accompany their mother by carriage to her inexpensive retirement at "the Charity" home.[25] On this occasion Stevie reacts to the unfortunate situation of both the impoverished cabby and his overworked horse the only way he can:

> He could say nothing; for the tenderness to all pain and all misery, the desire to make the horse happy and the cabman happy, had reached the point of a bizarre longing to take them to bed with him. And that, he knew, was impossible. . . . To be taken into a bed of compassion was the supreme remedy, with only the one disadvantage of being difficult of application on a large scale. (129)

Later, the narrator informs us that Stevie, "[b]eing no sceptic, but a moral creature," was "in a manner at the mercy of his righteous passions" (132). Contrariwise, the anarchists are portrayed as resolutely skeptical, immoral, and at the mercy of their unrighteous passions, their vanity. The claim that the revolutionists of *The Secret Agent* possess an avowed ideology and pronounced vanity — but not compassion — demands little substantiation. One need only think of Ossipon's brutal and deceptive treatment of Winnie — not to mention his betrayal of Verloc — after she murders her husband and has no place to turn.

To be sure, vanity, the mildest variant of narcissism, is more at issue for these anarchists than ideology: "in their own way the most ardent of revolutionaries," the Professor thinks, are "doing no more but seeking for peace in common with the rest of mankind — the peace of soothed vanity, of satisfied appetites, or perhaps of appeased conscience" (67). And the Professor imagines Heat's interest in him as centering not on justice but on winning the game — on his "superiors," his "reputation," the "law courts," his "salary," and the "newspapers" (58). At one point Mr. Vladimir even insists that the English as a group "are blinded by an idiotic vanity" (28), and at another Karl Yundt maintains that vanity is the "mother of all noble and vile illusions, the companion of poets, reformers, charlatans, prophets, and incendiaries" (46). It is also made clear that the "domesticated" Verloc is less sure of which side he is on in the great scheme of things than he is of his own great importance to it. Moreover, that the "anarchists" Michaelis and Ossipon pen studies like *Autobiography of a Prisoner* ("which was to be like a book of Revelation in the history of mankind" [94]), and *The Corroding Vices of the Middle Classes* ("a popular quasi-medical study" [41]), respectively, suggests that vanity, not social justice, guides their practical lives. In this sense, "justice," as Huizinga writes of archaic civilization, "is made subservient . . . to the rules of the game"; and hence "the idea of right and wrong . . . comes to be overshadowed by the idea of winning and losing, that is, the purely agonistic conception" (78–79). Huizinga also addresses the game as it is represented in Conrad's novel when he notes that "the innate desire to be first will still drive power-groups into collision and may lead them to incredible extremes of infatuation and frenzied megalomania," even when order breaks down. "At bottom it is always a question of winning — though we know well enough that this form of 'winning' can bring no gain" (101).

This final determination returns us to Eagleton's erroneous claim that the Professor "threatens" the smooth functioning of the game *from without.* For it is clear that the Professor is a part of the institutionalized game which, for each of this novel's inhabitants, is inescapable. It is not simply that the Professor wishes, like the rest, to prove his superiority at playing the game. Rather, it is that he is as much trapped within the game as anyone, a slave to "the India-rubber ball [the detonator in his pocket], the supreme guarantee of his sinister freedom" (67). Indeed, his critique of the other "revolutionists" is an apt assessment of his own unbreakable ties to the establishment: "You revolutionists," he tells Ossipon, "are the slaves of the social convention, which is afraid of you; slaves of it as much as the very police that stands up in the defence of that convention. Clearly you are, since you want to revolutionise it. It governs your thought, of course, and your action, too, and thus neither your thought nor your action can ever be conclusive" (*Secret Agent* 57–58). However, despite his claim that, contrary to the rest, he is not "bound in all sorts of conventions" (57), the Professor is depicted as equally a part of the greater game of civilization that determines the thoughts and actions of everyone. Like the "old terrorist" Yundt, for example, his thoughts too caress "images of ruin and destruction." Like Yundt he walks "frail, insignificant, shabby, miserable — and terrible in the simplicity of his idea calling madness and despair to the regeneration of the world" (231). Hence, although Caillois asserts that "the game is ruined by the nihilist who denounces the rules as absurd and conventional, who refuses to play because the game is meaningless" (7), the Professor is represented neither as the transcendent being nor as the game's spoiler that he takes himself to be — his only avenue of escape from the game being suicide itself.[26]

Thus, within the novel's "world of contradictions" — its fictional London "of marvels and mud, with its maze of streets and its mass of lights . . . sunk in a hopeless night" (203) — only the "gameworthy" survive. This insight is echoed in the Author's Note to *The Secret Agent* when Conrad speaks of his vision "of a monstrous town more populous than some continents and in its man-made might as if indifferent to heaven's frowns and smiles, a cruel devourer of the world's light" (6). As if responding to *Heart of Darkness*'s dismantling of the idea of civilization so cherished by the English, then, *The Secret Agent* reconstructs it as a lethal game. In both cases, however, London is represented not as the heart of light and center of civilization but as a "monstrous" and "duplicitous" place of darkness.

Avrom Fleishman writes that "something of the same duplexity must impress us as lying in the essence of Conradian landscapes, whether in the primal forests of *Heart of Darkness* or in the swarming modern townscape of *The Secret Agent* ("Landscape" 105). If this is true, it is at least in part due to the fact that these two works, when viewed in juxtaposition, expunge much of the presumed difference between their respective landscapes, rendering them metaphors for each other.[27] We should therefore reject readings of either work that maintain distinctions — such as "civilization" and "jungle" or "legal order" and "illegal anarchy" — the legitimacy of which the texts themselves refute. For this reason *Heart of Darkness* and *The Secret Agent* remain among the most uncannily disconcerting and cynical works of literary modernism.[28] Both of them, as Patrick Reilly notes of the former, clearly have been "squandered upon the reader who still feels secure" after reading them (68).

4

Civilization in Post–Great War Bloomsbury: Woolf's "Twenties" Novels and Bell's *Civilization* and *On British Freedom*

Civilization requires the existence of a leisured class, and a leisured class requires the existence of slaves — of people . . . who give some part of their surplus time and energy to the support of others. — Bell, CIVILIZATION

Does the progress of civilisation depend upon great men? Is the lot of the average human being better now than in the time of the Pharaohs? Is the lot of the average human being, however, . . . the criterion by which we judge the measure of civilisation? Possibly not. Possibly the greatest good requires the existence of a slave class. — Mr. Ramsay, in Woolf, TO THE LIGHTHOUSE

The text . . . is not equal to the work as a whole. . . . The work also includes its necessary extratextual context. The work, as it were, is enveloped in the . . . context in which it is understood and evaluated. — Bakhtin, "Toward a Methodology for the Human Sciences"

✳ Woolf and Bell in the 1920s

In the midst of the long June day of Virginia Woolf's *Mrs. Dalloway*, Peter Walsh muses on the passing ambulance which, unbeknownst to him, rushes suicide victim Septimus Smith to the hospital:

> One of the triumphs of civilisation, Peter Walsh thought. It is one of the triumphs of civilisation, as the light high bell of the ambulance sounded. Swiftly, cleanly the ambulance sped to the hospital, having picked up instantly, humanely, some poor devil. . . . That was civilisation. It struck him coming back from the East—the efficiency, the organisation, the communal spirit of London. (229)

Reminiscent of Marlow in Conrad's *Heart of Darkness*[1]—yet a less critical Marlow who, upon returning to the West, still clings to a sense of its greater humanity, "efficiency," "organisation," and "communal spirit"—Peter Walsh identifies an obsession of much of Woolf's writing, particularly in the wake of the Great War: the triumphs and discontents of English civilization. E. M. Forster underscores this notion when he writes that Woolf's novels "display unrest or disillusionment or anxiety" due to the war, that they are "the products of a civilisation which feels itself insecure" (*Two Cheers for Democracy* 272). Indeed, what Avrom Fleishman says of Woolf's *Jacob's Room* (1922) may be said of her other major works of the twenties: *Mrs. Dalloway* (1925), *To the Lighthouse* (1927), and *A Room of One's Own* (1929). "Having posited that *Jacob's Room* is a fiction in which an individual is shown partially constituted by his transactions with his society," Fleishman writes, "we are now prepared to see" this society, "in its largest sense, as Western Civilization" (*Virginia Woolf* 60). Yet, if Herbert Spencer's writings provide Conrad with the conventional wisdom about civilization at the turn of the century, Woolf's Bloomsbury milieu affords a considerably different perspective on "civilization" in the years following the Great War. In this connection, the speculations of Peter Walsh are instructive in yet another way. As Lucio Ruotolo first observed, many of Peter Walsh's "personal qualities" are shared by Clive Bell (115), one of Bloomsbury's foremost aestheticians, art and culture critics. What should be recognized is that not merely Bell's person but his controversial ideas as well are reflected in *Mrs. Dalloway*.

It is my contention that Bell's "theory of civilization," as expressed in *On British Freedom* (1923) and *Civilization* (1928), provides what Bakhtin calls "the necessary extratextual context" by which to better understand and evaluate the civilization represented in Woolf's *Mrs. Dalloway* and *To the*

Lighthouse. These novels invoke and critique, absorb and parody, Bell's "much read and much criticized" theory of civilization (Edel 284), not only because of its currency at the time but because Woolf herself remained deeply skeptical about many of its ramifications. As Alex Zwerdling reminds us, Bell's *Civilization* probably did "more to create the image of Bloomsbury as an exclusive cultural mafia than any other work" (102).

More specifically, I will argue that *On British Freedom* and *Civilization* inform Woolf's novelistic presentation of censorship, women, and class in civilization and that the appearance of Bell-like characters in the novels provides Woolf with a further method by which to express criticisms that could not, under the circumstances of their personal relationship, be voiced openly. Although Bell's notion of the present danger of censorship to civilization in *On British Freedom* is represented approvingly in *Mrs. Dalloway*, his notions of the function of women and class in *Civilization* are subverted by and treated parodistically in *To the Lighthouse* and *Mrs. Dalloway*. At issue is not simply that Woolf's fiction appropriates and transforms Bell's *On British Freedom* and *Civilization* in various ways but that our knowledge of this textual (and personal) relationship clarifies our understanding of this fiction's view of "civilization," that "key Bloomsbury word" (Dowling 137).

The Woolf–Bell relationship is even more complex than the Conrad–Spencer one given that the former pair were intimate acquaintances and relatives by marriage (Bell married Virginia's sister, Vanessa Stephen, in 1907). Although critics often allude to Woolf and Bell in one breath, as prominent members of the Bloomsbury Group,[2] little scholarly attention has been paid to any precise relationship, or dialogue, among their texts. Existing critical inquiry for the most part concerns their personal relationship, Bell's source for Terence in Woolf's first novel, *The Voyage Out*,[3] and the intersection of Bell's artistic theory and Woolf's artistic practice[4] — that "the basic attitude behind the aesthetico-philosophical theories of Woolf and Bell coincides with a profoundly sceptical view of western civilisation" (Heinemann 212).[5] The sole critic to notice any connection between Bell's and Woolf's visions of civilization is Philip Henderson who, in 1936, mentions in passing that "an indication" of "what Mrs. Woolf means by civilization" is "provided by Clive Bell" in "his book *Civilization*" (91). Until now Henderson's insight has remained unnoticed, unexplored, and untested.

That Woolf and Bell read each other's work is common knowledge. Theirs was a long-standing personal and intellectual relationship, lasting from 1899 until Woolf's death in 1941. Bell not only wrote about Woolf's fiction on a number of occasions — most notably in *Pot-Boilers* (1918), *Dial* magazine (1924), and *Old Friends* (1956)[6] — but made countless appearances in Woolf's letters and diaries (and at her lunch table). At one point, Woolf even contemplated writing a life of Bell.[7] In Bell's opinion, Woolf was, along with Hardy and Conrad, one of "our three best living novelists" (*Pot-Boilers* 11) and "one of the most beautiful [and] best bred women of her age" (*Old Friends* 99). Woolf's impression of Bell, on the other hand, tended to be ambivalent. She seemed unable to decide whether she found Bell to be a kindred spirit (*Diary* II, 195) whose opinion she greatly valued (*Letters* III, 69–70) or "intolerably dull" (*Letters* III, 219) and essentially unworthy of respect (*Writer's Diary* 18–19). In any case, Bell proved to be a force with whom Woolf, whether happily or not, felt she must reckon.

That Woolf had contact with Bell's tracts on civilization is also clear. For example, Woolf wrote to Bell in May of 1923 asking permission to see, and even to publish at her and Leonard Woolf's Hogarth Press, the completed manuscript of *On British Freedom* (*Letters* III, 33). Just exactly when Virginia gained access to *Civilization* remains somewhat less clear, but it is certain that she was aware of Bell's civilization project as early as 1906 (*Diary* II, 101). It is also clear that Woolf knew the general outline of Bell's theory long before its publication. Bell even dedicated *Civilization* to Woolf herself. "[S]he alone of my friends," Bell explains, was "in at the birth" and "followed the fortunes of this backward and ill-starred child." She alone knew "that it was the first conceived of all my brood, and that all the rest" have "come of it. Its conception dates from our nonage" (9). Further evidence that Woolf would have been familiar with Bell's civilization project years before it emerged in print is the echo of it found in *Jacob's Room*. Just as Bell refers to *Civilization* as a "light essay" (23) that pits present-day England against past "paragons of civilization," so too Woolf has Jacob Flanders consider writing "an essay upon civilization. A comparison between the ancients and moderns" (136). In his dedicatory letter to Woolf, Bell deems *Civilization* of a piece with *On British Freedom* and, except for changes introduced after the Great War, likens it to "the old familiar argument" (11) about which he chattered years before in Woolf's "workroom in Fitzroy Square" (10). At one point in *Civilization* Bell admits that his argument was originally sketched "20 years earlier" (157) — at a time comfortably after the two began exchanging ideas, and during the formative years of Bloomsbury. In April of 1927 Woolf even reports, in a letter to Vita Sackville-West from Cassis, France, that she watches Bell complete his *Civilization*: "Clive is seated at a rickety table writing on huge sheets of foolscap, which he picks out from time to time in red ink. This is the history of Civilisation. He has by him Chambers Dictionary of the English Language" (*Letters* III, 358).[8]

The development of Bell's theory of civilization is easily traced. The conclusion of *On British Freedom* is virtually identical to the introduction of *Civilization:* "It is for civilization — for which, by the way, we are supposed to have fought the war — that I am pleading: and though I am aware that liberty alone will not give it us, yet I am certain that no nation can be truly civilized till it possesses a far greater measure of personal freedom than is to be enjoyed in this or any other Anglo-Saxon community" (86). In *Civilization,* Bell is far more pointed in his formulation of the current "civilization problem":

> Since from August 1914 to November 1918 Great Britain and her Allies were fighting for civilization it cannot, I suppose, be impertinent to enquire what precisely civilization may be. . . . The story of this word's rise to the highest place amongst British war aims is so curious that, even were it less relevant, I should be tempted to tell it. . . . "You are fighting for civilization," cried the wisest and best of those leaders who led us into war, and the very soldiers took up the cry, "Join up, for civilization's sake." . . . I, in my turn, began to cry: "And what is civilization?" I did not cry aloud, be sure: at that time, for crying things of that sort aloud, one was sent to prison. (13)

From the vantage point of postwar safety Bell again posed this question and answered it in his "theory of civilization." "I must," he writes, "deduce the peculiar characteristics of civilization from a consideration of entities admittedly civilized and admittedly uncivilized" (21). Bell's conclusion: "My notion is that a Sense of Values and Reason Enthroned are the parent qualities of high civilization" (50–51) and that its "secondary qualities" are "a taste for truth and beauty, tolerance, intellectual honesty, fastidiousness, a sense of humour, good manners, curiosity, a dislike of vulgarity [and] brutality . . . in two words — sweetness and light" (120).

Bell's next move is a nostalgic one: to establish his "paragons of civilization" — fifth- and fourth-century Athens, Renaissance Italy, and France from Fronde to Revolution (49) — to which present-day England should aspire. However, for Bell civilization must never be defined as a nation-state but rather as a state of mind, a grouping of individuals (perhaps along the lines of the Bloomsbury Group) forceful enough to form a "nucleus which converts a passive culture into a civilizing force" (178). Indeed, it cannot be overemphasized that for Bell the "will to civilization" is individual and mental. Civilization "is the flavour given to the self-expression of an

age or society by a mental attitude: it is the colour given to social manifestations by a peculiar and prevailing point of view. . . . It is the mind, the
individual mind, which conceives, creates, and carries [it] out" (121–22).[9]
Bell next insists upon a strict social hierarchy to secure civilization: a
"civilizing elite" (149) beneath which must stand a service class to insure its
leisure. Whether or not one views Bell's *Civilization* as articulating "an
optimistic vision of culture" (Johnston 254) or an "extremely smug and
offensive" position characteristic of "Bloomsbury at its very worst" (Lee
10), it will become clear that Virginia Woolf's novels represent and worry
Bell's "theory" in striking ways that illuminate both.

✳ Censorship as a Threat to Civilization in *Mrs. Dalloway* and *On British Freedom*

On British Freedom (1923) and *Mrs. Dalloway* (1925) are the earliest books
by their authors to confront civilization — and the perceived threats to
civilization in the aftermath of the Great War — head on. With scathing
irony, each of these social satires explores the threats to English civilization
posed by various literal and figurative forms of censorship. Although it
would be an overstatement, even a distortion, to suggest that *Mrs. Dalloway*
simply mimes *On British Freedom*, the novel clearly derives numerous of its
insights, and even characterizations, from Bell's "pamphlet."

To be sure, *Mrs. Dalloway* does not share Bell's purposefully hyperbolic
bleakness on the subject of British freedom — that "Great Britain is one of
the least free countries in the world . . . quite the least free in Europe" (*On
British Freedom* 1), that the ordinary Englishman is "less free than a Roman
slave" (4), and that therefore Britain is "the laughing stock of the civilized
world" (10). Yet the novel does appropriate Bell's view that England is
"enslaved" by various "enemies of freedom": politicians, scientists, doctors,
and religious "goody rollers" who seek to legislate and to censor the
cultural fare consumed by the public.

Take Bell's condemnation of those doctors and moralists — adherents of
the "religion of health" and Church religion — who seek to limit public
freedoms. Whether post-Enlightenment scientists of the left or religious
moralists of the right, "the born enemies of liberty," Bell maintains, "cannot express themselves except by interfering with others. They are prey,"
he continues, "to an itch which renders them incapable not only of contemplation and appreciation but even of satisfying themselves with profitable work and harmless relaxation. To be happy they must be meddling"

(73).[10] A prime example of such meddling in *Mrs. Dalloway* can be found in the treatment of the shell-shocked and megalomaniac Septimus Smith by Doctors Holmes and Bradshaw. As much a victim of the doctors themselves as of the war, Septimus exemplifies Bell's claim that "organized medicine, were it allowed to have its way, would be fatal" (68). For Bell, while some doctors champion liberty, "[t]he common practitioner is made of poorer clay" (63). While modern science may have accomplished much, "a little science is a dangerous thing; and a very little is the common portion of an English general practitioner" (62). For Bell, doctors all too frequently "meddle" where they do not belong, possess a "bullying instinct," fetishize "health" and "normalcy," make a god of "proportion," repress feeling, and even contradict one another's diagnoses—apt characterizations of Septimus's dynamic duo of physicians.[11]

To consider Bell's final point first, Holmes and Bradshaw offer Septimus contradictory cures for an "ailment" that neither truly understands. Bell's charge that the doctrines of doctors "themselves change as rapidly and radically as fashions in frocks, while in their private opinions the doctors vary at least as much as the ladies do in their figures" (64), resurfaces in Septimus's observation that his two doctors are "different in their verdicts (for Holmes said one thing, Bradshaw another)" (*Mrs. Dalloway* 225). Holmes, a general practitioner for whom only the body, and not the psyche, is capable of suffering injury, holds that the despairing Septimus "was not ill"; in fact, "there was nothing the matter with him" (34). Prescribing "two tabloids of bromide" dissolved in water at bedtime, Holmes "brushed aside" Septimus's "headaches, sleeplessness, fears, dreams" as "nerve symptoms and nothing more" (138)—as figments of his imagination. By contrast, "the priest of science" (142) and specialist in "nerve cases" (144), the neurologist/psychologist Sir William Bradshaw, provides a different diagnosis and cure for Septimus's malaise after examining him for no more than "two or three minutes." "It was a case of complete breakdown," Bradshaw reasons, "complete physical and nervous breakdown, with every symptom in an advanced stage" (144), for which the cure "was merely a question of rest . . . of rest, rest, rest; a long rest in bed" (146). Bradshaw even thinks of Holmes, "those general practitioners! . . . It took half his time to undo their blunders. Some were irreparable" (145). Yet neither doctor truly speaks to Septimus's war experience, "that little shindy of schoolboys with gunpowder" (145), the real cause of his problem. In a rare instance when Septimus's two doctors agree, they unjustly view him as suffering from self-indulgence and narcissism. Holmes asks Smith to "take an interest in things outside himself" (31); and Bradshaw tells him, "try to think as little about yourself as possible" (149). Woolf's irony, of course, is clear: Holmes and Bradshaw are the real specialists in megalomania and egocentrism in *Mrs. Dalloway*.

Bell is also critical of the widespread medical fetishization of "health" and "normalcy" — an attitude Woolf's novel mirrors in its discussion of "proportion." "It is a curious ethical assumption," Bell writes, "that the proper study of mankind is health" (63). It is unfortunate that "[t]o differ from the commonplace . . . to be sensitive to beauty, or to care greatly for truth, in fact to be exceptional in any way, is to be abnormal" (63). With their "religion of health," Bell continues, doctors "claim to meddle with our lives and limit our freedom" based "on the entirely false assumption that health is an end in itself; that a world of perfectly 'normal' imbeciles, or at any rate of healthy general practitioners, is the ideal" (67–68). "Health," he insists, "is not the end: clear thinking and fine feeling are. . . . For it is just possible to have fine thought and feeling without health; but you can have neither without liberty to think and feel, and express too" (66–67).

Septimus's inability to "feel" anything, for which he believes himself "condemned" to "death" (*Mrs. Dalloway* 137), is only exacerbated by Holmes's and Bradshaw's moralizing and repressive prescriptions in the name of balance, health, normalcy, "proportion." *Mrs. Dalloway*'s ironic disquisition on these themes — that "health we must have; and health is proportion" (149) — further suggests how significant *On British Freedom* is to the novel's makeup. In this novel "proportion" is synonymous with the repression and atrophy of feeling, which comports with Bell's accusation that the medical practice of his time is censoring, repressive, and health-fetishizing. "If Dr. Holmes found himself even half a pound below eleven stone six, he asked his wife for another plate of porridge at breakfast," for "health is largely a matter in our own control" (138). Holmes even seeks to enforce the reign of his god of health through legislation. Because Septimus threatens suicide, "there was no alternative" to bed rest in one of Holmes's homes; "It was a question of law" (146). Similarly, Sir William Bradshaw, whom Alex Zwerdling aptly terms a "psychiatrist-policeman" (129), engages in social repression and worships "divine proportion." Reminiscent of one of Dickens's unreconstructed Utilitarians in *Hard Times*, Bradshaw insists that the one thing needful is "proportion": "Sir William said he never spoke of 'madness'; he called it not having a sense of proportion" (146). "To his patients he gave three-quarters of an hour; and if in this exacting science which has to do with what, after all, we know nothing about . . . a doctor loses his sense of proportion, as a doctor he fails" (149).

Bell's sense that doctors too often seek to censor their patients' behavior is also echoed in Holmes's and Bradshaw's aggressiveness. For Bell, too many doctors put their "smattering of science and the prestige of a great calling at the service of the bullying instinct" — "the attitude of these gentlemen who write to the papers and make speeches exhorting the Government to enforce their dogmas is about as unscientific as an attitude can be" (*On British Freedom* 63–64). "I do think it preposterous," Bell continues, "that a gang of arrogant and ignorant human beings should presume not only to lay down the law in a science where there is hardly a conclusion which goes unchallenged, but, as though they had discovered incontrovertible principles of universal application, to bully the Government into applying their nostrums" (65–66). How familiar this sounds when we consider Holmes's and Bradshaw's treatment of Septimus. Believing himself "condemned to death by human nature" (145), with Holmes and Bradshaw cast in the role of "human nature" (139, 141, 213), Septimus finally is driven to suicide not by the voices he hears but by Holmes's attempt, based on his legal right, physically to remove Septimus from his wife, Rezia, for bed rest in total isolation (226–27). Similarly, Bradshaw seeks to put bills "through the Commons" (278) promulgating censorship laws: "Worshipping proportion, Sir William not only prospered himself but made England prosper, secluded her lunatics, forbade childbirth, penalised despair, made it impossible for the unfit to propogate their views until they, too, shared his sense of proportion" (150). Clarissa Dalloway, at her long-awaited party, is aware of her own instinctual revulsion from Bradshaw's "forcing" of people's souls and making "life intolerable" (281). In *On British Freedom* as in *Mrs. Dalloway*, then, physicians are represented as the enemies of civilization when they coerce or censor thought and activity and when they worship at the shrine of "proportion" — complacent mediocrity incarnate.

Bell takes on not only the "religion of health" but religious fanatics as well, those "illiterate busybodies" who seek to control the public's "spiritual food" (19–20). More specifically, he castigates those proselytizing "goody rollers" for their will to censor. "This gang, the goody-goody, is extremely powerful — powerful enough to have *converted* what was once merry England into a place of proverbial gloom" (60; my emphasis). In *Mrs. Dalloway* too, "conversion" is railed against explicitly and is embodied in Miss Doris Kilman (with her suggestive family name) — a disaffected religious moralist with sympathies for Germany who attempts to convert Elizabeth Dalloway to her world view. Indeed, it is difficult not to see Miss Kilman in Bell's description of the domineering "petty tyrant":

You will find him, or more probably her, in the guise of a middle-aged woman of plain but energetic countenance, shaped sometimes like a lettuce gone to seed. . . . [O]ur modern tyrants sit, not in palaces, but in committee rooms, brooding over human wrongs and miseries and the odious frivolity and wickedness of those who are in any way unlike themselves. . . . By profession they are philanthropists; and, thus disguised, have contrived so far to escape most of that obloquy which tyrants deserve and get. (53–54)

Seeking to censor the public, such religious moralists, for Bell, want nothing less than "to impose, to arm their will or whim with the force of law, to have everything as they think it should be, to cut everyone's life to a pattern of their own design" (58).

In *Mrs. Dalloway*, Miss Kilman fits Bell's bill exactly. She is "philanthropic" ("for Miss Kilman would do anything for the Russians, starved herself for the Austrians, but in private inflicted positive torture, so insensitive was she" [16]), zealously "Christian" ("Then Our Lord had come to her. . . . The Lord had shown her the way" [187–88]), sits "on committees" (206), and is "one of those spectres who stand astride us and suck up half our life blood, dominators and tyrants" (16–17). Clarissa herself views Kilman's censoring will as a threat to one's "privacy of the soul" (192) and views Kilman as "clumsy, hot, domineering, hypocritical, eavesdropping, jealous, infinitely cruel and unscrupulous." "Had she ever tried to convert anyone herself?" Clarissa wonders of Miss Kilman. "Did she not wish everybody merely to be themselves?" (191). The diatribe against "conversion" in *Mrs. Dalloway*, of which Miss Kilman is one of the chief perpetrators, strongly echoes Bell's condemnation of it. It is linked, in the novel, with British imperialism in India and Africa; yet it also operates, like Miss Kilman herself, in "the perlieus of London":

Conversion is her name and she feasts on the wills of the weakly, loving to impress, to impose, adoring her own features stamped on the face of the populace. . . . [She] walks penitentially disguised as brotherly love through factories and parliaments; offers help, but desires power; . . . bestows her blessing on those who, looking upward, catch submissively from her eyes the light of their own. . . . But conversion, fastidious Goddess, loves blood better than brick, and feasts most subtly on the human will. (151–52)

Like *Mrs. Dalloway*, *On British Freedom* casts "conversion" in the image of a vain and power-mongering "old maid" disguised as a humanitarian (Miss Kilman "prayed to God. She could not help being ugly; she could not afford to buy pretty clothes" [195]):

In justice it should be added that the tyrant's temper, the passion to dominate and interfere, which is the steam that drives the goody-goody roller, is supplemented, not only by the disappointed coxcomb's vanity, but much more by the old-maid's envy and the acquired spite-fulness of a certain class of barren women. . . . You may see it any day of the week discolour the countenance of a philanthropic old maid. (*On British Freedom* 60–61)

Surprisingly, given Woolf's sensitivity to the portrayal of women in fiction, Kilman is depicted in precisely these terms. For example, Kilman considers her mental contest with Clarissa in this way: "it was not the body; it was the soul and its mockery that she wished to subdue; make feel her mastery. If only she could make her weep; could ruin her; humiliate her; bring her to her knees crying, You are right! But this was God's will, not Miss Kilman's. It was to be a religious victory" (189). Like the will to power of Bell's domineering petty tyrants, Miss Kilman's aspiration to convert and hold power over others is shrouded in the pretense of doing God's, and human-kind's, bidding.[12]

❋ Women and Civilization in *To the Lighthouse* and *Civilization*

In *A Room of One's Own* Woolf writes, "if one is a woman one is often surprised by a sudden splitting off of consciousness, say in walking down Whitehall, when from being the natural inheritor of that civilisation, she becomes, on the contrary, outside of it, alien and critical" (101). Woolf's ambivalent relationship to civilization as a female is posed by this comment and is reflected, with increasing intensity, in each subsequent of her "twen-ties" novels. It is particularly evident in *To the Lighthouse*, a less satiric but more critical work than *Mrs. Dalloway*. If *Mrs. Dalloway* closely adheres to *On British Freedom*'s depiction of the present danger to civilization of various forms of censorship, *To the Lighthouse* diverges sharply from Bell's conclusions on the role of women in civilization. Indeed, the later novel not only invokes and absorbs but ruthlessly critiques and parodies Bell's *Civilization* for its handling of the "woman question."

This rift between Woolf and Bell is best explained by Leonard Woolf and Quentin Bell. According to Virginia's husband, intellectuals of this period were still under the sway of cultural fallout from the Great War, which irrevocably changed Bloomsbury's expectations about the future of civiliza-tion. "We were," he writes of pre-1914 years, "mistaken in thinking that the world really might become civilized." But the war "postponed the danger of our becoming civilized for at least a hundred years" (*Beginning Again* 36–37). And in his monumental biography of Virginia Woolf, Quentin Bell argues that

> The variations in Virginia's comments upon Clive are in themselves an indication that her strictures should not be taken too seriously. But it was true that, since the war, Clive had become more worldly, and at the same time she herself had become both more interested in and more critical of worldliness. Being herself a snob she was able to understand the subtle corruption of values which she discerned in Clive and which she herself was to describe with some particularity in *Mrs. Dalloway.* (II, 85–86)

This postwar ambivalence in Woolf's feelings for Bell is even suggested in *Mrs. Dalloway,* when Woolf has Peter Walsh, the novel's Bell-like character, think, "Those five years—1918 to 1923—had been . . . somehow very important. People looked different. Newspapers seemed different" (108). Yet Woolf would not openly commit herself in print against Bell's positions. She would only do so privately in her diaries and indirectly in her fiction.

That Woolf would say one thing to Bell about *Civilization* in her letters to him and quite a different thing about it in her diaries is a manifestation of this ambivalence in her thinking about Bell's ideas during the twenties. Two examples of Woolf's subterfuge will suffice. In a letter to Bell in the fall of 1927, Woolf writes, "I've just finished your [*Civilization*] manuscript which indeed I couldn't stop reading. I think it most brilliant, witty and suggestive—I'm sure it's the best thing you've done—not a doubt of it. . . . It seems to me . . . full of really new and original things, and what a mercy to read anything so reasoned and written throughout" (*Letters* III, 438), while in a diary entry six months later she is dismissive of its merits: "Clive's book out—a very superficial one, L.[eonard] says" (*Diary* III, 184).[13] Bell picked up on Woolf's insincerity, which prompted another attempt on her part to flatter his work. In a subsequent letter to him she insists, "I had been really moved and stirred by [*Civilization*] and had tried to say so" (*Letters* III, 441), even though we know, from her most often quoted assessment of this book, that she deems Bell to have "great fun in the opening chapters but in the end it turns out that Civilisation is [merely] a lunch party at no. 50 Gordon Square" (Quentin Bell, *Virginia Woolf* II, 137).

The widest rift between Woolf and Bell centers on the role of women in civilization. As if offering his riposte to statements made by members of the women's movement, Bell argues in *Civilization against* the notion that "the measure of a people's civility is the position it accords to women" (27). For him, women are a "means to civility" (64) and not, the implication is clear, its "end." Bell's discussion of the role of women in civilization takes a form similar to all of his other discussions: he pits his nostalgia for ancient Athens against the debased present. The Athenians "appreciated the importance of the highly civilized woman — they appreciated her importance as a means to civilization," he writes. "They knew that without an admixture of the feminine point of view and the feminine reaction, without feminine taste, perception, intuition, wit, subtlety, devotion, perversity, and scepticism, a civilization must be lop-sided and incomplete" (164–65).[14] In addition to this offensive litany of clichés about women, Woolf undoubtedly would have found disturbing Bell's distinction between educated, intellectually and aesthetically developed women, on the one hand, and "housewives," on the other. "Truly," Bell continues, "the ordinary Athenian housewife was treated very much as though she were a highly respected slave. Naturally, for a housewife is a slave. And in this, as in most matters, the Athenians tried to see things as they are. They faced facts and called upon intellect to deal with them, thus elaborating a civilization in advance of anything that went before or has come after" (164). Although Bell admits that, "with exceptional luck, aptitude, and physique, a married woman may retain her civility" (168), he nevertheless maintains that those tasks associated with being a housewife "will tend generally to blunt the fine edge of her intelligence and sensibility, will indispose so delicate a creature for that prolonged study and serious application which to the highest culture are indispensable" (167).[15]

Bell's conception of the role of women in civilization is invoked only to be indicted in Woolf's *To the Lighthouse*, one of whose two "heroines" approximates that variety of woman Bell belittles: a "housewife." To the contrary, it is a "housewife," Mrs. Ramsay, who proves to be the chief "civilizing" force in the narrative — both before and after her death. Rather than being merely a "means to civilization" who provides men with "taste, perception, intuition, wit," Mrs. Ramsay, as one reader puts it, "does more to create and nurture civilization . . . than any other character" in the novel (Transue 89). It is Mrs. Ramsay's dinner, for example, and not Mr. Ramsay's refined philosophizing, that is depicted as reining in the "fluidity out there" (*To the Lighthouse* 147), as contributing, however momentarily, to a salutary intersubjectivity, to a coherent community of sensibility rarely achieved in everyday life. As Pamela Transue argues, "when the candles are lit at [Mrs. Ramsay's] dinner, they create a kind of sanctuary of civilization and order" (89). The same, moreover, can be said of Lily Briscoe's painting and, for that matter, Clarissa Dalloway's party: it is Woolf's heroines, as Jane Marcus first noticed, who constitute "the voice of civilization" (17).[16]

By contrast, Bell's archly "civilized" male in *To the Lighthouse* is maligned as petty, vain, and inveterately misogynistic. For example, Mr. Ramsay's protégé, Charles Tansley, at one point thinks, "It was the women's fault. Women made civilisation impossible with all their 'charm,' all their silliness" (129). He even goes as far as to insist that "women can't paint, women can't write" (75) — that is, cannot engage in those most civilized forms of artistic and intellectual endeavor.[17] "He was not going to be condescended to by these silly women," Tansley thinks. "He had been reading in his room, and now he came down and it all seemed to him silly, superficial, flimsy. . . . They did nothing but talk, talk, talk, eat, eat, eat" (129). Mr. Ramsay espouses a similar sentiment when he considers his wife's hope, weather permitting, to sail out to the lighthouse the following day: "The extraordinary irrationality of her remark, the folly of women's minds enraged him. He had ridden through the valley of death, been shattered and shivered; and now, she flew in the face of facts, made his children hope what was utterly out of the question, in effect, told lies" (50). He also repeatedly exaggerates his wife's "ignorance" and "simplicity," for "he liked to think that she was not clever, not book-learned at all" (182).

Not stopping at misogyny, however, Mr. Ramsay and Charles Tansley are also depicted as extremely vain for using women to feed their egos. As Woolf herself puts it of men in *A Room of One's Own* (published one year after Bell's *Civilization*):

> How is he to go on giving judgement, civilising natives, making laws, writing books, dressing up and speechifying at banquets, unless he can see himself at breakfast and at dinner at least twice the size he really is? . . . The looking-glass vision is of supreme importance because it charges the vitality; it stimulates the nervous system. Take it away and man may die, like the drug fiend deprived of his cocaine. (36)

In *To the Lighthouse* Mrs. Ramsay ventures a similar criticism of the role women play in male civilization, even if her tone is less accusatory: "Indeed, she had the whole of the other sex under her protection; for reasons she could not explain, for their chivalry and valour, for the fact that they negotiated treaties, ruled India, controlled finance" (13). Mr. Ramsay is characterized as taking immense "satisfaction in his own splendour" (48), and the Ramsay daughters notice that Tansley turns every subject of conversation toward himself in order to disparage others. "And he would go to the picture galleries," they complain, "and he would ask one, did one like his tie?" (16).[18] In *Mrs. Dalloway* too, Clarissa detects her own invisibility in the eyes of male civilization: "She had the oddest sense of being herself invisible; unseen; unknown; . . . this being Mrs. Dalloway; not even Clarissa any more; this being Mrs. Richard Dalloway" (14). In this earlier novel only a woman of Lady Bruton's status, who in any case "had the reputation of being more interested in politics than people; of talking like a man" (159–60), gains the full respect of her male acquaintants.

If the civilized male of *To the Lighthouse*, in Mrs. Ramsay's words, pursues "truth with such astonishing lack of consideration for other people's feelings" and rends "the thin veils of civilisation so wantonly, so brutally" (51), women like Lily Briscoe are shown to enhance civilization by seeking to make whole again, and hold together, this thin and torn fabric. As Lily muses at one point, "it was not knowledge but unity that she desired, not inscriptions on tablets, nothing that could be written in any language known to men, but intimacy itself" (79)—a quality of civilized life not accomplished by any of the novel's major male characters. Similarly, at one point Mrs. Ramsay thinks, "It didn't matter, any of it. . . . A great man, a great book, fame—who could tell? She knew nothing about it" (177), and at another "pitie[s] men always as if they lacked something" (129). Ironically, it is this same "housewife" who makes possible those civilized attributes Bell celebrates—the pleasant state of mind brought on by a congenial social atmosphere and good conversation (*Civilization* 131): "Flashing her needles, confident, upright, she created drawing-room and kitchen, set them all aglow; bade him take his ease there, go in and out, enjoy himself. She laughed, she knitted" (59). It is Mrs. Ramsay of all the novel's inhabitants who is capable of creating a "coherence in things, a stability; something . . . immune from change" amid a "flowing," "fleeting," "spectral" reality (158): "The room . . . was very shabby. There was no beauty anywhere. She forebore to look at Mr. Tansley. Nothing seemed to have merged. They all sat separate. And the whole of the effort of merging and flowing and creating rested on her. Again she felt, as a fact without hostility, the sterility of men, for if she did not do it nobody would do it" (126). In this respect, at least, Woolf's nameless housewife beats Bell's civilized male at his own game.

✳ Class in *Mrs. Dalloway* and *Civilization*

Woolf's criticism of *Civilization*—that Bell "has great fun in the opening chapters but in the end it turns out that Civilisation is [merely] a lunch party at no. 50 Gordon Square" (Quentin Bell, *Virginia Woolf* II, 137) — suggests another area in which Woolf's fiction challenges Bell's theory of civilization: for its insistence that members of an elite, leisure class, supported by a "slave" or service class, must compose this civilization. In the midst of *Civilization* Bell's emphasis on class difference betrays itself: "And after the handsome sample of savagery offered us between August 1914 and November 1918, we, nostalgic intellectuals, know that we have returned to the artificial pleasure of a fashionable dinner-party, where we can sit and rail in security against the unheroic quietude of civilized life, with a secret but profound sense of relief" (141). If *To the Lighthouse* mocks Bell's sense of the place of women in civilization, *Mrs. Dalloway* mocks Bell's sense of the role of class differences in civilization, depicting Bell's civilized elites as thinly disguised philistines with undisguised, and even crippling, wealth and power.

Leon Edel's judgment that *Civilization* is an "elitist's credo" (284), and Alex Zwerdling's that it is "a symptom of leisure-class anxiety and hostility in the wake of the General Strike and the democratization of British society since the war" (102), point to the kind of critique Bell's class-oriented "theory of civilization" meets in *Mrs. Dalloway*. In this novel, after all, theories are associated with naive youth: "Clarissa had a theory in those days — they had heaps of theories, always theories, as young people have" (231).

Bell argues that class stratification is necessary for the maintenance of civilization. In *Civilization* Bell expresses in no uncertain terms his disdain for the masses and the "flock instinct" (131) and laments the fact that the number of truly civilized beings in present-day England "is too small to form that operative nucleus which converts a passive culture into a civilizing force" (178). Writing in the wake of Thorstein Veblen's attack on "conspicuous leisure" in *The Theory of the Leisure Class* (1899),[19] Bell insists that "only a leisured class will produce a highly civilized and civilizing elite"; this, for him, is an opinion supported by "incontrovertible arguments and borne out by history" (150–51). Because "complete human equality is compatible only with complete savagery" (146), civilization requires the existence of a leisure class which, in turn, requires the existence of a service class (146).

> As a means to good and a means to civility a leisured class is essential; that is to say, the men and women who are to compose that nucleus from which radiates civilization must have security, leisure, economic freedom, and liberty to think, feel, and experiment. If the community

wants civilization it must pay for it. . . . This implies inequality — inequality as a means to good. On inequality all civilizations have stood. (149)

Bell next insists that "there has never been a civilized democracy" (156) and, moreover, that all civilizations have either been "imposed by the will of a tyrant or maintained by an oligarchy" (162). Although Bell does not go so far as to embrace "despotism" openly, he does maintain that "democracy, justice, and all that, are valuable only as means." "To discredit a civilization," he writes, "it is not enough to show that it is based on slavery and injustice, you must show that liberty and justice would produce something better" (161).

Given Woolf's class connections and her Bloomsbury intellectual and artistic milieu, it is likely that she would have embraced Bell's social vision.[20] Nevertheless, as Alex Zwerdling convincingly argues, she did not always, or even usually, adopt social positions that would have directly benefited her. Although Woolf was a "direct beneficiary" of certain Bloomsbury assumptions — among them that "culture, financial independence, and power were closely allied; that those at the top had earned their high station; that the network of family tradition best safeguarded the continuity of civilization" (93) — she did not necessarily adhere to this world view but rather was torn by contradictory feelings:

> Two diametrically opposed middle-class responses can thus be seen in Woolf's milieu — a sense of guilt about their own privileges, and a determination to justify and defend them. That Woolf felt both emotions, and felt them strongly, helps to account for the complexities and contradictions of her own social attitudes. Her guilt is recorded in the reactions of her fictional characters as well as in the more directly self-revealing works. (103–4)

Indeed, not only does Woolf deem Bell a class snob in her diary,[21] but *Mrs. Dalloway* itself effectively counters Bell's smug and self-interested insistence on social inequality. If, as Jane Marcus holds, Woolf's fiction is "always marked with socialist or class analysis" (17), then *Mrs. Dalloway*, in addition to whatever else it reacts against, responds negatively to Bell's elitist class analysis in a number of ways.

For one thing, the novel unleashes a critique not of the masses at all but of elites. The ironic characterization not of the working-class Septimus Smith but of the elite Lady Bruton is a case in point. A woman of aristocratic family connections ("She derived from the eighteenth century" [264] and "was very proud of her family . . . of military men, administrators, admirals . . . men of action, who had done their duty" [167]), Millicent Bruton, who invites Richard Dalloway and Hugh Whitbread to lunch and later makes a brief appearance at Clarissa's party (to hobnob with the prime minister [262–64]), is clearly the character with the most "leisure" in *Mrs. Dalloway*. Although a ranking member of "English society," she is decidedly uncivilized by Bell's standards, having never read Shakespeare (274), having "never read a word of poetry herself" (159), being incapable of writing "a letter to the *Times*" (275). Indeed, although "power was hers, position, income," and even though "she had lived in the forefront of her time," had "good friends," had "known the ablest men of her day" (169), Lady Bruton is depicted as completely cut off from civilization by her army of servants, as *deadened* by her leisure, by the "grey tide of service which washed around [her] day in, day out, collecting, intercepting, enveloping her in a fine tissue which broke concussions, mitigated interruptions, and spread around the house in Brook Street a fine net where things lodged and were picked out accurately, instantly, by grey-haired Perkins" (163). Rather than gaining "civilized" insight from the leisure her wealth affords, Lady Bruton instead remains caught up in the illusory and deceptive nature of this wealth:

> And so there began a soundless and exquisite passing to and fro through swing doors of aproned white-capped maids, handmaidens not of necessity, but adept in a mystery or grand deception practised by hostesses in Mayfair from one-thirty to two, when, with a wave of the hand, the traffic ceases, and there rises instead this profound illusion in the first place about the food — how it is not paid for; and then that the table spreads itself voluntarily with glass and silver . . . and with the wine and the coffee (not paid for). (157–58)

Such "leisure," in Woolf's novel, effectively hinders civilization, encourages that variety of philistinism so unpalatable to Bell.[22] Perhaps not surprisingly, Richard Dalloway, another member of the governing class (he is a Conservative M.P.), is taken in by Bruton's show of civility. At her luncheon he muses that he would like, "whenever he had a moment of leisure, to write a history of Lady Bruton's family" (167) and admits that "he had the greatest respect for her; he cherished these romantic views about well-set-up old women of pedigree" (159). Like R. H. Tawney who, in *Equality* (1931), castigates Bell's *Civilization* for its large dose of cleverness masquerading as wisdom (83), *Mrs. Dalloway* exposes the illusions of Bell's "civilized" class. As Tawney puts it in his riposte to *Civilization* (which also serves admirably as a critique of the Bruton ideology):

In order . . . to escape from one illusion, it ought not to be necessary to embrace another. If civilization is not the product of the kitchen garden, neither is it an exotic to be grown in a hot-house. . . . Culture may be fastidious, but fastidiousness is not culture; and, though vulgarity is an enemy to "reasonableness and a sense of values," it is less deadly an enemy than gentility and complacency. A cloistered and secluded refinement, intolerant of the heat and dust of creative effort, is the note, not of civilization, but of the epochs which have despaired of it. (82–83)

Whereas Bell's *Civilization* would find someone of Lady Bruton's leisure to be civilized, *Mrs. Dalloway* reveals her to be self-deceiving, genteel, and complacent, to be paradoxically refined yet uncultured. Like Quentin Bell's charge against *Civilization*, Lady Bruton is exposed to be "more concerned with the formalities of life than with its essential problems," with "how to order a good meal" rather than with "how to lead a good life" (*Bloomsbury* 93).

✳ Bell Ringers: Images of the Man in Woolf's Novels

To the extent that Woolf's fiction represents and critiques, appropriates and transforms Bell's theory of civilization, it also does so to the man himself. In *Jacob's Room*, for example, Jacob Flanders shares certain of Bell's important attributes, most notably that he too contemplates writing "an essay upon civilization. A comparison between the ancients and moderns" (136), and finds that "the ancient Greeks" best solved "the problems of civilization" (149). With his friend Timmy Durrant, Jacob at one point imagines that "civilizations stood round them like flowers ready for picking. Ages lapped at their feet like waves fit for sailing" (76). To be sure, the analogy does not entirely hold; Jacob Flanders becomes a Great War fatality.

Of course, in *Mrs. Dalloway* Peter Walsh most resembles Bell. Peter is the closest in circumstance to Bell himself of all Woolf's characters, in that he flirts with, might have married, and continues greatly to admire the Woolf-like character, Clarissa Dalloway. At one point, for example, Clarissa remembers that "She owed [Peter] words: 'sentimental,' 'civilised'; they started up every day of her life as if they guarded her" (53–54), and at another point thinks, "It was the state of the world that interested [Peter]; Wagner, Pope's poetry, people's characters eternally, and the defects of her own soul. How he scolded her! How they argued!" (9). And here sounding like Bell, Peter muses that "the future of civilisation lies . . . in the hands of young men . . . such as he was, thirty years ago; with their love of abstract principles" (75–76). Also like Bell, Peter possesses a smug pride in English civilization, even if he pretends to be among its severest critics: "Never had he seen London look so enchanting—the softness of the distances; the richness; the greenness; the civilisation, after India, he thought, stroll-ing across the grass" (107). It was "a splendid achievement in its own way, after all, London; the season; civilisation," Peter at another point muses; "[T]here were moments when civilisation, even of this sort, seemed dear to him as a personal possession; moments of pride in England" (82).

In *To the Lighthouse* Bell is represented far less directly, yet Mr. Ramsay echoes some of his ideas (see, for example, the epigraphs that introduce this chapter). Although undoubtedly modeled on Virginia's father, Leslie Ste-phen,[23] Mr. Ramsay nevertheless echoes certain arguments in *Civilization*. For one thing, Mr. Ramsay's pseudophilosophic speculations can be seen as a parody of Bell's two attributes of all civilizations: "a Sense of Values [a quality] and Reason Enthroned [a mental capacity]" (50). Might not Ram-say's thoughts on the "alphabet of human knowledge," in which he gets stuck at "Q" (quality) and "R" (reason), constitute Woolf's subtle attack on Bell's simplistic and sentimental thinking here?

> [His] was a splendid mind. For if thought is like the keyboard of a piano, divided into so many notes, or like the alphabet is ranged in twenty-six letters all in order, then his splendid mind had no sort of difficulty in running over those letters one by one, firmly and accu-rately, until it had reached, say, the letter Q. He reached Q. Very few people in England ever reach Q. . . . Qualities that in a desolate expedition across the icy solitudes of the Polar region would have made him the leader, the guide, the counsellor, whose temper, neither sanguine nor despondent, surveys with equanimity what is to be and faces it. . . . R—. . . . He would never reach R. (53–55)

Clearly, Ramsay is not Bell, yet there are similarities in their thought that appear to be more than merely coincidental.

In the publication year of *To the Lighthouse*, Woolf writes of Bell in her diary:

> I am once more at the stage of thinking Clive "second rate." It's all so silly, shallow, & selfish. Granted the charm of his vitality, still one would prefer a finer taste to it. How angry his "secondrateness" used to make me. . . . Now I think of it much less often, but I suppose the

feeling is there. All this summer he has twanged so persistently on the one string that one gets bored. Love love love — Clive, Clive, Clive — that's the tune of it. . . . Clive's love is three parts vanity. (III, 148–49)

Despite Woolf's repeated insistence that Bell is "vain" and "second rate," it is clear that she regarded his ideas to be "first rate" enough to merit a response. As Bakhtin argues, all utterances are in some measure responses "to what has already been said about the given topic, on the given issue, even though this responsiveness may not have assumed a clear-cut external expression." "Our thought itself," he writes, "is born and shaped in the process of interaction and struggle with others' thought" ("Problem of Speech Genres" 92). For while Woolf's complex, open-ended, and troubled fictions for the most part "struggle" with Bell's ideas, rendering them glib, dogmatic, and self-serving, we must not overlook the fact that both figures subscribed to the notion that civilization is more an individual than a collective phenomenon, more a state of mind than a nation-state. As Raymond Williams points out of Bloomsbury ideology at large, it was uninterested in notions of a "whole" society. "Instead it appealed to the supreme value of the civilized *individual*, whose pluralization, as more and more civilized individuals, was itself the only acceptable social direction." "The final nature of Bloomsbury as a group," Williams continues, "is that it was indeed . . . a group of and for the notion of free individuals" ("The Bloomsbury Fraction" 165, 169).[24] To the extent that Williams is correct, it is clear that the stakes between Woolf and Bell over the nature and function of civilization would have been high. And it is equally clear, given the complexities of their personal relationship, that Woolf's response to Bell's controversial theory of civilization would have taken the subtle and tacit form it takes in her post–Great War novels of the 1920s.

5

Discontent and

Its Civilization:

Rereading

Joyce's

"Paralyzed"

Dubliner

I seriously believe that you will retard the course of civilisation in Ireland by preventing the Irish people from having one good look at themselves in my nicely polished looking-glass. — Joyce, defending DUBLINERS, *in a letter to Grant Richards*

Evidently she had been unfit to live, without any strength of purpose, an easy prey to habits, one of the wrecks on which civilisation has been reared. — James Duffy on Emily Sinico, in "A Painful Case"

Their syphilisation, you mean says the citizen. To hell with them! . . . No music and no art and no literature worthy of the name. Any civilisation they have they stole from us. — The Citizen on England, in ULYSSES

It has long been a truism of Joyce studies that the critique of Irish civilization in Joyce's works centers upon its representative subjects: "paralyzed"

Dubliners.[1] Pointing to the author's avowed intention to "write a chapter of the moral history of my country" (*Letters* II, 134), critics typically view Joyce's fiction as "an attempt to represent certain aspects of the life of one of the European capitals" (*Letters* II, 109). Although Joyce insists that the raison d'être of a volume like *Dubliners* is "to betray the soul of that hemiplegia or paralysis which many consider a city" (I, 55) — Dublin seeming to him the very "centre of paralysis" (II, 134) — there has been little scholarly attention to the psychosocial and the broadly cultural nature and determinants of this crippling discontent.

Two notable expositions of Joycean paralysis in *Dubliners* and, by extension, other of Joyce's fictions have been advanced. The first, and still most popular, might be called the "thematic unity" theory: that "the theme of paralysis serves as a unifying concern which embodies the value of the material out of which the stories were shaped" (San Juan 17), that "the basic pattern underlying all others is a paralytic process: *Dubliners* has a pathological unity more subtle than is immediately apparent" (Walzl, "Pattern" 222). The second most popular explanation attributes this paralysis to spiritual enervation. Brewster Ghiselin argues this perspective succinctly: "When the outlines of the symbolic pattern have been grasped," he writes, "the whole unifying development will be discernible as a sequence of events in a moral drama, an action of the human spirit struggling for survival under peculiar conditions of deprivation, enclosed and disabled by a degenerate environment that provides none of the primary necessities of spiritual life" (318). Frequently accompanying this view is the insight that the Irish suffer inexorably simply because they deserve it: that "the timelessness of Irish paralysis reinforces . . . mythic, religious and legendary patterns that Joyce seems to place so frequently at the very center of each story" (Torchiana 9). Yet both of these perspectives neglect the fact, in Florence Walzl's words, that "Joyce's picture of Dublin social life is solidly based on historical reality" ("*Dubliners:* Women" 53). Moreover, both of these explanations, although convincing up to a point, fail to address the psychosocial dimension of the paralysis represented in Joyce's fiction.

To this end, I seek to bring late-Freudian theory and related Frankfurt School ideas to bear on the paralysis represented in *Dubliners* (1914) and *Ulysses* (1922). Let me state at the outset that I advance ideas from Freud's *Future of an Illusion* (1927; hereafter cited as *FI*) and *Civilization and Its Discontents* (1930; cited as *CD*), and from Max Horkheimer and Theodor Adorno's *Dialectic of Enlightenment* (1947; cited as *DE*), neither unqualifiedly to apply these critiques to Joyce's fiction nor, still less, to argue any (chronologically impossible) influence between these theoretical works and the fiction. Instead, I will discuss *Dubliners* and *Ulysses* in light of Freud's and Adorno/Horkheimer's critiques of civilization in order to reveal what might be called a Joycean critique of modern Irish civilization. Moreover, by bringing Joyce's texts to bear on this tradition in the "hermeneutics of suspicion,"[2] the critical limitations, as well as the critical power, of this tradition can be broached. If Conrad represents civilization as a game, one constituted, paradoxically, of self-interested yet self-deceiving discourse, and if Woolf depicts civilization as a mental state, ideally androgynous if in practice all too often patriarchal, Joyce represents it as a paralyzed and paralyzing collectivity, a social organization dependent for its existence on the threat of "enemies" without its borders and "traitorous citizens" within.

✳ The Illusion of a Future: Gerty MacDowell and Little Chandler

Freudian interpretations of Joyce's texts have tended to concentrate either on character or author psychology, on what Joyce thought of Freud, or on speculations of what portion of Freud's work was known to Joyce.[3] This has led to the critical neglect of certain important intersections of Joycean and Freudian thinking. For one thing, both writers view the path of individual development as a trope for the process of civilization — that "civilization," as Patrick Brantlinger characterizes late-Freudian thought, "is no more than the mature individual writ large" (*Bread and Circuses* 163). "I perceived even more clearly," Freud himself declares late in life, "that the events of human history" and of "cultural development" are "no more than a reflection of the dynamic conflicts between the ego, the id, and the super-ego . . . are the very same processes repeated on a wider stage" (quoted in Levi 174). Likewise, Joyce opens his essay "Ireland, Island of Saints and Sages" with the statement that "Nations have their ego, just like individuals" (154) and, in his 1904 sketch "A Portrait of the Artist," speaks of paralysis not in individual terms but in terms of the "general paralysis of an insane society" (266).

  Second, both Joyce and Freud unceremoniously reject the possibility of autonomous subjectivity. As Gerald Levin succinctly puts it of Freud's work, the individual therein is "a diminished being, ridden with conflicts that civilization heightens rather than alleviates" (142–43). And Jeremy Hawthorn argues of Joyce's fiction, "few novels show their characters less as free, autonomous beings or more tied to their society and its history" (116). Whatever else one may say of the characters who inhabit Joyce's *Dubliners*, *A Portrait of the Artist as a Young Man*, *Exiles*, *Ulysses*, and *Finnegans Wake*, none of them, it is clear, accomplishes that task set by Stephen Dedalus: to "fly by those nets" of "nationality, language, religion" (*Portrait* 203) — indeed, these fictions are among other things *about* this impossibility.[4]

Third, both Joyce and Freud indicate the possibility of a mental "liberation" which their works can provide their readers. "By withdrawing their expectations from the other world and concentrating all their liberated energies into their life on earth," Freud, here reminiscent of Marx, optimistically asserts of his readers toward the end of *The Future of an Illusion*, "they will probably succeed in achieving a state of things in which life will become tolerable for everyone and civilization no longer oppressive to anyone" (50). Joyce is equally direct about the therapeutic function of *Dubliners*, even if his rhetoric is smug and self-serving: "I believe that in composing my chapter of moral history in exactly the way I have composed it I have taken the first step towards the spiritual liberation of my country" (*Letters* I, 62–63). However, more important than this common ground between them — and despite Joyce's avowed disdain of Freud (whom he at one point refers to as "the Viennese Tweedledee" [*Letters* I, 166])[5] — is the great degree to which late-Freudian thinking supplies us with the tools to uncover a neglected critique of civilization in Joyce's fiction.

The Future of an Illusion and *Civilization and Its Discontents* are of particular interest to me here because it is in these works that Freud's theory is more a social than an individual psychology. Although Freud's approach to the problem of civilization is not "historical" in any thoroughgoing way — to the extent that he psychoanalyzes civilization much as he would a patient — these two texts, unlike the majority of Freud's earlier ones, take up the health of Western civilization as a whole rather than that of individuals within it.[6]

But what, for Freud, is civilization? His answer: "the whole sum of achievements and the regulations which distinguish our lives from those of our animal ancestors and which serve two purposes — namely to protect men against nature and to adjust their mutual relations" (*CD* 36). For Freud this first purpose concerns our capacity to extract wealth from nature in order to satisfy human needs, and the second one concerns the regulations used to adjust human relations, particularly with respect to the distribution of available wealth (*FI* 6). Although one might expect that this civilizing trend leads to a harmonious human community that can devote itself at last to the acquisition and enjoyment of wealth, in fact, for Freud, "It seems rather that every civilization must be built up on coercion and renunciation of instinct" (*FI* 7). And herein lies the true purpose of religion for Freud: by maintaining the illusion of a divine order, civilization can continue to demand the instinctual renunciations necessary for its survival. In this way, for him, religious ideas amount to little more than expressions of childhood neurosis and illusion.

For Freud, however, it is not religion alone but what he calls "the narcissism of minor differences" as well by which civilization is able to dispel aggressive feelings generated by its own repressiveness. This concept is particularly valuable for our purposes as it suggests an important link between civilization and narcissism—a link represented repeatedly in Joyce's fiction. In *The Future of an Illusion*, Freud maintains that

> The narcissistic satisfaction provided by the cultural ideal is . . . among the forces which are successful in combating the hostility to culture within the cultural unit. This satisfaction can be shared in not only by the favoured classes, which enjoy the benefits of the culture, but also by the suppressed ones, since the right to despise the people outside it compensates them for the wrongs they suffer within their own unit. No doubt one is a wretched plebeian, harassed by debts and military service; but, to make up for it, one is a Roman citizen, one has one's share in the task of ruling other nations and dictating their laws. This identification of the suppressed classes with the class who rules and exploits them is, however, only part of a larger whole. For, on the other hand, the suppressed classes can be emotionally attached to their masters; in spite of their hostility to them they may see in them their ideals; unless such relations of a fundamentally satisfying kind subsisted, it would be impossible to understand how a number of civilizations have survived so long in spite of the justifiable hostility of large human masses. (13)[7]

In *Civilization and Its Discontents* Freud puts this phenomenon in even plainer terms: "It is always possible to bind together a considerable number of people in love, so long as there are people left over to receive the manifestation of their aggressiveness" (61). It is difficult to overestimate the importance of Freud's concept of a culturally encouraged narcissism—as a means of diffusing aggressive feelings within civilization—when attempting to understand Joyce's representation of Irish paralysis.[8]

Gerty MacDowell in the "Nausicaa" episode of *Ulysses* (and her two predecessors in *Dubliners* who closely resemble her: Eveline, in the story of that name, and Maria, in "Clay") is a case in point.[9] While it is hardly innovative to attribute to her a narcissistic perspective—Kimberly Devlin deems her "narcissistic and yet highly self-conscious" (141), and Mark Shechner speaks of her as "the narcissistic phase of Irish Catholic adolescence" (161) — none has linked Gerty's narcissism, as late-Freudian thinking would urge, with the preservation of civilization: as a means of allaying the discontent that arises from its contradictions. Indeed, most attention to Gerty's narcissism has settled on the style of narrative discourse associated with her. Fritz Senn, for example, notes that this discourse "is manifestly unable to characterize anything outside itself." "It reflects only its own vacuity," he continues, "it hardly illuminates or communicates, its glitter is narcissistic, its essence is self-gratification" (309). Apt though this assessment is, the psychosocial context that necessitates Gerty's text demands further clarification.[10]

To say the least, Gerty, like Eveline and Maria, experiences her "present naively, as it were, without being able to form an estimate of its contents" (*FI* 5), due to her need to dress an otherwise unbearable existence in the narcissistic garb of self-celebratory discourse. Consider the images in "Nausicaa" that suggest Gerty's narcissistic delusion: her placement on Sandymount Strand like Narcissus, "near the little pool by the rock" (*Ulysses* 292), and her memory of standing before the bedroom mirror — "what joy was hers when she tried [new attire] on then, smiling at the lovely reflection which the mirror gave back to her!" She "knew how to cry nicely before the mirror. You are lovely, Gerty, it said" (287–88).[11] Introduced as self-absorbed, "lost in thought, gazing far away into the distance" (285), Gerty accepts a narcissistic orientation toward her experience in order, as Freud would have it, "to re-create the world; to build up in its stead another world in which its most unbearable features are eliminated and replaced by others that are in conformity with [her] own wishes." The victim "corrects some aspect of the world which is unbearable" to her, Freud continues, "by the construction of a wish and introduces this delusion into reality" (*CD* 28). Because Gerty is not able, despite her avowed desire, to "throw my cap at who I like because it's leap year" (297), she therefore resorts to slighting her friends Cissy Caffrey and Edy Boardman — engaging in the narcissism of minor differences — in order to keep potentially crippling realizations about her future amatory life at bay.

Gerty's narcissism of minor differences manifests itself in her suspiciously fluctuating appraisals of her friends. Sometimes finding Cissy "a girl loveable in the extreme" (285) and "sincerity itself, one of the bravest and truest hearts heaven ever made" (290), and other times finding her a "confounded little cat" (297) (and Edy a "little spitfire" [289], an "Irritable little gnat" [295]), Gerty attempts to deflect the misery of her experience onto others: no matter how bad it is for her it is worse for her friends; no matter how good they look she looks better. Gerty's new clothes, she reasons at one point, will "take the shine out of some people she knew," and her shoes, "the newest thing in footwear," will also contribute to her unparalleled beauty ("Edy Boardman prided herself that she was very *petite* but she never had a foot like Gerty MacDowell, a five, and never would" [287]). Gerty's narcissism—because of the blinders it applies and the limited focus it therefore enforces—allows her to evade, or at least to ignore, the dimensions of her own material hopelessness. It allows her to explain away her competitiveness with Cissy and Edy as due to *their* "jealousy," to the "little tiffs" that "from time to time" afflict even the best of "girl chums" (286). Further, she can insist on her superiority over her "fallen women" friends because they date "soldiers and coarse men" (299) whereas she is "adored" exclusively by "gentlemen" (like Bloom). However, Gerty's narcissism of minor differences pertains not only to physical appearance but to religious difference. She makes much out of the difference between Catholics, who know "Who came first and after Him the Blessed Virgin and then Saint Joseph" (287), and Protestants, such as the mysterious "gentleman" (Bloom is Jewish), who nevertheless might "convert" if they "truly loved her" (293). By fetishizing the difference between Catholics and Protestants, rather than focusing on her own social oppression, Gerty's self-knowledge remains severely limited. Gerty will keep her mind off of that which oppresses her as long as other distracting tensions, religious and otherwise, exist to claim her attention.

While the nature of Gerty's narcissistic delusion is, above all else, sexual, it is also related to her internalization of religious rhetoric, its "external coercion gradually becom[ing] internalized" (*FI* 11). As Joyce himself insists in "Ireland, Island of Saints and Sages," "individual initiative is paralysed by the influence and admonitions of the church" (171). Freud would explain this phenomenon by suggesting that Gerty feels that she will enjoy, if she only has patience, the perfection that she is presently being denied. Because—as Freud explains the Western religious understanding—"In the end all good is rewarded and all evil punished," Gerty can assume that "all the terrors, the sufferings and the hardships of life are destined to be obliterated" (*FI* 19). This is represented most clearly in Gerty's description of the "men's temperance retreat conducted by the missioner," in which the assembled men, "after the storms of this weary world, kneeling before the immaculate"—as in death—are "*gathered together without distinction of social class*" (*Ulysses* 290; my emphasis). For Gerty this socioeconomic equality is clearly the final and just state of things for which she must patiently wait.

Freud's critique of eros and civilization speaks to Gerty's sexuality as well. Indeed, Freud himself asks the question, "[I]s it not the case that in our civilization the relations between the sexes are disturbed by an erotic illusion or a number of such illusions?" (*FI* 34). His answer, of course, is a resounding yes: "I am . . . speaking of the way of life which makes love the centre of everything, which looks for all satisfaction in loving and being loved" (*CD* 29). In his "On Narcissism: An Introduction" Freud makes clear, in his characteristically misogynistic prose, the role narcissism plays in this illusion: "Strictly speaking, such women love only themselves with an intensity comparable to that of the man's love for them" (46). Yet what better way to characterize Gerty's obsession than this way: her obsession with "loving and being loved" ("Nothing else but love mattered. Come what may she would be wild, untramelled, free" [299]), both as tantalizing lover ("a womanly woman" [293]) and as nurturing daughter/mother ("A sterling good daughter was Gerty just like a second mother in the house" [291]). Indeed, for Gerty, love is "a woman's birthright" (288), "her dream" and "master guide" (299). "[S]he could make him fall in love with her" (294), Gerty at one point thinks of Reggy Wylie, for "he who would woo and win Gerty MacDowell must be a man among men" (288). As for Bloom, the "mystery man on the beach," Gerty can miraculously tell "without looking" that he never takes "his eyes off of her" (295). Replete with "sweet flowerlike face" (301), with the most seductive "bluest Irish blue" eyes, and with her "wealth of wonderful hair" (286), Gerty Mac-Dowell fancies herself no less than "as fair a specimen of winsome Irish girlhood as one could wish to see" in "God's fair land of Ireland" (285–86). In this way Gerty mistakes Bloom's lust for love, his "passionate gaze" for "undisguised admiration": "It is for you, Gerty MacDowell, and you know it" (296).

Freud's critique of love centers on the contradictory and ambiguous role of eros within civilization, on the "careless way in which language uses the word 'love.'" "People give the name 'love' to the relation between a man and a woman . . . but they also give the name 'love' to the positive feelings between parents and children, and between the brothers and sisters of a family" (*CD* 49). For Freud, because "love comes into opposition [with] the interests of civilization," on the one hand, and because "civilization threatens love with substantial restrictions," on the other, the relation of love to civilization becomes ambiguous (*CD* 50). For him, whereas the commandment to "Love thy neighbor as thyself" is fundamental to the development of civilization, it is nevertheless "impossible to fulfill; such an enormous inflation of love can only lower its value, not get rid of the difficulty." "Civilization pays no attention to all this," Freud continues; "[I]t merely admonishes us that the harder it is to obey the precept the more meritorious it is to do so" (*CD* 90). If Gerty MacDowell's perspective on love can be seen as the ideal fictionalized representation of Freud's revealed contradiction, then the narrator's perspective on it in "Cyclops" can be seen as its ideal parody:

> Love loves to love love. Nurse loves the new chemist. Constable 14A loves Mary Kelly. Gerty MacDowell loves the boy that has the bicycle. M. B. loves a fair gentleman. . . . Jumbo, the elephant, loves Alice, the elephant. . . . You love a certain person. And this person loves that other person because everybody loves somebody but God loves everybody. (*Ulysses* 273)

Trite, sentimental, and defensive, this narcotic view of love, Joyce's text seems to be suggesting, cannot help but encourage Gerty's placid acceptance of the hopelessness that she faces.[12]

To the extent that Freud's critique of civilization provides insights into the paralysis of Joyce's female subjects, it sheds light on the discontent of Joyce's male subjects as well. In the case of Little Chandler, the protagonist of "A Little Cloud," for example, late-Freudian theory reveals a related aspect of Joyce's critique of Irish civilization. Beyond the conventional wisdom that Little Chandler's state of paralysis is due to his own sentimentality and delusions of grandeur,[13] this discontent is more convincingly explained in psychosocial terms.

R. B. Kershner has pointed out that "Little Chandler's story, more than that of any other character, works upon a framework of massive oppositions." "Of all the Dubliners," Kershner continues, "he and his opposite number, Gallaher, are perhaps the closest to stock characters; the two seem to exist only in order to complement one another" (*Joyce, Bakhtin, and Popular Literature* 96). To be sure, such oppositions as East/West and England/Ireland dominate the symbolic and metaphoric architecture of the narrative.[14] The story of an encounter, after eight years, between "two friends" who meet at Corless's — a Continental-style hotel and restaurant in Dublin — "A Little Cloud" opens by suggesting the nearly total opposition of Thomas ("Little") Chandler, a thirty-two-year-old clerk (and would-be poet) at the Kings Inns, and Ignatius Gallaher, a successful, expatriate journalist of the London press who returns home for a business visit.

Whereas the "divide" that separates Chandler and Gallaher — derivative poet versus derivative journalist — is ultimately engulfed in irony, it is not undercut so completely as to negate the relevancy of this distinction between them. Little Chandler (so nicknamed because "though he was but slightly under the average stature" nevertheless "gave one the idea of being a little man" [*Dubliners* 70]) has remained a petty clerk in "old jog-along Dublin" (78) with its "poor stunted houses," a "band of tramps" (73), and its "horde of grimy children" who populate the street "like mice," like "minute vermin-like life" (71). Gallaher, on the other hand, who years ago Chandler thought possessed a "future greatness" (72) and rare "talent" (71), has since escaped to "great city London" (70) in order to pursue his "triumphant life" (80). In comparison with Gallaher's "travelled air, his well-cut tweed and fearless accent" (70), his "large gold watch" (80), and his career, which takes him not only to London and Berlin but to Paris with its "gaiety, movement, excitement" (76), Chandler cuts a pious and a "modest figure" (71), is a "melancholy" (73) and timid man who merely "pull[s] along" (74), vacationing no farther from "dull" Dublin than the Isle of Man. In contrast to Gallaher, Chandler feels he possesses a "sober inartistic life" (73) of "tiresome writing" (71). Whereas Little Chandler allows his whiskey to be "very much diluted" (75) and sips at the drink (76), Gallaher finishes his "boldly" (76), drinking it "neat" (75). Dublin, Little Chandler comes to feel, is a slow, small, and watered-down version of London, a still backwater for those too weak to leave. To Little Chandler's "stale" marriage (82), unromantic and constraining (he now regards Annie as cold and passionless), Gallaher speaks of his freedom to sample from among the wealthy, exotic, passionate, and voluptuous women of Europe, "Hot Stuff!" (76).

While Hélène Cixous is certainly correct to note that " 'A Little Cloud' symbolizes the fallen dream, the idea of powerlessness" (90), it is Freud's insights into the mystifying powers of civilization that best explain the paralysis represented in "A Little Cloud." For what better way than through "the narcissism of minor differences" to explain Little Chandler's newfound discontent at the prospect of seeing Gallaher again? "For the first time in his life he felt himself superior to the people he passed. For the first time his soul revolted against the dull inelegance of Capel Street. There was no doubt about it: if you wanted to succeed you had to go away. You could do nothing in Dublin" (73).[15] Too close for comfort in wealth and station to the Dubliners around him, Little Chandler can distinguish himself only by patronizing Ireland ("the old country" [75]) as Gallaher does him ("old hero" [74]). Despite the fact that Chandler is anything but satisfied with his lot, he nevertheless vainly attempts to contrast his "refined" manners, appearance, and literary sensibility with those base ones of the "crowd" (70, 74). Perhaps he has little to boast about, but his compatriots have even less.

Freud's critique of civilization also speaks to Little Chandler's resignation to fate and his "dull resentment against his life" (83): "He felt how useless it was to struggle against fortune, this being the burden of wisdom which the ages had bequeathed to him" (71). Germane to this attitude, Freud writes that in addition to the constraints imposed by civilization on the individual "are added the injuries which untamed nature — he calls it fate — inflicts on him. One might suppose that this condition of things would result in a permanent state of anxious expectation in him and a severe injury to his natural narcissism" (*FI* 16). For this reason, Little Chandler (like Gerty, Eveline, and Maria) conjures an escape fantasy ("Could he not escape from his little house? . . . Could he go to London?" [83]), even though his narcissistic impulse, which limits options rather than makes them possible, checks this notion immediately ("It was useless, useless! He was a prisoner for life" [84]). Despite the fact that he comes to "feel somewhat disillusioned" with Gallaher (76–77), he nevertheless proceeds to engage in self-victimization by internalizing his own aggression, by making himself his own enemy. As Theodor Adorno puts it, linking Freudian narcissism with the internalization of social sanctions, "This repression of . . . powerlessness points not merely to the disproportion between the individual and his powers within the whole but still more to injured narcissism and the fear of realizing that [individuals] themselves go to make up the false forces of domination before which they have every reason to cringe" ("Sociology and Psychology" 89). In Adorno's Freudian scenario, the civilization-inspired superego is triumphant, rendering the subject his or her own jail-keeper.[16]

In Little Chandler's case, not only does civilization, as Freud would view it, master the individual's dangerous desire for aggression by weakening it and by setting up an agency within him to guard it, "like a garrison in a conquered city" (*CD* 70–71), but civilization offers two other means of evading its own shortcomings, both of which are reflected in "A Little Cloud": isolation and intoxication (*CD* 24–25). Robert Boyle has described Little Chandler's fundamental solitude — "he cannot emerge from the hell of loneliness in which he is trapped" (92) — yet neglects to point out that it is a feeling of isolation verging on paranoia: "The bar seemed to him to be full of people and he felt that the people were observing him curiously" (*Dubliners* 74). The function of intoxication in this story is even more obvious. Not only does Chandler become "warm and excited," the "three small whiskeys" having "gone to his head" and the cigar having "confused his mind" (80), but earlier Gallaher is described as "emerging after some time from the clouds of smoke in which he had taken refuge" (78). Hence, Joyce's fiction suggests, "intoxicants" too function as mystifiers of Ireland's imposed contradictions. They permit Little Chandler, paradoxically, both to admire and to despise Gallaher. In spite of Chandler's hostility toward Gallaher, he sees in the expatriate the English ideal he (and Ireland) seeks but cannot embody. He can only lamely wish to "vindicate himself in some way, to assert his manhood" (80) — even if he remains fundamentally "paralyzed."[17]

✳ The Myth of Enlightenment: The Experience of Leopold Bloom

Cheryl Herr has argued powerfully that, "given the culture that Joyce shows us, what we normally mean by the term 'freedom' is at best a theory and an illusion" (*Anatomy* 25). Although Freud provides important insights into this aspect of the fiction, other aspects of Joyce's representation of civilization are best revealed through a post-Freudian framework of understanding. To this end, work by members of what is loosely called the Frankfurt School — comprising such figures as Theodor Adorno, Walter Benjamin, Erich Fromm, Max Horkheimer, and Herbert Marcuse — is most useful. Particularly appropriate is Horkheimer and Adorno's *Dialectic of Enlightenment*, a work that extends and deepens Freud's late critique of civilization while incorporating pertinent Marxist and Nietzschean insights. Sometimes aphoristic, always paradoxical and polemical, *Dialectic of Enlightenment* is of particular relevance to readings of *Ulysses* in that a sizable portion of this study is devoted to Homer's *Odyssey*, the "basic text of European civilization" (*DE* 46) and "earliest representative testimon[y] of western bourgeoise civilization" (*DE* xvi).[18]

Although important points of divergence exist between Freud's late works and *Dialectic of Enlightenment* — most important, that at root the former two are "psychological" whereas the latter one is "sociological," and that Freud promotes scientific (psychoanalytic) reason as a means of shedding illusion whereas Horkheimer and Adorno link such rationality with the century's most catastrophic myth, nazism — Freud's conclusion in *The Future of an Illusion* and *Civilization and Its Discontents* is essentially Horkheimer and Adorno's premise: that "the history of civilization is . . . the history of renunciation" (*DE* 55).[19] Fredric Jameson clarifies the relationship between late-Freudian theory and *Dialectic of Enlightenment* when he argues that "One fundamental psychoanalytic inspiration of the Frankfurt School derives . . . from *Civilization and Its Discontents*, with its eschatological vision of an irreversible link between development . . . and ever-increasing instinctual renunciation and misery." "Henceforth," he continues, "for Horkheimer and Adorno, the evocation of renunciation will function less as psychic diagnosis than as cultural criticism" ("Imaginary" 79). Late-Freudian theory also supplies *Dialectic of Enlightenment* with the psychological sources of the individual's self-surrender to civilization's repressiveness.[20]

The raison d'être of *Dialectic of Enlightenment* is to explain a key paradox of this century: that the myth-oriented phenomenon of nazism could flourish in a nation presumed to be the bastion of Enlightenment-rational ideas. Its authors note instead that "the fully enlightened earth radiates disaster triumphant" (*DE* 3). For Horkheimer and Adorno this paradox is the fault and culmination of the rational tradition in Western thinking dating from antiquity. Further, they argue that reason has always been split between "abstract idealism" and "crass materialism," instead of being holistically conceived and exercised. Consequently, "Ideals, values, [and] ethics," as C. Fred Alford succinctly articulates their argument, "are removed to the abstract realm of the intellect and the spirit, where, like religion . . . they are applauded in the abstract." "However," he continues, "precisely because they come to be seen as an expression of our higher selves, they are split off from everyday life, which is then given over to a crass materialism that tolerates no opposition to the merely given" (105). For Horkheimer and Adorno, the human need defined by Freud to construct civilization in order to dominate nature necessitates this dependence on material over idealistic reason. Hence, for all practical purposes, "reason" becomes synonymous with "instrumental reason" — the reason behind science, technology, and industrialism — whose goal is to dominate nature. Yet this "manipulation" spreads from the natural to the human realm: Enlightenment rationality, as the existence of a "culture industry" and anti-Semitism suggest, ends in the domination of people — "enlightenment" proves to be "as totalitarian as any system" (*DE* 24) and "progress" proves to be "regression" (*DE* xv). Hence the paradox, or "dialectic," at the heart of Horkheimer and Adorno's thesis: in the twentieth century "enlightenment returns to mythology, which it never really knew how to elude" (*DE* 27), whereas in the ancient world (as represented by the *Odyssey*) "myth is already enlightenment." Reminiscent of Walter Benjamin, Horkheimer and Adorno here explicitly link "terror and civilization," barbarism for them being little more than "the other face of culture" (*DE* 111–12).

The thesis of *Dialectic of Enlightenment* is essential to an understanding of Horkheimer and Adorno's notion of a "culture industry," which in turn reveals an aspect of Leopold Bloom's experience in the "Lotuseaters" and "Nausicaa" episodes of *Ulysses*.[21] For Horkheimer and Adorno, the problem with mass culture is that it is no longer norm-breaking. Instead, it functions affirmatively and must be "understood as a process whereby otherwise dangerous and protopolitical impulses are managed and defused" (Jameson, *Political Unconscious* 287). Insisting that "the whole world is made to pass through the filter of the culture industry" (*DE* 126) and that this industry is "a system which is uniform as a whole and in every part" (*DE* 120), Adorno maintains that, "insofar as the culture industry arouses a feeling of well-being that the world is precisely in that order suggested by the culture industry, the substitute gratification which it prepares for human beings cheats them out of the same happiness which it deceitfully projects." Moreover, for Adorno, "It impedes the development of autonomous, independent individuals who judge and decide consciously for themselves" ("Culture Industry Reconsidered" 18–19). For Horkheimer and Adorno, advertising has a special place within the culture industry: it is its "elixir of life" (*DE* 162). For them, the mark of advertising's success in the culture industry is that "consumers feel compelled to buy and use its products even though they see through them" (*DE* 167). Moreover, its method is similar to that of any other propaganda effort: "the mechanical repetition of the same culture product" (*DE* 163).

It is hardly news, however, to suggest that advertising helps shape subjectivity in *Ulysses*.[22] For years critics have noted that Gerty's is a "media-controlled self-image" (Henke 135) and that the "haphazard life of commodities in Gerty's narrative partially derives its significance from the manner in which an Irish common reader of the early twentieth century experienced material objects in their most hyperbolically available form: through advertisements" (Richards 765). For Bloom, himself an ad canvasser, the significance of advertising is even clearer. Yet Bloom's experience is further elucidated by Horkheimer and Adorno's notion of the culture industry as "civilized" manipulator. Indeed, *Dialectic of Enlightenment* helps clarify the connection between Bloom's experience of Dublin advertising and the discontented civilization at large represented in Joyce's fiction.

Bloom himself presages the advertising insights of *Dialectic of Enlightenment*, yet extends it to cover Church liturgy as well as political and commercial propaganda. Consider Horkheimer and Adorno's notion that the culture industry "consists of repetition" (*DE* 136). In "Cyclops" Bloom notes this "effect" and "trick," the "isolated repeatable device" (*DE* 163). "Because, you see, says Bloom, for an advertisement you must have repetition. That's the whole secret" (*Ulysses* 265). Moreover, in "Nausicaa," on Sandymount Strand, Bloom muses on the church service he has just overheard: "Mass seems to be over. Could hear them all at it. Pray for us. And pray for us. And pray for us. Good idea the repetition. Same thing with ads. Buy from us. And buy from us" (309). Bloom's "Freudian" recognition that "the effect of religious consolations may be likened to that of a narcotic" (*FI* 49) is here linked with advertising strategy: that religion, like ads, exercises a narcotic effect upon, as well as appeals to the narcissistic side of, the masses.[23] "Drugs age you after mental excitement," Bloom thinks. "Lethargy then" (69). This four-way relationship among religion, advertising, narcotics, and narcissism—which for Horkheimer and Adorno culminates in "the mere illusion of happiness, a dull vegetation, as meager as an animal's bare existence, and at best only the absence of the awareness of misfortune" (*DE* 63)—takes on flesh in *Ulysses* when Bloom observes that the "best place for an ad to catch a woman's eye [is] on a mirror" (304), and when he asks the question, "What do [women] love? Another themselves?" (311).

Dialectic of Enlightenment reveals another significant phenomenon in *Ulysses*: that "[t]he culture industry as a whole has molded men as a type unfailingly reproduced in every product" (*DE* 127). Whether in reference to the "Belfast and Oriental Tea Company," with its "choice blend, finest quality, family tea" (*Ulysses* 58), or to "Plumtree's Potted Meat," without which one's home is "[i]ncomplete," yet with it, "an abode of bliss" (61), the same abstract promise—in this case a harmonious family life—is tendered as if it were a concretely purchasable commodity. In *Ulysses* the lack of differences between teas and canned meats is exceeded only by the lack of differences among the various "messages" of the culture industry.

In "The Universal Literary Influence of the Renaissance," Joyce writes of the "modern city" (with its "electric tram, telegraph wires, the humble and necessary postman, the newsboys, the large commercial businesses"): "in the midst of this complex and many-sided civilization the human mind, almost terrified by materialistic vastness, is bewildered, forsakes itself, and withers" (19–20). Given this image of what modern cities can do to individuals, it is not surprising that Bloom, in the midst of Dublin's "materialistic vastness," would fall victim to the culture industry.[24]

Indeed, it can be argued that in "Nausicaa" Bloom succumbs to the narcissistic gratifications of the culture industry to the extent that he fails to move beyond a sense of Gerty as advertising image, as sexual culture product. Although much has been written about the nature of Bloom's "objectification" of Gerty,[25] the notion that Bloom perceives her as a sexually provocative advertising image amid an entire "culture industry" remains in need of further elaboration.

To be sure, Bloom's judgment after noticing that Gerty is lame, "see her as she is spoil all" (303), reveals that he sees her as a contrived image, a surface phenomenon lacking depth, from the pages of a magazine or from the stage of a theater ("Must have the stage setting, the rouge, costume, position, music" [303]). Gerty herself seems to grasp Bloom's sense of her for what it is and, echoing the rhetoric of advertising, insists that Bloom "had eyes in his head to see the difference for himself" (295). Gerty is an ad "come-to-life" much as Bloom, correctly, imagines he appears to her: "She must have been thinking of someone else all the time" (303). Indeed, neither finally attains what is presumably being "sold" in their encounter: the promise of romance and mystery, followed by matrimony and an "abode of bliss." As Horkheimer and Adorno explain,

> The culture industry perpetually cheats its consumers of what it per-petually promises. The promissory note which, with its plots and staging, it draws on pleasure is endlessly prolonged; the promise, which is actually all the spectacle consists of, is illusory: all it actually confirms is that the real point will never be reached, that the diner must be satisfied with the menu. (*DE* 139)

Think not only of Bloom in this connection — whose self-effacing paralysis prohibits him from completing his message to Gerty in the sand ("Mr. Bloom effaced the letters with his slow boot" [312]) — but of Gerty too, who fulfills the function of pornography in the idiom of an advertising image, yet who refuses to speak of underwear other than as "unmentionables," and who "crimsons" at the slightest provocation. Like the culture industry itself, Gerty "is pornographic and prudish," possessing a conception of love "downgraded to romance" (*DE* 140).

When one considers the "kind of language between" Bloom and Gerty here (similar to that between Bloom and Martha Clifford, by mail, in "Lotuseaters"), *Dialectic of Enlightenment* is once again illuminating. "The culture industry does not sublimate; it represses," Horkheimer and Adorno write. "There is no erotic situation which, while insinuating and exciting, does not fail to indicate unmistakably that things can never go that far" (140). In Bloom's epistolary encounter with Martha his advertising image, his packaging, renders him a lie — one "Henry Flower." Likewise, Martha's letter to him (*Ulysses* 63–64) holds out a sexual promise that will never be kept; it too remains a nuanced "image" without material substance (save for the enclosed narcissus flower).[26]

If the "Nausicaa" and "Lotuseaters" episodes provide us with the clearest picture of Bloom's participation in a "culture industry," then "Cyclops," as James H. Maddox puts it, is the episode "which most persistently regards Bloom as a social being . . . forced into a hostile confrontation not with citizens but with The Citizen, who is in grotesque form the Spokesman for the community" (85). *Dialectic of Enlightenment* is also useful for this type of social inquiry in that it sheds light on Bloom's experience of anti-Semitism and Irish ultranationalism.[27] Just as Horkheimer and Adorno, in the "Elements of Anti-Semitism" portion of their study, are "concerned with the actual reversion of enlightened civilization to barbarism" (xvi–xvii) and view anti-Semitism to be no less than "a ritual of civilization" (*DE* 171),[28] so "Cyclops" represents Irish civilization as paralyzed by modes of thinking that render a "utopian" anti-Semitism to be the product not of *mythological* but of *rational* modes of understanding. Arguing that "the ruthless unity in the culture industry is evidence of what will happen in politics" (*DE* 123), Horkheimer and Adorno maintain that in a world of mass series production stereotype replaces individual judgment and blindness replaces genuine reflection (*DE* 201).

Horkheimer and Adorno's use of the tropes of blindness, unreflectiveness, and paranoia in their discussion of anti-Semitism holds particular relevance for our discussion of "Cyclops." Beyond Clive Bell's assertion that "a completely civilized person will not be of the single-eyed sort" (*Civilization* 123), Horkheimer and Adorno argue that "anti-Semitic behavior is generated in situations where blinded men robbed of their subjectivity are set loose as subjects" (*DE* 171). "The morbid aspect of anti-Semitism," they write, "is not projective behavior as such, but the absence from it of reflection. When the subject is no longer able to return to the object what he has received from it, he becomes poorer rather than richer. He loses the reflection in both directions: since he no longer reflects the object, he ceases to reflect upon himself, and loses the ability to differentiate" (*DE* 189–90). What better way than this to characterize Bloom's experience with the Fenian Citizen in "Cyclops"? Surrounded in Barney Kiernan's pub by talk of the "little Jewy" (240), "Shylock" (257), "The Whiteeyed Kaffir" (274), the "bloody dark horse" (275), the "perverted Jew," a "defraud[er] of widows and orphans" (276), the "wolf in sheep's clothing" (277), and "the bloody Jewman" (280), Bloom is viewed by the crowd as stereotypically both "clever and stupid," as lagging "behind advanced civilization" yet "too far ahead of it" (*DE* 186). Against Bloom's "both/and" orientation (his "moderation" [*Ulysses* 266] and his "but on the other hand" [251]), "the public eye" (256) in Barney Kiernan's is depicted as possessing an "either/or" one. Indeed, it is because this anti-Semitic voice is a collective one that, despite evidence to the contrary, it can maintain its favorite myths ("I'm told those Jewies does have a sort of a queer odour coming off them" [250]). For Horkheimer and Adorno, anti-Semites gather together to celebrate the moment when authority permits what is normally outlawed. Further, their pathological hatred of Jews is not curable precisely because there can be no convincing argument against their materially false judgments. Like other paranoiacs, anti-Semites perceive the world around them only to the extent that it corresponds to their "blind purposes" (*DE* 184, 193, 190). For this reason "[t]he compulsively projecting self can project only its own unhappiness — from the very basis of which it is cut off by reason of its lack of reflective thought" (*DE* 192).

Bloom is accused of being a member not of the "Gaelic league" but of the "antitreating league" — the "curse of Ireland" (*Ulysses* 255) — which suggests the real basis of the anti-Semitic feeling against him: he cannot be both Jewish and Irish. "The Nationalist brand of anti-Semitism," Horkheimer and Adorno write, "ignores religious considerations and asserts that the purity of the race and the nation is at stake" (*DE* 176). Indeed, for the Citizen as for the I-Narrator ("a collector of bad and doubtful debts"), the will to national purity is taken to its logical — and narcissistic — conclusions. Whether these patriots speak of "Irish games" (*Ulysses* 259), the "Irish language" (255), "Irish industries" (275), the "tribal images of many Irish heroes and heroines of antiquity" (244), or the "muchtreasured and intricately embroidered ancient Irish facecloth" that is Joe Hynes's noserag (272), there is the sense that legitimate Otherness is unthinkable, much less acceptable, and that all individuals should be classified either as wholly for the cause or wholly against it. In "Cyclops" this historical revisionism clearly takes on narcissistic dimensions: "There's no-one as blind as the fellow that won't see, if you know what that means. Where are our missing twenty millions of Irish should be here today instead of four, our lost tribes? And our potteries and textiles, the finest in the whole world. And our wool that was sold in Rome in the time of Juvenal" (267–68). Moreover, the assembled patriots speak of the United States as "our greater Ireland beyond the sea" (270), rendering Horkheimer/Adorno's critique of anti-Semitism in Nazi Germany all the more relevant to an understanding of "Cyclops." In both cases "illness is socialized," and the "intoxication of joint ecstasy" culminates in "horror or fright" for the victims (*DE* 197). In both instances members of the crowd engage in "false projection" such that "all words become part of the delusive system, of the attempt to possess through the mind everything for which experience is inadequate, to force meaning on a world which makes [them] meaningless" (*DE* 195). At the conclusion of "Cyclops" the violence attempted by the Citizen against Bloom is depicted in proliferating verbiage as a parody of biblical legend — "And they beheld Him even Him, ben Bloom Elijah, amid clouds of angels ascend to the glory of the brightness at an angle of fortyfive degrees" (283)—even if the "terror" of genuine communal "blindness" and "ecstasy" is readily apparent between the lines.

Phillip Herring argues that the Citizen is a bigot and a "petty Irish chauvinist who cares little whom he strikes with the boulders he hurls" ("Joyce's Politics" 3), and Joyce comments that his Citizen "unburdens his soul about the Saxo-Angles in the best Fenian Style" (*Letters* I, 126). Beyond these insights, however, *Dialectic of Enlightenment* helps reveal Joyce's representation of the mechanism by which Jews (or any other marginal group) are used to hold together a civilization otherwise on the verge of collapse. Indeed, Freud, Horkheimer, and Adorno collectively indicate the great extent to which anti-Semitism and narcissism function together in Joyce's fiction, as the interrelated means by which civilization displaces aggressive tendencies in its members.[29]

To be sure, Horkheimer and Adorno's point that "the blind murderer has always seen his victim as a persecutor against whom he must defend himself" has roots in *Civilization and Its Discontents*. There, Freud argues that, far from gentle, people are instinctually aggressive. "As a result, their neighbour is for them not only a potential helper or sexual object, but also someone who tempts them to satisfy their aggressiveness on him . . . to humiliate him, to cause him pain" (*CD* 58). In "Cyclops" it is Bloom who becomes the dangerous neighbor, the "threatening other" against whom the community's aggression is directed. It is he who is associated with Ireland's European neighbors, likewise enemies of "the fair hills of Eire" (268), making the paradox of external enemy and internal victim complete: "The friends we love are by our side," the Citizen warns Bloom, "and the foes we hate before us" (251). Insisting that "foreign wars is the cause of" Ireland's economic problems (243), that foreigners come "over here to Ireland filling the country with bugs," and that "[w]e want no more strangers in our house" (265), the Citizen, as Bloom correctly notes, perpetuates both "national hatred among nations" and "persecution" within Ireland (271). As Freud argues, and as the Citizen exemplifies, the "civilized" commandment to "Love thy neighbour as thyself" is "really justified by the fact that nothing else runs so strongly counter to the original nature of man" (*CD* 59):

> —Well, says John Wise. Isn't that what we're told. Love your neighbour.
> —That chap? says the Citizen [of Bloom]. Beggar my neighbour is his motto. (*Ulysses* 273)

As Freud, Horkheimer, and Adorno would argue, the Citizen here projects his own "civilized" aggressiveness onto Bloom, providing this Fenian (and civilization at large) with the two "threats" necessary to continue under present contradictory circumstances: an inferior group within and a barbarous one without the glorious yet besieged homeland.

W. J. McCormack has most vociferously bemoaned the widespread "refusal to acknowledge the metaphorical nature of Joycean 'paralysis'" (94). To begin to redress this critical imbalance, my reading of Bloom, the Citizen, Gerty, Little Chandler, and Ignatius Gallaher seeks to demonstrate the extent to which Joycean "paralysis" is part and parcel of an entire critique of Irish civilization, rather than simply a thematic unifying principle or an attack on the "inherent spiritual enervation" of Dubliners. Yet Joyce's texts are far more knowing than Freud's in at least one respect: for their understanding and demonstration of the complex relationship between the discourse of culture and the language of the mind, between the "social text" and the "streaming of consciousness."[30] To be sure, one of this fiction's most provocative qualities is that it forcefully shows us just how much an impoverished public discourse can effect, detrimentally, the subjects who speak and think it. Helmut Bonheim argues that "Joyce's style is indeed admirably suited to his central theorem: that the more positive and creative aspects of civilization are developed by those who, by fighting against society as it is, fight for it, by those who envision the future as substantially different from the present" (15). If Bonheim is correct, then it is arguable that such "paralyzed" Dubliners as Eveline, Maria, Chandler, Gerty, and the Citizen represent for Joyce various extremes to which the "civilized" will go, not in fighting society but in fighting themselves.

6

The Sense of an Ending: Spenglerian Decline and the Mexican Novels of Lawrence and Lowry

The history of humanity has no meaning whatever and . . . deep significances reside only in the life-courses of the separate cultures. Their inter-relationships are unimportant and accidental. —Spengler, THE DECLINE OF THE WEST

Countries, civilisations, empires, great hordes, perish for no reason at all, and their soul and meaning with them. — Geoffrey Firmin, in Lowry, UNDER THE VOLCANO

She had a strange feeling, in Mexico, of the old prehistoric humanity. . . . Then there was a mysterious, hot-blooded, soft-footed humanity with a strange civilisation of its own. — Kate Leslie, in Lawrence, THE PLUMED SERPENT

✳ The Literary Fate of *The Decline* between the Wars

"Forgotten," Theodor Adorno aphoristically warns, Oswald "Spengler takes his revenge by threatening to be right" — his "oblivion is the product of evasion" ("Spengler" 54). In a similar vein Erich Heller observes that "in a remarkably short time [Spengler, 1880–1936] has achieved a kind of highly topical oblivion" (159). Like Spencer's "typology of civilization" and Bell's *Civilization*, Spengler's *Decline of the West* (*Der Untergang des Abendlandes*, 1918, rev. 1922, Eng. trans. 1926) today is often dismissed as reductive, deterministic, and overly schematic, a quirky mix of "theory" and "prophecy" (Hale 139). And, like Bell's *Civilization* and Freud's *Civilization and Its Discontents*, Spengler's theory of civilization is clearly a response to the Great War, however much its author would like to disguise this fact. But here the similarities end. As opposed to Spencer's linear, progressive, and unified vision of civilization, Bell's rarefied, parlor-room vision of it far from the heat of world events, and Freud's repression-oriented psychosocial vision of it, Spengler's vision of civilization is cyclical, multiple, and, as Fredric Jameson holds, "catastrophic" in nature (*Political Unconscious* 28).

However, there existed a period, roughly between the wars, when *The Decline of the West* was taken to be a masterwork in the theory of civilization — and not just in Germany and Europe but in North America and the Soviet Union as well.[1] Although of less concern after World War II, the fallout from *The Decline*'s impact could still be felt in 1959 when Helmut Werner would conclude that "Spengler has decisively influenced [Germany's] view of the world and of history" and "continues to do so" (xxiii). In 1970 Mikhail Bakhtin notes that "Spengler's ideas about closed and finalized cultural worlds still exert a great influence on historians and literary scholars" ("Response to *Novy Mir*" 6), and as recently as 1989 Tomislav Sunic argues that Spengler's "analyses, in light of the disturbing conditions in the modern polity, again seem to be gaining in popularity" and that "Spengler probably best succeeded in spreading the spirit of cultural despair to his own as well as future generations" (51, 52). However, more significant to me than Spengler's impact on historiography and cultural history — his work having evinced distrust in historians and philosophers from the moment of its publication[2] — is *The Decline*'s importance to those "encyclopedic" novels and long poems of the 1920s–1940s that depict a civilization shaken by political, social, economic, scientific, artistic, and philosophic revolutions and wars.[3] Spengler's study is clearly the bible of what Frank Kermode terms "the modern apocalypse" — "a pattern of anxiety" that recurs in various "stages of modernism" (*Sense of an Ending* 96) — and of what George Watson calls "the myth of catastrophe," the "nearly universal myth of literary intellectuals between the wars" (100).

The surprising popularity of Spengler's magnum opus is perhaps best explained by Northrop Frye's observation that *The Decline* is more a creative than a scholarly achievement. Like poetry, for Frye, *The Decline* represents "civilized life" as "assimilated to the organic cycle of growth, maturity, decline, death, and rebirth in another individual form" (*Anatomy* 160). With Frye's archetypal criticism (or Hayden White's typology of historiography)[4] in mind, we might even say that Spenglerian civilization is to Spencerian civilization what "tragedy" and "satire" are to "comedy" and "romance" and that these two disparate theories of civilization stand at opposite poles of all modernist conceptions of the story of civilization.[5] As the progress–retrogression debate detailed in Chapter 1 suggests, narratives of civilization in this century conclude either with integration and the overcoming of all problems (comically, like Spencer's) or with disintegration and the triumph of these problems (tragically, like Spengler's). In either case, however, fate plays an essential role in determining the course of civilization.

Given the reception of Spengler's "tragic" text of civilization, then, it is not difficult to imagine its relevance to D. H. Lawrence's *Plumed Serpent* (1926) and Malcolm Lowry's *Under the Volcano* (1947), both of which are set in Mexico and represent Western civilization in the tragic, decadent, and "Faustian" terms of *The Decline*. Indeed, Lawrence's and Lowry's major Mexican novels are ideal for exploring Spengler's intersection with modernist British fiction in that *The Plumed Serpent* comes at the beginning of *The Decline*'s force in English culture and *Under the Volcano* comes at its end. The two novels also bear consideration together on this score because they demonstrate opposed appropriations of and responses to Spengler's determinations. Whereas Lawrence's novel, at one with the voice of heroine Kate Leslie, invokes but then repudiates Spenglerian pessimism, countering its tragic impulse with a utopian myth of rebirth, Lowry's novel, through its hero Geoffrey Firmin, succumbs to this impulse and seeks to make a virtue of necessity by "aestheticizing" this decline, turning it into poetry. Nevertheless, Lowry's text depicts the Consul in an ironic light, undermining his all too effortless and narcissistic acceptance of Spenglerian fatalism. Further, *Under the Volcano* exhibits an awareness of *The Plumed Serpent* itself, engaging Lawrence's novel in a dialogue. But the connections and interconnections do not end here. All three of these texts adhere to Edward Mendelson's characterization of "encyclopedic" novels — attempts to "incorporate representative elements of all the varieties of knowledge their societies put to use" (9) — and stand as romantic and religious works of prophecy.[6] Similar to Conrad's appropriation of Spencer, Woolf's use of Bell (and possibly even Joyce's close proximity to Freud), Lawrence and

Lowry invoke Spengler to place the events of their novels within the larger framework of Western decline familiar to their readers.

Lawrence and Lowry scholars have on a number of occasions recognized but have never rigorously defined, elaborated upon, or tested this textual relationship. Although the only direct reference to Spengler in Lawrence's major works appears in a draft of *Lady Chatterley's Lover*,[7] readers have noted the presence of *The Decline* in *The Plumed Serpent* and, achronologically as it happens, in *The Rainbow* and *Women in Love* as well. In "Oswald Spengler and D. H. Lawrence," for example, J. Barry claims that in these two earlier novels "Lawrence comes closest to creating, within the three generations of the Brangwens, a microcosm of the Spenglerian world-picture wherein the old Hellenic ideals give way to a Faustian existence characterized by an intense spirituality, a duality of mind and body" (151). Baruch Hochman sees Spengler's fatalistic affirmation of the "decadence of Western civilization on grounds of necessity" in the "later Lawrence, but especially the Lawrence of *The Plumed Serpent*" (238), and Wyndham Lewis castigates Lawrence for attributing to American Indians qualities in fact deriving from the ideas of Spengler and other Europeans (quoted in Draper 18).[8]

The Decline is mentioned explicitly in *Under the Volcano* at only one point — when Hugh Firmin exclaims of journalistic "prostitution," "That's one point on which I'm in complete agreement with Spengler" (100) — yet its importance to the novel is far greater than the single allusion would suggest. Anthony Kilgallin, for example, identifies Spengler as "an important functional reference throughout *Under the Volcano*" and argues that "Geoffrey's death is fully in accord with Spengler's theory of the determinism of inevitable decline for the Faustian spirit of Western man in the twentieth century" ("Faust" 33). David Markson maintains that Spenglerian concepts, among many others, "all function *operatively* to become part of the texture of [the novel's] events themselves" (7), and Michael Cripps writes that, "following Spengler, Lowry sees in the Consul's inability to live in the world he had inherited, the death-wish of an entire civilization" (91). Ackerley and Clipper argue that Lowry was attracted "by Spengler's cyclic view of history [and] by his use of Faustian imagery to define the condition of western man" (153). In an early unpublished draft of the novel they even discover Hugh Firmin accusing half-brother Geoffrey of "quoting Spengler" at him (387).[9]

Although not conclusive in themselves, these judgments and discoveries collectively constitute a point of departure from which to explore Lawrence's and Lowry's appropriations of Spengler, and to explore the means by which their novels subvert or "dialogize" *The Decline* when meditating on the relative merit of "saving civilization" or of "aestheticizing" its demise.

✳ The Spenglerian Shape of Civilization in *The Plumed Serpent* and *Under the Volcano*

In a letter of 17 November 1915 Lawrence writes, "I think there is no future for England, only a decline and fall." "That is the dreadful and unbearable part of it," he continues, "to have been born into a decadent era, a decline of life, a collapsing of civilization" (*Letters* II, 441). This letter, written three years before the publication of *The Decline*, suggests why Spengler's thesis would eventually become so attractive to Lawrence. As K. K. Ruthven points out, it is around this time that "Lawrence took a renewed interest in the Decadent theme that Europe is in the final stages of its decline" (47). This leads to the question of how we are to understand *The Plumed Serpent*'s appropriation of Spengler given Lawrence's predilection to see things in this way anyway, there being so many theories of decline and degeneration then in currency. I believe that an answer to this question is suggested in a letter by Malcolm Lowry to Jacques Barzun. There, responding to Barzun's negative review of *Under the Volcano*, Lowry defends his use of other literary works in crafting his fiction. "A young writer will naturally try to benefit and make use of what he has read," he writes, "as a result of which . . . 'design-governing postures' are from time to time inevitable" (*Selected Letters* 143). Although Lowry is speaking here primarily of technical matters, it is nevertheless in this same sense that we may understand *Under the Volcano* and *The Plumed Serpent* to be incorporating *The Decline of the West:* as the tragic and fatalistic theory of civilization to provide the "design" for the civilizations represented in these novels.

A detailed examination of the appropriation and subversion of this design first requires a look at Spengler's influential "morphology" of civilization itself. Following in the wake of Giambattista Vico's and Nikolai Danilevsky's cyclical theories, on the one hand, and Max Nordau's and Brooks Adams's theories of Western "degeneration" and "decay," on the other, Spengler's two-volume *The Decline of the West* argues that there have been eight civilizations in human history — Egyptian, Babylonian, Indian, Chinese, Classical (Greco-Roman), Arabian (Magian), Mexican, and Western (Faustian) — all of which have been organically determined. For Spengler, each culture-civilization must pass through a cycle of four stages, collectively extending over 1,000 years: the spring or infancy of a culture in which its history is first recorded and its religions and myths are born; the summer or youth of a culture in which its philosophy and critical spirit are born and its religious reformations occur; the fall or adulthood of a culture in which it experiences its enlightenment (its rule of reason) and the flowering of its artistic and intellectual creativity (for the West, approximately 1800); and the winter or old age and decline of a culture — "civilization" itself — "the organic-logical sequel, fulfillment and finale of a culture" (*The Decline* I, 31). For Spengler, the decline of the West "comprises nothing less than the problem of *Civilization*," for "every culture has *its own* civilization." Spengler next explains that the terms "culture" and "civilization," which previously expressed an ethical distinction, are used in his work "in a *periodic* sense, to express a strict and necessary *organic succession.*"[10] "Civilizations," he writes, "are the most external and artificial states of which a species of developed humanity is capable. They are a conclusion . . . death following life, rigidity following expansion, intellectual age and the stone-built, petrifying world-city following mother-earth. . . . They are an end, irrevocable, yet by inward necessity reached again and again" (I, 31). As Wellek and Warren note, "in Spengler we arrive at the idea of closed cultural cycles developing with fatal necessity: self-enclosed, though mysteriously parallel" (122). Further, for Spengler, civilization represents the withering of artistic, intellectual, and religious vitality, the rise of the mob out of the "folk" and society out of community. Civilization also spells the rise of imperialism, science, technology, and skeptical philosophy, all while democracy is supplanted by "Caesarism," the cult of an omnipotent emperor. Finally, after the demise of civilization its inhabitants exist as they were before the advent of culture: "historyless" and "formless." In short, for Spengler, civilization is to culture as something stale, corrupt, and alienated is to something vital, genuine, and integrated.[11]

Past-civilization-oriented though *The Decline of the West* is, we must not lose sight of its primary mission, at least as far as its author was concerned: to explain the *hic et nunc* realities of Western civilization, however out of our control they may be. Indeed, Spengler claims of his own project, "it is not merely a question of writing one out of several possible and merely logically justifiable philosophies, but of writing *the* philosophy of our time, one . . . dimly presaged by all" (Preface xv). Whereas Spengler fluctuates between the position that *The Decline* is a "Copernican system of history" that renders no civilization superior to any other and the position that his study arms Westerners with information of their own fate to which no other civilized group has ever been privy, Spengler's caveat that "the present is a civilized, emphatically not a cultured time" (I, 40) pervades his study.

Numerous aspects of Spengler's "tragic" theory of civilization are represented in *The Plumed Serpent*. For one thing, the novel is laden with Spenglerian assumptions about civilization's fated demise and with images of "the exhaustion of an entire mode of civilization" (Hochman 254). For example, Mexico is repeatedly referred to as "doomed," "deadly," "inescapable," "violent," "barren," "hopeless," and "decayed" ("the buildings [of Mexico City] were either new and alien, like the Country Club, or cracked and dilapidated, with all the plaster falling off" [*Plumed Serpent* 31]). The novel's protagonist, Kate Leslie, feels "that Mexico lay in her destiny almost as a doom" (24) and attributes to native Mexicans a bizarre "fatality" (24, 50). Worse off even than Mexico, however, the Irish Kate derides her native Europe for its "hopelessness," "ugliness," "cynicism," and "emptiness," for being the "dry-rot of the world's sterility" (103). Frequently sounding like Spengler, Kate ridicules "the pallid wanness and weariness of her world" (122).

Spengler's view that the course of civilization is organically determined and cyclical is also ubiquitous in *The Plumed Serpent*. Although L. D. Clark is certainly correct to point out the importance of Aztec notions of circles and circularity in *The Plumed Serpent* (129),[12] many of the novel's evocations of cyclicality point more toward Spengler's historical sense of it. For example, references to the "cycle of humanity" (148), the cycle of races ("Every dog has his day. And every race" [400]), and the cycle of deities ("Even the gods must be born again" [59]) pervade the novel, echoing Lawrence's determination in *Fantasia of the Unconscious* (1922), in words that strongly recall Spengler, that "civilization" is in its "winter period," a period of "death and denudation" (quoted in Hochman 239). At one point Kate considers how "monstrous" she finds the "rolling and unfolding of the life of the cosmos" (243), which underscores the novel's sense that the course of civilization is controlled by cosmic, not human forces. As Baruch Hochman observes, history in *The Plumed Serpent* "is largely a reflex of nature, or of the cosmic life." Speaking of the "almost deterministic force" of nature in Lawrence's novel, Hochman points out that "the life of civilizations — any civilization — depends on the cosmic life outside it and is ultimately controlled by that life" (237).

Moreover, *The Plumed Serpent* invokes *The Decline*'s perception of our "great crisis of the present": that "*Pure* Civilization, as a historical process, consists in a progressive exhaustion of forms that have become inorganic or dead" (I, 32).[13] In this scenario cosmopolitanism supplants provincial values, and "mechanical" and intellectual modes replace "organic" and intuitive ones. Lawrence's novel ceaselessly maligns what it takes to be the debased "mechanical world" and the "horrible machine of the world," in which the individual is reduced to an automaton (104–5). Even the "freest" of people, Don Ramon at one point muses, are "slaves to the industrial machine" (72). Like Spengler, *The Plumed Serpent* counterposes the provinces (the Sayula countryside where the redemptive religion of Quetzalcoatl is reborn) and the "world-city" (Mexico City) in order to celebrate the former at the expense of the latter. In Lawrence's novel the Mexican capital is repeatedly referred to as violent and evil, a "mongrel city" full of "loutish men" (20) with inferiority complexes ("There are all sorts of inferiority complex, and the city Mexican has a very strong sort" [13]).[14] As Baruch Hochman aptly notes, Lawrence "blames the corruption of civilization itself for the violence its denizens undergo" (255).

Spengler's claim that it is no longer the "folk" but the "mob" who inhabit the civilized world-city is also echoed in *The Plumed Serpent*. For Spengler, this mob's "uncomprehending hostility to all the traditions representative of the Culture," and its "keen and cold intelligence that confounds the wisdom of the peasant," "betoken the definite closing-down of the Culture and the opening of a quite new phase of human existence — antiprovincial, late, futureless, but quite inevitable" (I, 33–34). In *The Plumed Serpent* too, we read of "the degenerate mob of Mexico city" (11) who constitute "the rabble": "It was the cold, collective lust of millions of people," Kate thinks, "to break the spirit in the outstanding individuals" (136).

Yet what frameworks of understanding guide this civilized "mass" man? For both *The Decline* and *The Plumed Serpent* the answer is the same: Christianity, socialism, and imperialism. "Socialism," Spengler writes, is "the Faustian world-feeling become irreligious; 'Christianity' so called . . . is always on the lips of the English Socialist, to whom it seems to be something in the nature of a 'dogma-less morale'" (I, 358–59). Viewing socialism to be a late Western civilized outgrowth of Christianity — albeit a "trivial" and "superficial" version of it — Spengler charges that socialism is "*not* a system of compassion, humanity, peace and kindly care [as Christianity would take itself to be], but one of will-to-power." "The Stoic takes the world as he finds it," Spengler continues, "but the Socialist wants to organize and recast it," to "fill it with *his own* spirit" (I, 361–62). In the world of *The Plumed Serpent* too, the unenlightened succumb either to the Scylla of socialism or to the Charybdis of Christianity. Don Ramon's wife, Carlota, for example, is a devout Catholic who represents adherence to Christianity. Repeatedly disparaged as a "pure European" who has no place in the new Mexico of aristocrat Ramon Carrasco and military general Cipriano Viedma (she dies when Don Ramon turns the Catholic church in their village into a church for the religion of Quetzalcoatl), Carlota Carrasco's Christian perspective is continually undercut in the novel.[15] At one point, for example, Kate thinks, "Jesus is no saviour to the Mexicans. He is a dead god in their tomb." In this way, for her view, "whole nations become entombed under the slow subsidence of their Past" (136). Socialism is also maligned in the novel as an inherently hypocritical and "bullying" (73) creed of bad faith. Deemed a terror, the "logical" child of "materialism" (112), and an "infectious disease, like syphilis" (101), bolshevism is portrayed as tainting all individuals who come in contact with it. Kate's American cousin, Owen Rhys, for example, is portrayed as a "great socialist" who, while disapproving of the inhumanity of bullfights, happily and eagerly goes to see one (7). The hypocritical Owen also disapproves of Kate's disdain for "common people," yet is shown to hate "common rowdiness as much as [does] Kate" (10). Moreover, Owen's acquaintance, Villiers, is said to watch the bullfight for the "thrill of it, without emotion, coldly and scientifically" (16). Kate even ridicules the frescoes of socialist painter Diego Rivera on the grounds that his depictions of the Indians are merely "symbols in the weary script of socialism and anarchy" (52). For Don Ramon, Carlota's "Charity" and the popular "Socialism" are both "Anti-Christ[s]" (209).

Finally, *The Plumed Serpent* echoes Spengler's determination that "Imperialism is Civilization unadulterated"; that "In this phenomenal form the destiny of the West is now irrevocably set" (I, 36–37). The novel also underscores Spengler's belief that "the great Cultures are entities" that "arise out of the deepest foundations of spirituality," that "the peoples under the spell of a Culture" are "its products and not its authors," and, hence, that groups may legitimately be divided up by "nation" (II, 170). In *The Plumed Serpent* too, national and racial purity is celebrated, and the mixing of races is said to lead to "the homogeneity of death" (77) in the form of "mongrel" individuals.[16] Moreover, the introduction into Mexico of "mechanical foreigners" (404–5) with their "European ideas" (54) is repeatedly said to cost Mexico its "soul." Cipriano maintains that "the foreigners seem to make the Mexicans worse than they are" (23), and Owen admits that Mexicans remain "in the grip of outsiders, as they have been for hundreds of years" (63). Freeing Mexico from these stultifying foreign influences is precisely the work of Ramon and Cipriano's religion of Quetzalcoatl. In Ramon's fourth hymn, "What Quetzalcoatl Saw in Mexico," for example, Mexicans are exhorted to throw off the yoke of their foreign exploiters (256–60).

By the same token, many aspects of Spengler's "tragic" theory of civilization are appropriated by *Under the Volcano*.[17] For one thing, the novel depicts Spengler's correlation of the rise of Caesarism and "the end of Democracy." "In the late Democracy," Spengler writes, "*race* bursts forth and either makes ideals its slaves or throws them scornfully into the pit," but "in no other civilization has the will-to-power manifested itself in so inexorable a form as in . . . ours." "The thought, and consequently the action, of the mass[es]," he continues, "are kept under iron pressure" while "the parties become the obedient retinues of a few, and the shadow of coming Caesarism already touches them." "Through money," Spengler concludes, "democracy becomes its own destroyer, after money has destroyed intellect." At this point "Caesarism *grows* on the soil of Democracy, but its roots thread deeply into the underground of blood tradition" (II, 463–64). This democracy–Caesarism dynamic echoes throughout *Under the Volcano:* in the novel's allusions to the imminent Second World War,[18] to the "Caesars" who produce it (Hitler, Mussolini, Stalin, and Franco), to the Mexican fascists who end Geoffrey's life, and, perhaps most importantly, to the "blood-money" used by the fascist "Sinarchistas" to purchase loyalty from dispossessed "Pelados." In this final instance Geoffrey, Hugh, and Yvonne watch in horror as the "Pelado's smeared conquistador's hands, that had clutched the melon, now clutched a sad bloodstained pile of silver pesos and centavos. The Pelado had stolen the dying Indian's money" (250). That the three do not and cannot aid in any way the dying Indian by the roadside is of course precisely the point.

To consider the microcosmic level rather than the macrocosmic one, Spengler's depiction of this present state of affairs is also embodied in Geoffrey Firmin's personal tragedy, which becomes a trope for his tragically fated civilization. Spengler himself suggests the forcefulness of this relation between self and civilization, public and private realms, when he remarks that "nothing can eliminate this duality from the world" because "it is radical, founded in the essence of the animal that is both microcosm and participant in the cosmic" (II, 329). Like Yeats's Spenglerian *A Vision* (1925), which attempts to construct a myth of self and civilization ("a civilization is a struggle to keep self-control, and in this sense it is like some great tragic person" [268]), *Under the Volcano* emphasizes this correlation between decadent self and declining civilization.[19] As Stephen Spender puts it in his introduction to *Under the Volcano*, the Consul's neurosis "is the dial of the instrument that records the effects of a particular stage of civilisation upon a civilised individual" (xiii). For Ronald Binns, who deploys curiously Spenglerian rhetoric, "the Consul *is*, to an extent, England, and the contemporary historical context forms an inescapable part of his decline" (44).

Even Lowry himself, in his preface to the French edition of *Under the Volcano*, insists that "the destiny of my hero can be considered in its relationship to the destiny of humanity" ("Preface to a Novel" 14).

This invocation of "destiny" brings us to what is perhaps the Consul's most salient trait: his surrender to a deadly fate he seems to ascertain in advance. And this is precisely what Spengler believes his theory to afford: "No culture is at liberty to *choose* the path and conduct of its thought," he writes, "but here for the first time a Culture can foresee the way that destiny has chosen for it" (I, 159). Moreover, Geoffrey Firmin, because he is convinced of his own imminent demise, chooses to luxuriate in the aesthetic appreciation of it — Narcissus-like[20] — rather than attempt to alter his situation. As Hugh sees it, the Consul blindly surrenders himself to what he believes to be an inescapable destiny (*Under the Volcano* 183). Thinking of the events of his day as he moves closer to his suicide-murder in the Farolito, Geoffrey, as Stephen Tifft puts it, "dedicates himself to the tragic destiny which — he is convinced — is his" (47):

> And he saw dimly too how Yvonne's arrival, the snake in the garden, his quarrel with Laruelle and later with Hugh and Yvonne, the infernal machine, the encounter with Senora Gregorio, the finding of the letters, and much beside, how all the events of the day indeed had been as independent tufts of grass he had half-heartedly clutched at or stones loosed on his downward flight, which were still showering on him from above. (*Under the Volcano* 362)

Not only does this passage share *The Decline*'s totalizing and deterministic thrust, but it even captures the rhythm of Spengler's prose and evokes his sense of nostalgic melancholy. Thus, although Tifft asserts that "Lowry never fully reveals the origins of the Consul's tragic fatalism" (48), a glance at the Spenglerian rhetoric of this novel provides an important clue.

Also significant is the degree to which Spengler's theory of civilization informs the representation of Mexico and imperialism in *Under the Volcano*, even if the novel denigrates Spengler's conclusions about the interrelation of civilizations. For Spengler, of the eight civilizations that have existed, Mexican civilization is unique in having been "murdered" by the West before it could self-destruct. "For, as it happens," Spengler writes, Mexico "is the one example of a Culture ended by violent death." "It was not starved, suppressed, or thwarted," he continues, "but murdered in the full glory of its unfolding, destroyed like a sunflower whose head is struck off by one passing" (II, 43). Whether or not this trope of the murder of one civilization by another is echoed in Geoffrey's act, as a European in Mexico, of decapitating a flower — "the consul decapitated a dusty coquelicot poppy growing by the side of the gutter with his stick" (61) — it is clear that the "tragic Mexico" of *Under the Volcano* ("How merrily Mexico laughed away its tragic history, the past, the underlying death!" [254]) possesses an unmistakably Spenglerian, and even Laurentian, cast.

The "various tragedies of Mexican history" (248) alluded to in Lowry's novel all relate to literal and figurative invasion by outside civilizations — whether Cortez's Spain, Napoleon's France, the United States, or, as is suggested of the present, Hitler's Germany. In this sense, the novel's four major characters (all of French, English, or American origin) collectively represent Mexico's encounter with the West, which for *The Decline* ends in conquest. This "forceful young civilization," Spengler writes, covers the old one "with ever-thickening layers of West-European-American life-forms under which, slowly, the ancient native form disappears" (II, 46).[21] Similarly, Lowry's Cuernavaca is composed of "three civilizations" (10), the ghosts of two of them sedimented beneath the present one: "There was Cortez Palace," Yvonne muses, "and there, high on the cliff, a man standing gazing over the valley who from his air of martial intentness might have been Cortez himself" (56). And Hugh insists — directly echoing Speng-ler — that the conquest of Mexico "took place in a civilisation which was as good if not better than that of the conquerors, a deep-rooted structure" (300). Indeed, Spengler credits the Aztecs with "a comprehensive policy, a carefully ordered financial system," a "highly developed legislation," and "a wealth of literature in several languages, an intellectually brilliant and polite society in great cities to which the West could not show one single parallel" (II, 43). Even the repression of the "memory" of conquest to which Spengler alludes is reflected in the idealizing caption of an illustrated calendar that hangs on the wall of a cantina in Lowry's novel: "The last Aztec emperor . . . Moctezuma[,] and Hernan Cortes, representative of the Spanish race, meet face to face: two races and two civilizations which had attained a high degree of perfection unite to form the nucleus of our present national character" (27; trans. Ackerley and Clipper 46).

Ronald Binns's insight that history in *Under the Volcano* "is merely a perpetual process of betrayal and exploitation, of conquerors and victims" (51), suggests a final way in which Spengler's theory of civilization informs the depiction of civilization in Lowry's novel: as a commentary on the nature of imperialism. For Spengler, a distinguishing characteristic of the "Western soul" is its Faustian "expansion-power": "it was this, in the last resort, that killed and even annihilated the Mexican and Peruvian culture" (II, 46). Moreover, for him, imperialism is not a matter of choice but is instead an inherent dimension of "the late mankind of the world-city stage"

(I, 36–37). This aspect of Western civilization is illustrated in Lowry's novel time and again (as it is in *The Plumed Serpent*). In the argument among Geoffrey, Hugh, and Yvonne on the subject of intercultural exploitation, for example, Spengler's sense of the inevitability of imperialism is discernible: "first, Spaniard exploits Indian, then, when he had children, he exploited the halfbreed, then the pure-blooded Mexican Spaniard, the criollo, then the mestizo exploits everybody, foreigners, Indians, and all. Then the Germans and Americans exploited him: now the final chapter, the exploitation of everybody by everybody else" (*Under the Volcano* 299–300). Like *The Plumed Serpent* — in which Kate muses that Mexico "would have its victim. America would have its victim. As long as time lasts, it will be a continent divided between Victims and Victimisers. What is the good of trying to interfere!" (218) — *Under the Volcano* captures *The Decline*'s sense of the violence and exploitation central to all intercultural encounters. For Lowry, as for Spengler, the history of civilization is the history of cultural victimization writ large.

✳ Spengler Dialogized: The Resistance to Civilization and the Aesthetics of Decline in *The Plumed Serpent* and *Under the Volcano*

If Spengler's theory of civilization provides a "design-governing posture" for Lawrence's and Lowry's novels, it is equally clear that it is problematized, parodied, or, as Bakhtin would put it, "dialogized" in them as well. Indeed, as the epoch's key text to proclaim the impossibility of saving (or even altering) civilization and to presage the Second World War, *The Decline* is central to, yet does not finally determine, either novel's representation of civilization. Both Kate Leslie and Geoffrey Firmin find it impossible to leave Mexico; but whereas the former ultimately embraces Ramon's renewal of the Quetzalcoatl religion as a means of escaping the decline of the West, the latter instead perishes "accepting" Spengler and revels in the aesthetic appreciation of his own, and of his civilization's, demise. Thus, whereas *Under the Volcano* succumbs to *The Decline*'s apocalyptic appeal and, like Spengler's text, turns it into decadent, overblown romantic poetry, *The Plumed Serpent* resists this appeal and instead counters with a utopian, theocratic narrative of rebirth.

In *Fantasia of the Unconscious* (1922) Lawrence already appears to challenge Spengler's conclusions:

> This time . . . we have consciously and responsibly to carry ourselves through the winter-period, the period of death and denudation. . . .

For there are not now, as in Roman times, any great reservoirs of energetic, barbaric life. . . . This time the leading civilization cannot die out. . . . It must suffer a great collapse, maybe. But it must carry through all the collapse the *living clue* to the next civilization. (Quoted in Hochman 241)

In his essay of two years later, "On Human Destiny," Lawrence again seems to allude challengingly to *The Decline:* "They know our civilisation has got to smash, sooner or later. . . . They say glibly: 'Oh, well, every civilisation must fall at last'" (251). And in a draft of *Lady Chatterley's Lover* Tommy Dukes counters Spenglerian ideas when he asserts: "[T]here will be a new civilisation, the very antithesis of tabloids and aeroplanes. . . . There will be a civilisation based on the mystery of touch, and all that that means" (quoted in Martz 119). F. R. Leavis addresses this tension between Lawrence and *The Decline* when he describes Spengler's "idiom" as "curiously Laurentian," but then goes on to insist that "the likeness between Lawrence and Spengler goes no further: the comparison ends in contrast. For Lawrence is in himself the strongest argument against Spengler's 'philosophy'" ("D. H. Lawrence" 140). Leavis is correct here, but for the wrong reasons. It is not so much, as Leavis imagines, that Lawrence's personal example as a writer repudiates Spengler. Rather, it is that Lawrence's writings challenge Spengler's verdicts, that works like *The Plumed Serpent,* however chimeric they may be, offer a blueprint to revivify the civilization both Spengler and Lawrence take to be in its death throes. As J. Barry puts it in a different context, "Spengler's *Decline of the West* is but prelude to the reincarnation of primitive values" (151).[22]

After the Great War Lawrence is known to have sought physical escape from "the murderous influence of European civilization" (Sanders 136). From this perspective *The Decline* itself may be seen as a part of the Western disease that *The Plumed Serpent* seeks to cure. To be sure, one way of understanding Ramon's and Cipriano's new-old religion is that it seeks, in Spengler's terms, to turn "civilization" back into "culture." Ramon is the reincarnated Quetzalcoatl, Cipriano the reincarnated Huitzilopochtli — ancient gods who have returned to Mexico to save it from sterility and death. Ramon maintains that "We *must* change back to the vision of the living cosmos; we *must.*" "The oldest Pan is in us," he continues, "and he will not be denied" (316). When Ramon speaks of civilization, he deploys Spengler's organic tropes to do so: "Men are still part of the Tree of Life, and the roots go down to the centre of the earth," he insists. "Loose leaves, and aeroplanes, blow away on the wind, in what they call freedom. But the

Tree of Life has fixed, deep, gripping roots" (80). Yet, unlike Spengler, Ramon insists that cultures live on even if civilizations must die.

The Aztec cult of Ramon and Cipriano merits only brief treatment here, so often has it been discussed and explicated.[23] Moreover, readers of *Women in Love* and *Lady Chatterley's Lover* will find much familiar about this new-old Mexican culture-religion, whose symbol is a plumed serpent. This creed seeks "to bring the great opposites into contact and into unison again" (*Plumed Serpent* 418) — such "opposites" as mind and body, culture and nature, male and female, the rational and the sensual — the separation of which for Spengler and Lawrence typifies "civilization" at its very worst. Hence the symbol of Quetzalcoatl (*quetzal*/bird and *coatl*/serpent), which embraces the "opposites" of earth and sky, high and low, and so on. At one point Kate muses on "[t]he magnificence of the watchful morning-star, the watcher between the night and the day, the gleaming clue to the two opposites" (93–94); and at another she celebrates her provincial lakeside retreat as "not too savage, and not over civilised" (108). Still later, Cipriano's face strikes her as "the face at once of a god and of a devil" (311). Civilization, on the other hand, is viewed as fetishizing one opposition over the other — intellect over feeling, mind over body, and so forth — to the detriment of all.

The Quetzalcoatl ritual's pagan quality clearly is meant to help replace civilization with culture. It is purposefully "uncivilized"; dozens of references to "savagery," "barbarian consciousness," and "the ancient barbaric world" are used by Lawrence's narrator to flatter, not denigrate, the Mexicans of both aristocratic and peasant classes who join the movement. Kate sees in Cipriano "the secret savage coming into his own" (316) and wonders at the "deep, full, almost martial singing of men, savage and remote, to the sound of the drum" (349): "This was what they were, these people! Savages, with the impossible fluid flesh of savages, and that savage way of dissolving into an awful black mass of desire" (400). Kate notes that they consciously revert to savagery (138) and, after initially thinking it "evil," later views it, like her wedding clothes when she is dressed to marry Cipriano, as "strange and primitive, but beautiful" (330) — opposite to the familiar, sophisticated, and ugly European civilization she leaves behind. The novel ends with Kate's complete acceptance of this new-old culture, which becomes the official state religion of Mexico.

Ramon's challenge to European civilization (and Lawrence's to Spenglerian pessimism) is problematic in at least two respects. First, it remains an open question just how authentically Aztec and un-European this old-new church really is. All we see is one church hierarchy replace another; the real differences enacted by Ramon and Cipriano seem to make little actual difference. Moreover, the very ideas these two Mexicans espouse are perhaps more European — specifically, the romantic notion of noble savagery — than anything else. One reader, for example, asserts that "Don Ramon seems to speak for Lawrence's view of Western Civilization itself" (Hochman 234). Wyndham Lewis is even blunter in his criticism, complaining that Lawrence's Indian "is pure Spengler" — "I daresay the Aztecs themselves would scarcely recognize Mr. Lawrence's account of their beliefs" (177, 252). And Katherine Anne Porter, in her 1926 review of *The Plumed Serpent*, takes Lawrence to task for "pretentiousness," for "having invaded a mystery that remained a mystery to him." "His Indians are merely what the Indians might be if they were all D. H. Lawrence's," she continues; "The three characters who act as his mouthpieces are simply good Europeans at bottom" (quoted in Draper 271). This becomes clear when we consider the close proximity of Ramon's thought to, say, Mellors's thought in *Lady Chatterley's Lover* or Birkin's in *Women in Love:* each of these men favors sensuality over intellect, individual instinct over social convention, and mystery over reason.

Second, Ramon's (and seemingly Lawrence's) "solution" is problematic for its autocratic and even protofascist tenor, for its appeal to an irrational, mass response, and for its total inability to question its own mode of understanding; there is no room for difference, dissension, or debate in the new-old religion of Quetzalcoatl. After Ramon flings "his right arm tense into the air" the "men of the ring did the same, and the naked arms were thrust aloft like so many rockets," after which "involuntarily the men in the crowd twitched, then shot their arms upwards, turning their faces to the dark heavens" (197). Even more troubling, the novel appears to celebrate Ramon's ability, with "words," to "put the power of his heavy, strong will over the people. The crowd began to fuse under his influence. As he gazed back at all the black eyes, his eyes seemed to have no expression, save that they seemed to be seeing the heart of all darkness in front of him, where his unknowable God-mystery lived and moved" (337). Lines like these tempt one to agree with John R. Harrison's contention that *The Plumed Serpent*'s "emphasis on ritual and symbol," its "casting off of mental consciousness," its "belief in the power of a natural leader, in 'dark gods,' in irrationalism and racialism" lead "straight to the mass hysteria of the regimes of Hitler and Mussolini" (188).

By comparison, *Under the Volcano* takes *The Decline* to its logical conclusions and eschews the kind of "solution" reflected in *The Plumed Serpent*. Rather than challenging Spengler's determinations, Lowry's novel fleshes out Western decline so graphically and horrifyingly that many have found the novel unbearably pessimistic, not to mention unreadable. Nevertheless, *Under the Volcano* is far from a mouthpiece for Spengler. If the Consul incarnates Spenglerian decline, the novel as a whole throws this decline into question. Hence, Alfred Kazin's estimation of *Under the Volcano* as "in the best sense a novel" of "politics" (Lowry, *Selected Letters* 438) tells only half the story. Kazin's comment neglects the novel's preoccupation with political *in*activity and masochistic escape. From this perspective Ronald Binns's statement that "*Under the Volcano* counterposes two basic political positions: to change the world (through socialism or art) or to accept it" (47) is nearer to the truth; yet it seems to me that the polarity in the novel even more closely approximates the romantic tension between aesthetic escape and worldly action, aesthetic order and worldly disorder, and aesthetic versus ethical responsibility.[24]

Spengler's "historical pessimism" (Arendt 155) and his fatalistic and deterministic world prophecy have been accused of being "secretly conservative" (Mann, "Theory of Spengler" 225) (just as the Consul has been accused of simply accepting the "status quo" [Cripps 95]). "The image of man which lurks behind Spengler's vast historical canvas," Erich Heller argues, "is perverted, and could only be accepted by a hopelessly perverted age. For Spengler has no idea of the true stature of the problem of human freedom" (169). "As it is," Heller continues, speaking of Spengler (but convincingly of Geoffrey Firmin as well), "there is no terror and no pity in his acceptance of Destiny" — Spengler "appears merely concerned with lending Destiny a hand in the business of destruction" (170) (just as Lowry views the Consul to be "a man that is all destruction" [*Selected Letters* 200]). For this reason, F. R. Leavis wonders if we should listen to Spengler's "admonition to cease bothering about the inevitable future[.] That is impossible," he reasons. "Ridiculous, priggish and presumptuous as it may be, if we care at all about the issues we cannot help believing that, for the immediate future, at any rate, we have some responsibility" ("Mass Civilization" 170). Whether or not one agrees with Heller's and Leavis's judgments, their questioning of the usefulness of Spengler's (or for that matter *Under the Volcano*'s) suggestions remains poignant: "What, then, according to Spengler, are the values left to us?" Heller asks. Must not his "tempestuous" insights rob these values "of their power to guide our actions" (171)? Spengler's answer to such charges also speaks well for the Consul:

> It will no doubt be objected that [my] world-outlook, which . . . cuts off all far-reaching hopes, would be unhealthy for all and fatal for many,

once it ceased to be a mere theory and was adopted as a practical scheme of life by the group of personalities effectively moulding the future. Such is not my opinion. . . . I fail to see that it is any disadvantage to discover betimes that some of these hopes must come to nothing. And if the hopes thus doomed should be to those most dear, well, a man who is worth anything will not be dismayed. (*The Decline* I, 40)

Geoffrey "escapes" this problem by turning his decline and demise into poetry — by savoring his own death as if it were a work of art.

In a letter written one year prior to the publication of *Under the Volcano*, Lowry writes that "our house [in British Columbia] is still here but civilization, so called, is closing in upon us a little too much for our liking" (*Selected Letters* 90). This association of civilization and decadence suggests that Lowry has absorbed both Spengler's rhetoric and disdain for civilized "corruption." As Jeffrey Satinover asserts of our own time, Spengler's Faust "may be thought of as the great anti-myth of the West": the tragedy of a culture or individual self-consciously pursuing greatness at all costs (109). By these lights Geoffrey's "surrender to fate" and his obsession with self are two sides of the same coin. As Theodor Adorno explains, "in a world of brutal and oppressed life, decadence becomes the refuge of a potentially better life by renouncing its allegiance to this one." What can "oppose the decline of the West is not a resurrected culture but the utopia that is silently contained in the image of its decline" ("Spengler" 72). This insight aptly characterizes Geoffrey's "decadence": his utopia is located not in a redeemed or redemptive civilization but in the very "image of its decline." Indeed, the Consul revels in an "aesthetics of decline" throughout his long final day of life, from Yvonne's return in chapter 2 to the novel's last line, where the decline becomes literal: "Somebody threw a dead dog after him down the ravine" (375). Geoffrey's ironic cry of "poor little defenceless" China, Ethiopia, Flanders, Belgian Congo, Latvia, and Russia (310) soon becomes "poor little defenceless me" (313), revealing the Consul's fixation on the artistic form his own decline is taking, in which he himself plays the role of both artist-creator and art object. Although a number of opportunities to "reverse his doom" present themselves, Geoffrey eschews them all and chooses instead to "watch" himself go under with great fascination. An aphorism of Spengler's nicely illustrates the allure of the Consul's "aesthetics of decline": "He who does not experience history as it really is — tragic, pervaded by fate, and thus meaningless, aimless and amoral — is not in a position to make history," Spengler writes. "The life of the individual is important to no one but himself; from the standpoint of history what matters is whether he attempts to escape from history or to sacrifice to it" (*Aphorisms* 52). In this paradoxical way Geoffrey's decline becomes both an "escape from history" and the ultimate "sacrifice to it." For "When the doomed are most eloquent in their sinking," Lowry writes in a poem, "It seems that then we are least strong to save" (*Selected Poems* 75). Clearly, whatever else we might say about him, the Consul chooses his art over his life.

This stated, we must not overlook the fact that whereas Spengler's (and Lawrence's) conclusions are rhetorically definitive, complete and final, Lowry's are not. Indeed, *Under the Volcano* may be said to "dialogize" Spengler's theory — putting the Consul's Spenglerian discourse in conflict with other discourses — in order to render Geoffrey's world view partial and limited. Although we might agree with Mann's critique of Spengler — "if there is anything more appalling than fate, it is the human being who bears it without lifting a finger" ("Theory of Spengler" 222–23) — we cannot quite so easily conclude this of Lowry's fiction, which at many points depicts Geoffrey's discourse in an ironic light.

Bakhtin's notions of "dialogism" and the "polyphonic novel," particularly as he considers Dostoyevsky, are germane to an understanding of Lowry's subversion of Spenglerian rhetoric in *Under the Volcano*.[25] For Bakhtin, whereas many novels present completely final arguments summarized from the author's standpoint (think, for example, of *The Plumed Serpent*),[26] Dostoyevsky's works present incomplete and uncompletable arguments, genuine dialogues. Paramount in Dostoyevsky's novels, for Bakhtin, is their "plurality of independent and unmerged voices and consciousnesses, a genuine polyphony of fully valid voices." Instead of presenting us with "a multitude of characters and fates in a single objective world illuminated by a single authorial consciousness," Dostoyevsky depicts a multiplicity of equally compelling world views (*Dostoyevsky's Poetics* 6). Further, Dostoyevsky's characters are not circumscribed by authorial ideology but take on a life of their own; they are *"subjects of their own directly signifying discourse"* (7). Writing on "the idea in Dostoyevsky," Bakhtin attributes to the Russian author "an extraordinary gift for hearing the dialogue of his epoch, or, more precisely, for hearing his epoch as a great dialogue," both "the loud, recognized, reigning voices of the epoch" and the "voices still weak, ideas not yet fully emerged" (90). It is in this sense that *Under the Volcano* dialogizes *The Decline of the West*, rendering it but one of the epoch's many voices. In Lowry's fiction Spengler's text becomes the ideology of merely one character which, far from authorially underwritten, exists only as a part of an incomplete and uncompletable conversation.

Before examining *Under the Volcano*'s polyphony, it will be useful to discuss again that creed Spengler's monologic theory of civilization most seeks to quell: socialism, the preeminent doctrine of altering the world through political action at that time. Thomas Mann has commented on the inexorable tension between Marxism and Spenglerism, maintaining that next to Spengler's "leaden historical materialism the materialism of a Marx is sheer blue-sky idealism" ("Theory of Spengler" 226). Varying between conceptions of socialism as the "cause" and the "symptom" of Western decline since 1900, Spengler in either case views socialism as chimeric, as contrary in spirit to the fate of all civilizations.[27] As if responding to Marxist progressivism, Spengler insists that "the future of the West is not a limitless tending upwards and onwards for all time towards our present ideals, but a single phenomenon of history, strictly limited and defined as to form and duration, which covers a few centuries" (*The Decline* I, 39). For Spengler socialism forgets that the West itself is fated, like all civilizations, to wither and die. So what remains "for us," according to Spengler, at the conclusion of *The Decline*, "whom a Destiny has placed in this Culture and at this moment of its development [is that] our direction, willed and obligatory at once, is set . . . within narrow limits." "We have not the freedom to reach to this or to that," he continues, "but the freedom to do the necessary or to do nothing. And a task that historic necessity has set *will* be accomplished with the individual or against him" (II, 507). Clearly, for Spengler, the individual cannot help but march in step to the drumbeat of civilization's destiny.

Another way of stating Lowry's relationship to *The Decline* is that, whereas the Consul is strongly Spenglerian, *Under the Volcano* is not. The "dialogization" of Spenglerian ideas is most evident in chapter 10 of the novel where, in the argument between the Consul and Hugh, pseudo-Spenglerian meets pseudosocialist.[28] In contrast to Hugh's defense of communism as "a new spirit, something which one day may or may not seem as natural as the air we breathe" (304), the Consul's rhetoric here is distinctly Spenglerian. Insisting that there is no such thing as "freedom" (312), Geoffrey angrily declares of history, "Go back a thousand years. What is the use of interfering with its worthless stupid course?" "Countries, civilisations, empires, great hordes, perish for no reason at all," he continues, "and their soul and meaning with them" (310). The Consul further argues that "all this . . . about going to fight for Spain" and "poor little defenseless China! Can't you see there's a sort of determinism about the fate of nations? They all seem to get what they deserve in the long run" (309). However, as resolute as the Consul may be in his own mind (and clearly he is not), the novel undercuts his Spenglerian discourse by placing it in dialogue with

Hugh's socialism and other ideologies. As Bakhtin argues of Raskolnikov's discourse in *Crime and Punishment*, it engages other positions, thereby losing its monologic, finalized quality, and "acquires the contradictory complexity and living multi-facedness of an idea-force, being born, living and acting in the great dialogue of the epoch" (*Dostoyevsky's Poetics* 89). Similarly, Lowry's novel reduces Spengler's "encyclopedia" — one key voice in the "great dialogue of the epoch" — to the status of a polemic.

When we also realize that the argument between the Consul and Hugh in chapter 10 is "a verbatim report of an argument between" Malcolm Lowry and Conrad Aiken, "with the positions reversed" (Aiken quoted in Ackerley and Clipper 387), it is even clearer that Lowry's novel is polyphonic in the most literal sense. Like Dostoyevsky, Lowry is capable of fully representing the ideas of others while preserving a distance from them, neither confirming nor incorporating them into a finalized belief system (Bakhtin, *Dostoyevsky's Poetics* 85). Further, in *Under the Volcano*, *The Decline* is not only placed in dialogue with other texts, it is rendered "internally dialogic, adorned with polemic, [and] filled with struggle" (*Dostoyevsky's Poetics* 32). Note, for example, how closely the Consul's thoughts at one point approximate Spengler's freewheeling comparison of the religions, architecture, social practices, conquerors, and prophets of various civilizations. This stream-of-consciousness passage in *Under the Volcano* demonstrates the extent to which Geoffrey's self-parody also stands as a parody of *The Decline of the West*:

> [T]he Consul was talking about the Indo-Aryans, the Iranians of the sacred fire, Agni, called down from heaven . . . by the priest. He was talking of Soma, Amrita, the nectar of immortality, praised in one whole book of the Rig Veda . . . he was talking of Norwegian architecture, or rather how much architecture, in Kashmir, was almost, so to speak, Norwegian, the Hamadan mosque for instance, wooden, with its tall tapering spires, and ornaments pendulous from the eaves. . . . The Consul was talking . . . of Archimedes, Moses, Achilles, Methuselah, Charles V and Pontius Pilate. The Consul was talking furthermore of Jesus Christ. (307–8)

Not only is this a brilliant parody of Spengler's clotted, Germanic prose and penchant for comparing seemingly disparate figures and cultures, but the Consul's Spenglerian voice here is dialogized: the novel refuses to allow it closure, finality, or ultimate authority (unlike *The Plumed Serpent* in which these qualities are granted to Ramon and Cipriano).[29] As the Consul's own dialogue with *The Decline of the West* suggests, "everything must touch the *character* to the quick, provoke him, interrogate him, even polemicize with him and taunt him" (Bakhtin, *Dostoyevsky's Poetics* 64). In this way, Lowry's novel exposes Spengler's theory to be merely one more fiction, no matter how powerful an explanatory fiction it is, just as the novel exposes its own obsession with catastrophe to be a special fetish of the era. As George Watson puts it of this crisis mongering of the period, "catastrophe, in the end, was only a toy for intellectuals to play with, if one can conceive of a toy being put to such passionate uses" (109).

Although I would not go this far in condemning *Under the Volcano*'s use of Spengler, it is clear that the fetish of Lowry's day was "civilized crisis," just as the fetish of Conrad's day was "civilized progress" and that of Woolf's, Joyce's, and Lawrence's high modernist moment was "civilized recovery." That the fictions of Conrad, Lawrence, Joyce, Woolf, and Lowry at many points reveal these intellectual fashions to be clichés attests both to this fiction's sensitivity to prevailing theories of civilization and to its ability to appropriate and subvert the dominant discourses of its culture — to expose the blinding torch for what it is.

✹

7

The Subject of Civilization: Narcissism as Disease in Lowry's Early Fiction

[C]ivilization is itself but a mixed good, if not far more a corrupting influence, the hectic of disease, not the bloom of health. — Coleridge, ON THE CONSTITUTION OF CHURCH AND STATE

Good God, if our civilization were to sober up for a couple of days it'd die of remorse on the third. — Hugh Firmin, in Lowry, UNDER THE VOLCANO

✸ Narcissus under the Volcano

Malcolm Lowry's *Under the Volcano* has been termed "modern literature's most powerful account of doom" (Falk 213), a suitable appellation given the novel's manifold Faustian dimensions.[1] However, if Faustianism—in incarnations from Marlowe to Spengler—is primary to the text's makeup, narcissism is closely secondary to it. Indeed, these two tropes combine in Lowry's fiction to depict what might be called "the narcissistic tragedy of Faust" (Satinover 109). In Chapter 6 I addressed the Spenglerian elements of civilization in *Under the Volcano* while only glimpsing the "narcissistic" ones. Here I wish to demonstrate the degree to which civilization and the subjects of civilization are represented in Lowry's early fiction to be suicidally narcissistic—to be fatally enamored of their own distorted reflections. If Joyce depicts civilization as paralyzed by the "narcissism of minor differences" and anti-Semitism, Lowry represents civilization as narcissistic to the core, as a blinding torch at once dazzling and deceptive, magnificent and mystifying. By Lowry's "early fiction" I refer to the two novels he lived to see published, *Ultramarine* (1933) and *Under the Volcano* (1947). Together, these texts constitute one of the richest legacies of the romantic tradition—dating at least as far back as Coleridge—to view civilization as "the hectic of disease" rather than "the bloom of health."[2] Lowry's fiction, along with Joyce's, echoes Edward Carpenter's claim that "the word Disease is applicable to our social as well as to our physical condition" (2), but Joyce's fiction glimpses macrocosmic-microcosmic interaction whereas Lowry's fiction focuses more narrowly on the subject within civilization. Indeed, so resolutely narcissistic are the characters in Lowry's fiction that the representation of civilization itself becomes eclipsed: the only story these subjects can fashion is their own, while civilization seems to "disappear." It is therefore only when we recognize that Lowry's major characters are metaphors for civilization at large that his critique of civilization betrays itself.

In an early draft of *Under the Volcano* it becomes clear that narcissism is represented as a pervasive disease of the civilized individual. At one point in this draft, for example, Hugh Firmin muses on his half-brother Geoffrey's surprisingly fine appearance while watching the dipsomaniac "gazing at himself in the mirror":

> It was as though the passionate narcissism which drinking and his almost purely oral response to life entailed had fixed his age at some time in the past, at that unidentifiable moment, perhaps, when his persistent objective self, weary of standing askance and watching his downfall, had silently withdrawn from him altogether, like a ship secretly leaving harbour at night. (Quoted in Day 263)

Unlike this early draft of the novel, the published text of 1947 bears no explicit reference to narcissism. Although perhaps a strategy to distance the work (and author) from this issue,[3] the weight of narcissism on the final version of *Under the Volcano* is nevertheless acutely felt. In Lowry's reworking of the above passage, for example, the presence of narcissism is hardly a subtle one, even if the term itself is absent: "Yet it was as though fate had fixed his age at some unidentifiable moment in the past, when his persistent

objective self, perhaps weary of standing askance and watching his downfall, had at last withdrawn from him altogether, like a ship secretly leaving
harbour at night" (183–84). The hint of narcissism here is not difficult to
discern: the self-absorbed ex-Consul "gazing at himself in the mirror," the
invocation of fate, doom, and the refusal to mature, and the vision of a
bifurcated self, with one portion watching the other deteriorate (with
aesthetic fascination).

In its allusion to this phenomenon the above passage is not unique to the
novel. Indeed, I will argue that the presence of narcissism in *Under the
Volcano*—as psychological condition explored and critique of civilization
revealed—is all-pervasive and that an examination of the ways in which
narcissism appears in the literature of psychoanalysis and cultural criticism
significantly enriches our understanding of Lowry's work. Whereas David
Markson identifies Ovid as one source for the novel, pointing out that
Geoffrey Firmin "becomes" Narcissus (among other figures) (6), and
though Lawrence Thornton briefly treats Lowry's text in his study on
narcissism and the modern novel, maintaining that "at the deepest levels of
consciousness the Consul is aware that his anguish is founded on an inability to love" (35), the great extent to which *Under the Volcano* represents
civilization as narcissistically diseased, both on microcosmic and macrocosmic levels, remains in need of elaboration.[4] This is all the more
surprising when we remember that in the 1930s and 1940s of the novel's
genesis, civilization at large was often viewed as "neurotic," much like
individuals (Fine 128). Although Lowry's *Ultramarine* focuses even more
than does *Under the Volcano* on the narcissistic subject within civilization, it
nevertheless merits discussion for illuminating aspects of Lowry's master-
piece that otherwise might remain obscure.

Before exploring Lowry's complex representation of civilization, however, it is worth pointing out that *Under the Volcano*, in its broadest outline,
reworks Ovid's "Echo and Narcissus" from *Metamorphoses*, the story of one
"who refused to love anyone but himself, and thereby loved himself to
death" (Zweig v). Lowry's tale of the final day in the lives of Geoffrey Firmin
and Yvonne Constable is undoubtedly informed by Ovid's 170 lines of Latin
verse, the most detailed classical rendering of the myth and "most important
source for the theme" (Vinge 11). Most obviously, both Ovid's and Lowry's
tales are accounts of "rejected wooing" and "frustrated passion," and the
inevitable decompensation and death that ensue in a setting best described
as "chthonic"—in the shadowy, moist, infernal realm of the dead.[5]

Further, Geoffrey Firmin is depicted as a latter-day Narcissus, fascinated
by his own reflection at which he gazes in a pool surrounded by natural
splendor: "The Consul saw himself again, hovering over the parapet,

gazing down at the swimming pool below, a little turquoise set in the garden. Thou art the grave where buried love doth live. The inverted reflections of banana trees and birds, caravans of clouds, moved in it" (143). Allusions to the object of Narcissus's love (his own reflection "where buried love doth live") and to the deadliness of such desire ("the grave") are manifest here, just as they are earlier that day when, by his own pool's edge, Geoffrey hallucinates an image later identified as himself: an "object shaped like a dead man . . . which seemed to be lying flat on his back by his swimming pool" (91). The Consul's Narcissus-like fate is reflected not only in swimming pools, however, but in mirrors, such as the one in the Cantina Farolito from which, an hour before his death, Geoffrey's "face silently glared at him, with stern, familiar foreboding" (337).

Yvonne Constable plays Echo to her ex-husband's Narcissus even if, like Hugh Firmin and French filmmaker Jacques Laruelle, she is both Echo to the Consul and a narcissist in her own right. Like Narcissus, Geoffrey feels, but easily overcomes, the magnetic pull of this affectionate other: "Nevertheless the desire remained — like an *echo* of Yvonne's own — to find her" and to "reverse their doom. . . . The desire passed" (214–15; my emphasis). Just as Echo feels incomplete without the Narcissus whom she shadows (she eventually becomes incorporeal voice and can only echo him), so too Yvonne feels herself to be Geoffrey's "consoling unwanted shadow" (63) and in a letter to her ex-husband laments, "without you I am cast out, severed. I am an outcast from myself, a shadow" (364). Just as the fates of Echo and Narcissus are symbiotically linked — the former pining away for want of the latter, the latter's condition defined in his spurning of the former — so too are those of the ill-starred divorced couple, as Yvonne suggests, once more in a letter to Geoffrey: "if I only knew that you wanted me, you know I would have long since been with you. For my life is irrevocably and forever bound to yours. Never think that by releasing me you will be free. You would only condemn us to an ultimate hell on earth" (366–67). It is precisely a "hell on earth" to which both Narcissus and Geoffrey are condemned: the former "watching his image in the Stygian water" of hell (73) and the latter frequently noting that he lives in a hell of his own making (36, 38, 199, 314).[6]

✳ Self as Civilization: Psychoanalytic Matrices of Narcissism in *Under the Volcano*

In *Civilization and Its Discontents*, Freud forges an analogy between civilization and the subject within civilization, reasoning that, "If the development of civilization has such a far-reaching similarity to the development of the individual and if it employs the same methods, may we not be justified in reaching the diagnosis that, under the influence of cultural urges, some civilizations, or some epochs of civilization . . . have become neurotic?" (91) Freud's answer, of course, is a resounding yes; and subsequent to *Civilization and Its Discontents* an entire tradition of psychosocial criticism arose seeking to relate the state of civilization to the subjects within it.[7]

Freud's linking of psychological and sociological realities is of particular relevance to Lowry's novel, which stands as a keen psychological investigation into the narcissistic personality structure. Indeed, *Under the Volcano* represents the self as a microcosm of the diseased civilization. As one critic notes, Lowry's "protagonists are haunted by the accumulated guilt of civilization" (Epstein 16). "For Lowry," another maintains, "the private life and the public world are never disjoined, and he sees in the self-absorption of the Consul the same inability to engage external realities and the same failure of will that led Chamberlain to Munich" (Cripps 93). To be sure, *Under the Volcano* repeatedly links Geoffrey's symptoms of narcissism — his alcohol addiction, sexual difficulties, and sadomasochistic raging — with the West's warmongering, escapism, and self-destruction. In this connection Sherrill Grace argues that Lowry's "great theme, for which alcohol is a metaphor, is human isolation and the collapse of Western Culture" (*Voyage* 35), and Lowry himself, in his famous letter to Jonathan Cape in defense of *Under the Volcano*, relates "the Consul's self-destruction" to "the theme of war" (*Selected Letters* 82). Moreover, at one point Hugh refers to a snoring Geoffrey as "the muted voice of England long asleep" (*Under the Volcano* 98), evoking Britain's impotence in dealing effectively with the rise of threatening European dictatorships of the left and right. Lowry's novel suggests that, if the narcissist is solely self-regarding, then he cannot defend himself against even the most nefarious of external threats.[8] No one who wishes to come to grips with *Under the Volcano*, therefore, can afford to neglect those civilized dilemmas represented in the Consul's experience of problems rooted in narcissism: his incessant need to drink, his failure to make love with Yvonne (yet success a few hours later with a prostitute), and his "self-destructive instinct" (Dodson 30).

An inquiry into Firmin's infirmity might begin with Freud's 1914 work, "On Narcissism: An Introduction," the "agreed-upon starting point for all psychodynamic studies of narcissistic personality disorders" (Chessick 28). In this paper, Freud distinguishes between individuals who are capable of loving "objects" other than themselves, and narcissists who have regressed to the point of total "libidinal investment of the self" and for whom object love becomes impossible because the boundary between "self" and "world" is blurred. Freud defines "Primary narcissism" as a normal infantile stage of development between autoeroticism and object relations, in which the newborn invests all of its libido in its own ego, recognizing neither that the mother is anything more than a need-satisfying extension of the self nor that there is any world at all beyond the self. "Secondary narcissism," on the other hand, represents a step backward to the point at which the infant, due to pain and frustration felt from unmet needs, defensively withdraws its slowly developing object libido and redirects all sexual energy toward the self (even though the child by this time is aware of a reality beyond the self).[9]

Recent theorists of narcissism — Heinz Kohut and Otto Kernberg among the most important — have stressed not primary narcissism and oedipal conflict but secondary narcissism and preoedipal conflict. Kohut characterizes this change of emphasis as reflecting a shift from the pathology of the "Guilty Man" of Freud's day, who suffers castration anxiety and incestuous wishes and whose id-oriented "aims are directed toward the activity of his drives," to that of the "Tragic Man" of the past half-century (including the 1930s and 1940s of Lowry's writing career), who instead suffers disintegration anxiety (feelings of fragmentation, identity loss, emptiness, boredom, and absurdity) and whose ego-oriented "aims are toward the fulfillment of the self" (*Restoration* 132). Instead of being victimized by too much parental and societal authority and by guilt feelings relating to the family romance, narcissists of more recent times suffer from "object relations" (Kernberg) or "selfobject" (Kohut) failures originating in parental empathic deficiency. "Acting out" instead of "repressing" their conflicts, the "grandiose" of recent generations harbor intense feelings of rage toward themselves and others, underscoring Kernberg's judgment, contra Freud, that "normal narcissism and normal object investments go hand in hand, while pathological investments of the self and of objects . . . go together" ("Narcissism" 130). Explaining this cultural shift in conditions from Freud's to Kohut's day, Jeffrey Berman comments, "Culture defines psychopathology, and as the forms of society change, so do the forms of mental illness" (48).[10]

Despite the great theoretical differences between Kohut and Kernberg,[11] the conclusions they share suggest much about the Consul's motivations and behavior — and about the civilization that "encourages" his narcissism. Perhaps most important, they shed light on Geoffrey's narcissistic personality structure originating in an empathically deprived youth. Although this experience is nowhere described in intricate detail, the novel supplies us with enough information to piece together an etiology of his psychic injury. For one thing, the Consul lacks the attention of parents during much of his childhood, parents whom he could "idealize" and from whom he could derive the empathy and positive mirroring necessary for healthy development. His mother died when he was young, his remarried father "scandalously" disappeared into the Himalayas never to return, and his stepmother also died an untimely death (19), all in quick succession; these contribute to his feeling of anger and abandonment (197–98). "[S]o touched by any kindness done to him" (19), Jacques remembers of the young Geoffrey, he would even "burst out crying if you mentioned in his presence the word 'father' or 'mother' " (16). More than what his past tells us, however, it is the Consul's present condition that most immediately suggests his pathological narcissism.

To be sure, the most noticeable of the Consul's afflictions is his rampant dipsomania. As William H. New observes, "At an overt level, *Under the Volcano* is probably more than anything else an arrestingly vivid evocation of an alcoholic state of mind" (33), with references to drinking, as Dale Edmonds has tabulated, occurring on 252 of the novel's 377 pages ("Mescallusions" 278). Although many explanations of Geoffrey's alcoholism have been ventured,[12] readers have not yet recognized the extent to which this disorder is a compensation for the deprivation of parental and partner empathy, a defense against the desire to rage at others and at the self for such deprivation, and a means of escape from a reality that cannot fulfill grandiose (or even ordinary) needs.

In a book-length study of alcoholism and narcissism, Gary G. Forrest echoes Kernberg's finding that "the addictive potential is maximum . . . for narcissistic personality structures" (*Borderline* 222), noting that "like Narcissus, the alcoholic is egotistically preoccupied with the self" (26) and that "Narcissistic injury" is generally "a *consistent* and *chronic* experiential reality in the case of persons who develop alcoholism" (18). Moreover, when Forrest writes that the dipsomaniac's purview "is in many respects limited to self-orientation" (42) and that his "basic narcissistic security operations are eventually centered around the matters of drinking and alcohol" (43), he accurately characterizes Geoffrey Firmin's condition. Described at one point in the novel as "oozing alcohol from every pore" (284), the Consul exhibits a self-ironic obsession with alcohol; he can focus on little but "the drink situation" (303).

Kohut adds that drug addiction "serves not as a substitute for loved or loving objects, or for a relationship with them, but as a replacement for a defect in the psychological structure" brought about by the trauma of "defective empathy with the child's needs" (*Analysis* 46)—all of which characterizes accurately the way alcohol functions in Geoffrey's life. Associating his "abandonment" by his parents when a child with that by Yvonne during the past year, the Consul thinks,

> such desolation, such a desperate sense of abandonment, bereavement, as during this last year without Yvonne, he had never known in his life, unless it was when his mother died. But this present emotion he had never experienced with his mother: this urgent desire to hurt, to provoke. . . . It was hard to forgive. . . . Harder still, not to say how hard it was, *I hate you.* (197–98)

"Hurt" become "hate," Geoffrey seeks to vent his frustration on his surrogate parents, Yvonne and Hugh, who are in Cuernavaca to help him escape his nightmarish predicament (yet who have possibly betrayed the Consul together). Because Yvonne, as Richard K. Cross writes, "cannot give him the unconditional love for which he yearns" (55), the Consul punishes her through drinking. Posing the rhetorical question, "Could one be faithful to Yvonne and to the Farolito both?" (201), Geoffrey, throughout his final day of life, abjures Yvonne's advances only to proclaim of alcohol what he never could of her: " 'I love you,' he murmured, gripping the bottle with both hands" (91).

If alcohol functions for Geoffrey as a compensation for past narcissistic injuries, it also functions as "his chief avenue of escape" (Tifft 51) from a world that cannot sate his grandiose needs. "In the case of Narcissistic personalities," Kernberg explains, "alcohol or drug intake may constitute a predominant mechanism to 'refuel' the pathological grandiose self and assure its omnipotence and protection against a potentially frustrating and hostile environment in which gratification and admiration are not forthcoming" (*Borderline* 222). Quite obviously, the Consul's dipsomania provides him with frequent respites from a painful and unsatisfying existence — in the form of hallucinations, blackouts, and pleasing disorientations — and with countless moments "of being drunk in which alone he was sober" (85). Moreover, Geoffrey uses alcohol to "shut out all thought of Yvonne" (337) and to escape his familial, social, and vocational shortcomings. He even comes to equate his alcohol-induced feeling of security with the cantinas themselves: "[W]hat beauty," he asks himself at one point, "can compare to that of a cantina in the early morning?" (50). Later he admits that "all [my] love is the cantinas now: the feeble survival of a love of life now turned to poison" (65). Contrasting Hugh's and Yvonne's threatening "sober and non-alcoholic paradise" (313) with the "peace" of the Farolito, which fills him "with an almost healing love" (200), the Consul chooses "companionship in drink" rather than interaction with "loved ones" who can only fail to gratify him. Robert B. Heilman comes the closest of any critic to suggesting the narcissistic basis of Geoffrey's alcoholism, deeming this drinking "an escape, an evasion of responsibility, a separation from life, a self-worship, a denial of love" (23). "If one cannot alter civilization," we hear the Consul asking, "why not alter the self?"

In addition to his addiction, however, Geoffrey's bouts of narcissistic rage help explain his sexual difficulties and suicidal urge. Kohut writes that "it is easily observed that the narcissistically vulnerable individual responds to actual (or anticipated) narcissistic injury either with shamefaced with-drawal" or "with narcissistic rage" ("Thoughts" 636–37). Arguing that narcissistic rage differs from ordinary anger and aggression in that it is directed at "selfobjects" (seen as flaws in a narcissistically perceived reality) instead of at "objects" (experienced as separate from ourselves), Kohut maintains that this rage seeks to destroy the source of the narcissistic insult itself through revenge, even if an entire war is lost for the sake of the battle. For "the enemy is a recalcitrant part of an expanded self over which the narcissistically vulnerable person had expected to exercise full control" ("Thoughts" 644). Hence, if the Consul's drinking represents a movement of withdrawal, his sexual practice and self-destructive tendency represent movements of rage ("The Consul was fighting off an all but irresistible, senseless onrush of wild rage" [303]).[13]

Geoffrey's refusal/inability to have sexual relations with Yvonne ("Sorry, it isn't any good I'm afraid" [90]) while accepting the entreaties of a prostitute, Maria, only hours later, can in part be explained in these terms; neither his alcoholism nor any "anxiety of performance" can explain his contradictory sexual behavior. Because Yvonne does not constitute a viable "approving-mirroring selfobject," the Consul will punish her both through sexual rejection and through having relations with Maria shortly thereafter (he even refers to his contact with the prostitute as "the final stupid unprophylactic rejection" [348]). Geoffrey also expresses his desire for revenge when, shortly before he departs alone for the Farolito, he wails at Yvonne, "Mummy, let me go back to the beautiful brothel" (313). Even when the Consul is alone with Maria he thinks of Yvonne. Admitting to himself that "miserably he wanted Yvonne and did not want her" (347), Geoffrey, during this sexual encounter with the prostitute, envisions an encounter with his ex-wife instead: "Lightning silhouetted against the window a face, for a moment curiously like Yvonne's. . . . Her body was Yvonne's too" (348–49). Hence, what is at issue for Geoffrey, more than any personal satisfaction to be gained from this encounter, is the punish-ment he can inflict on a delusional construct, himself-as-Yvonne, in the attempt to destroy the offense perpetrated against the grandiose self.

However, the Consul hopes to punish not only Yvonne but himself as well. Forrest explains that "the alcoholic male quite frequently punishes his wife (mother substitute) for the entirety of the marriage in retaliation for his mother's primary role in early life narcissistic injury," and that he "at the same time . . . masochistically punishes himself . . . for somehow being so unlovable, inadequate, and worthless initially within the context of mother–self . . . relationships" (269). Indeed, the masochistic side to his encounter with Maria is everywhere apparent. Geoffrey associates his own "lust" with "death" and the groans of love with those of the dying. He even wonders if it is "possible to suffer more than this": out of "this suffering something must be born, and what would be born was his own death" (349). Perceiving in the encounter with Maria "a crisis without possession, almost without pleasure finally" (351), the Consul masochistically severs the one potentially significant relationship reopened to him: "He couldn't go back to Yvonne if he wanted to," he realizes, "for brutal hygienic reasons alone" (353). And yet, in other ways too, Geoffrey articulates his narcissistic rage turned inward, his will to self-destruction that is "an ultimate form of masochistic behavior" (Forrest 173). Despite the fact that the Consul's death is technically a murder, it is nevertheless clear that by 2 November 1938 he actively seeks his own demise. Drinking mescal, which he takes to be lethal, and ignoring the warnings of two Mexicans who urge him to leave the Farolito before it is too late, Geoffrey glimpses the true identity of his Unión Militar murderer: "the Chief of Gardens might have been the image of himself" (359). There are moments in the Farolito when the Consul considers extricating himself from the fatal course he is on with the intoxicated, armed killers, but his suicidal urge, rooted in a will to gain revenge for narcissistic injuries sustained, wins out in the end: "the Consul felt neither serious nor like escaping" (355). As Kohut remarks, people "sometimes would rather die than live with narcissistic injury" ("The Self in History" 773). In this way, Geoffrey Firmin gains the ultimate Pyrrhic victory that is his own death.[14]

✳ Narcissistic Civilization in *Under the Volcano* and *Ultramarine*

Freud's linking of "neurotic" individuals and civilizations also suggests the inverse of what I have been exploring: that civilization as a whole experiences the developmental problems of individuals. In a book on narcissism, the self, and society, Reuben Fine explains that "the broad view"

> of neurosis as part of the burden of civilization, together with the idea that whole civilizations can become neurotic, epitomized the farreach-

ing expansion of the whole idea of neurosis that [Freud] had built up in such a painstaking way for forty years. The culture imposes intolerable demands on the individual, demands so great that in the effort to accede to them the individual falls into neurotic conflicts of one kind or another. This point of view was quite common in the thirties and early forties. (128)

Under the Volcano, a novel of the forties, suggests precisely this phenomenon: that civilization is a disease of major proportions and that the West shows "symptoms of decay and impending catastrophe" (Binns 44). Indeed, I hope to show that *Under the Volcano* and *Ultramarine* represent civilization itself to be narcissistic, even as civilization "disappears" in the narcissistic self-narratives of Lowry's subjects.

Malcolm Lowry is known to have commented that "the real cause of alcoholism is the complete baffling sterility of existence as *sold* to you" (Spender xxvii); and Stephen Spender, in his introduction to *Under the Volcano*, writes that the Consul reflects "an extreme external situation within his own extremity." Geoffrey's "neurosis becomes diagnosis," he continues, "not just of himself but of a phase of history" (xiii). Lowry's and Spender's comments reveal a further aspect of *Under the Volcano*: that it not only investigates the personality structure of narcissism but represents civilization itself to be narcissistic — in tropes similar to those found in Christopher Lasch's *Culture of Narcissism*. Registered in the psychological condition of the novel's major characters and in their relation to the manifold institutions of civilization, *Under the Volcano* depicts civilization as narcissistic in the extreme, exploring the ways in which "the sentimental politics of the Anglo-Saxon world is reduced to impotence" (Dodson 18). Although Lasch's controversial work at points clearly succumbs to polemical oversimplifications, it nevertheless delineates a sustained feature of contemporary civilization represented in Lowry's novel.[15]

Based explicitly upon the analyses of Kohut and Kernberg (yet at the same time providing the sociohistoric determinants and consequences of narcissistic pathology),[16] and appearing in the wake of Richard Sennett's exploration of the social dimensions of narcissism in *The Fall of Public Man*, Lasch's *Culture of Narcissism* holds that

> Narcissism appears realistically to represent the best way of coping with the tensions and anxieties of modern life, and the prevailing social conditions therefore tend to bring out narcissistic traits that are present, in varying degrees, in everyone. These conditions have also transformed the family, which in turn shapes the underlying structure of personality. (50)

Agreeing with Sennett that "narcissism may be encouraged by cultural developments" (220) Lasch maintains that "every society reproduces its culture — its norms, its underlying assumptions, its modes of organizing experience — in the individual, in the form of personality" (34).

Moreover, for Lasch, modern Western culture "reproduces" in its individuals an ethics of hedonism, a disregard of history, an obsession with appearance and fame, and the experience of reality as a mirror of the self. Similar to Horkheimer and Adorno's notion of the "culture-industry," Lasch finds the causes of narcissism in runaway "bureaucracy, the proliferation of images" in advertising and film, "the rationalization of the inner life, the cult of consumption," and "changes in family life" (*Culture* 32); and Sennett's position is similar. For Sennett the phenomenon of cultural narcissism, representing the triumph of "the very opposite of strong self-love" (324), develops as a result of the blurring of the boundaries between private and public life, self and other. "Narcissism," he writes,

> is self-absorption which prevents one from understanding what belongs within the domain of the self and self-gratification and what belongs outside of it. . . . This absorption in self, oddly enough, prevents gratification of self needs; it makes the person at the moment of attaining an end or connecting with another person feel that "this isn't what I wanted." Narcissism thus has the double quality of being a voracious absorption in self needs and the block to their fulfillment. (8)

Lasch sees the symptoms of this inability to find contentment in the "prevailing passion" of living for the moment, the permissive sexual attitudes that nevertheless do not proffer "sexual peace," and the "survivalist mentality" in which "self-preservation" replaces "self-improvement as the goal of earthly existence" (*Culture* 53).[17]

One might legitimately raise the question of how these critiques of culture apply to Lowry's Cuernavaca of the late 1930s, or of why the novel's critique of culture resembles Lasch's and Sennett's. One answer is that the works speak to one another due to their overlapping purviews. Sennett, for example, dates the beginning of the predicament he analyzes with "the entrance of personality into the public realm in the last century" (221), and Lasch argues that the phenomenon of cultural narcissism "first took shape in the twenties" ("Politics and Social Theory" 201). As the subtitle of Lasch's book erroneously suggests, the "culture of narcissism" is not merely the story of "American life in an age of diminishing expectations" but a reality of "international" dimensions: "Bourgeois society seems everywhere to have used up its store of constructive ideas," and the "political crisis of capitalism reflects a general crisis of Western culture" (*Culture* xiii).[18]

Under the Volcano represents civilization as narcissistically diseased through its depiction of the thoughts and actions of its four major characters, who suffer less from too much "authority" than from the lack of any raison d'être. Whether it is their reaction to the impending world war, to the dying Indian on the roadside, or to each other's uncommunicated needs, each "sees the world as a mirror of himself and has no interest in external events except as they throw back a reflection of his own image" (Lasch, *Culture* 47). Each of these escapist and enervated exiles is haunted by an ideal self-conception which, clashing against the reality of what he or she has become, is a source of pain. Be it Yvonne's desire to be "Hollywood's greatest dramatic actress" (*Under the Volcano* 264), Jacques's to make "great films" that would change the world (9), or Hugh's to repair the world through his own stunning presence, it is quickly apparent how little is actually being done to realize these ends. As the Consul points out, "Nobody seemed to be doing anything important; yet everything seemed of the utmost hectic importance" (142). In this way the four "self-elegists" can ponder their contributions to humanity while, as Richard K. Cross notes, "the dictates of self-preservation and personal convenience" (50) guide their practical lives. In *Ultramarine* too, protagonist Dana Hilliot is depicted as capable of loving (and hating) only himself. The rest of the world exists only as a backdrop against which his narcissistic self-fashioning takes place.

Yvonne's indifference to politics and Hugh's passion for it finally amount to the same obsession with the self. By contrast, the elder Jacques and Geoffrey betray a disinterest in the world outside themselves that is astonishingly direct. Imagining that others see him as an "aesthete" (*Under the Volcano* 8), Jacques is revealed to have "few emotions about the war, save that it was bad. One side or the other would win. And in either case life would be hard," and "in either case one's own battle would go on" (9). The Consul's escapism is equally pronounced. He repeatedly seeks to dissociate himself from all worldly strife and political responsibility in order, like William Blackstone "who went to live among the Indians," to escape all "interfering" people with their "ideas." Michael Cripps puts the Consul's position charitably: Geoffrey devalues the social world "by the absolute primacy he assigns his own spiritual life" (86).

The younger Yvonne and Hugh are depicted with even more subtlety and irony, which accounts for the equal measures of sympathy and antipathy they evoke. For their many great differences, they share a relationship to the novel's representation of civilization that is surprisingly similar. The former an ex-actress of Hollywood films and the latter a radical journalist and "member" of the Spanish anarchists, both are Goffmanian individuals par excellence, "performing selves" who exist only in the adopted roles they present to others. Moreover, both demand immediate gratification and live in a state of perpetually unsatisfied desire, and are unable to relate to others without seeing them as extensions of themselves (Lasch, *Culture* xvi, 86). Yvonne and Hugh both seek admiration for works achieved, yet each finally lives out "the fantasy of narcissistic success which consists of nothing more substantial than a wish to be vastly admired" (Lasch, *Culture* 232).

Yvonne's self-infatuation, for example, is among other things an evasion of her profound insecurity about, and dissatisfaction with, existence. This is most apparent in her fabrication of a Hollywood magazine article in which her "glamorous" life and (as yet unobtained) rise to cinema stardom are traced. Reminiscent of Joyce's Gerty MacDowell, whose description is rendered from a perspective she herself would consider flattering, and in the insipid, idealized style of a fin-de-siècle, mass-distribution women's magazine, Yvonne constructs her identity directly out of "materials furnished by advertising and mass culture, themes of popular film and fiction" (Lasch, *Culture* 91):

> Look out, you sarong sirens and glamour girls, Yvonne Constable, the "Boomp Girl," is back in Hollywood! . . . But she's twenty-four now, and the "Boomp Girl" has become a poised exciting woman who wears diamonds and white orchids and ermine. . . . I found her the other day at her beach home, a honey-tanned Venus just emerging from the surf. (Under the Volcano 261–62)

This passage alone reveals a number of the "new narcissist's" manias: the obsession with appearance, aging, wealth, and with one's own life history (Sennett 5), and the need to see one's " 'grandiose self' reflected in the attentions of others" (Lasch, *Culture* 10). However, when "the disparity between romance and reality, the world of beautiful people and the workaday world," becomes apparent to Yvonne, she is crippled by an "ironic detachment" (Lasch, *Culture* 96) that stifles her very will to go on: "For the first time," she writes Geoffrey in a letter after leaving him, "I understand the meaning of suicide . . . God, how pointless and empty the world is!" (346). Thus, although Richard H. Costa fittingly notes that Yvonne's "loving is mainly of herself" (18), we must also consider the fact that she is immersed in a social reality which, as Lasch holds, "far from fostering private life at the expense of public life, has made deep and lasting friendships, love affairs, and marriages increasingly difficult to achieve" (*Culture*

30). Perhaps Yvonne, like Gerty, must mentally "rewrite" her life in order to survive a culture that fails to provide fundamental needs.

Hugh's dissimilarity from Yvonne as "the political conscience of the book" (Dodson 33) is superficial rather than deep. Like Lord Jim, whose actions on behalf of others are clearly "part of a purely personal battle to escape self-condemnation" (Cripps 85), Hugh proclaims a desire to change the world even though his behavior and outlook, as Dale Edmonds notes, seems to derive "as much from a desire to gratify personal romantic whimsy as from genuine love for humanity" ("Immediate Level" 102). Laruelle initially views him as "an irresponsible bore, a professional indoor Marxman, vain and self-conscious really, but affecting a romantic extroverted air" (*Under the Volcano* 8). Hugh's interest in politics, like his interest in seafaring ("it was not a ship he was steering now, but the world, out of the western ocean of its misery" [104]), guitar playing, song writing, womanizing, and bullfighting, is little more than a thinly disguised search for narcissistic gratification. Lasch explains that when the boundaries between self and world blur, as they do for Hugh, "politics degenerates into a struggle not for social change but for self-realization," a spectacle of "dramatic gestures" and "style without substance" (*Culture* 28, 82). Conceiving of "the desire to be, to do, good, what was right," in terms of "the passionate, yet so nearly always hypocritical, affirmation of one's own soul," and of his feeling of "boundless impatience" and "immeasurable longing" (*Under the Volcano* 124), Hugh betrays a variety of *engagé*, for all of his sincerity and good intentions, that is little more than self-engagement.

Indeed, Hugh is the Political Man par excellence for a narcissistic culture in that he is politically disarmed as a result of his incessant need to romanticize his actions. At one point, for example, he envisions the following scenario:

> Hugh made a speech. Stalin gave him a medal and listened sympathetically while he explained what was on his mind. "True . . . I wasn't in time to save the Ebro, but I did strike my blow" — He went off, the Star of Lenin on his lapel; in his pocket a certificate; Hero of the Soviet Republic, and the True Church, pride and love in his heart. (239–40)

Like the events of Yvonne's fabricated movie magazine article, those of Hugh's imagined award clash profoundly with the reality, as the Consul bluntly puts it, of one who turns "out to be a bragging degenerate obviously convinced after he'd been drinking that he was doing something heroic" (311). His action in the Spanish Civil War limited to falling out of an ambulance with "two dozen beer bottles and five journalists on top of

[him], all heading for Paris" (102), the ineffectual Hugh, "unbrave but wanting to be brave, unloving but hoping to love," as Douglas Day notes, can only bang out "songs of martial brotherhood on a cheap guitar" while his half-brother and Yvonne are killed nearby (324).

Hugh's other avocations are also practiced in an attempt to gain narcissistic gratification. He seeks to present "a dashing fellow" (150–51) to the world and keep himself in the "limelight" (179) at all times. Referring to his guitar as "a pretty important symbol in his life" (154) ("it was due to a guitar he'd become a journalist," a "song-writer," that "he had first gone to sea" [155–56]), the younger Firmin's fixation on the instrument suggests his obsession with fame and with the audience necessary to secure it. A Kohutian "selfobject" of sorts, Hugh's guitar and the women he attracts with it are seen primarily as extensions of himself, as mirrors to reflect back the sense of self-worth he craves. However, not merely instruments of "seduction" (177), his guitars function as surrogate women generally—both lovers he can easily manipulate and impress ("Hugh could play almost any kind of guitar," and "his numerous instruments declined with his books in basements or attics in London or Paris" [154–55]), and mothers behind whom he can hide (one artist portrays Hugh "as an immense guitar, inside which an oddly familiar infant was hiding, curled up, as in a womb" [177]). Even Hugh's almost phallic appearance suggests his need for an always-approving audience. He is described as "stretching himself to his full mental height of six feet two (he was five feet eleven)" (104) and as possessing an "erect and careless bearing" (143). He dons a cowboy outfit replete with "too-tight trousers" and "pistol . . . holster lazily slapping his thigh" (95, 94), of which he is "secretly enormously proud" (96).

Hugh's short-term relationships with married women also suggest his need to attach himself to someone "for constant infusions of approval and admiration," only to break things off for fear of becoming emotionally dependent (Lasch, *Culture* 40). "In the realm of sexuality," Sennett maintains, "narcissism withdraws physical love from any kind of commitment, personal or social." "Every sexual relationship under the sway of narcissism," he continues, "becomes less fulfilling the longer the partners are together" (9). In the attempt to escape responsibility and his "largely negative, selfish, absurd and dishonest" past (*Under the Volcano* 152), Hugh, the "incurable 'love-object,'" at one point admits that he is "incapable finally of love altogether" (179). Whether it is Hugh's bullfighting in the Arena Tomalín ("Hugh calmly walked off" the bull and "bowed to the cheering spectators" [279]), his "call" to the sea (at one point he admits to possessing "an enormous unquenchable pride" to "be buried in the [sea]"

[167]), or his song-writing career (of which this "prodigy" [150] is later exposed to be a "plagiarist" [172]), the younger Firmin's every exploit is carried out as if it were a spectacle worthy of the stage.

Hugh's earlier "incarnation" in Lowry's *Ultramarine* (1933) as protagonist Dana Hilliot is also instructive here.[19] An almost parodic combination of Joyce's *Portrait of the Artist as a Young Man*, Melville's *Billy Budd*, and any number of Conrad's sea stories of initiation, *Ultramarine* centers on a few days in the life of Hilliot when aboard the *Oedipus Tyrannus* while docked at Tsjang-Tsjang. Interior monologue and remembered experience extend the time frame to include Dana's Norwegian youth and recent courtship with Janet Travena, his English "girl." Like Hugh, the narcissistic Hilliot turns all experiences of the world into experiences of the self. Referring to himself as a "soiled Narcissus" (117) — "I put down my glass noisily then picked it up again, and gazed mournfully at my reflection. Narcissus" (92) — Dana, like Hugh, can only imagine himself in the idealized world of pulp romances or in the world of Kipling's *Captains Courageous*, which he currently reads (133). A man who believes "himself to live in inverted, or introverted, commas" (18), Dana, like Conrad's Jim, cannot help but view himself, no matter how trivial his activities, as if in the stirring plots of "light holiday literature":

> *Seaman*, with bucket on his arm, with singlet on his back, with sweat rag round his neck, Dana Hilliot, nineteen, enters the messroom. . . . While he scrubs he thinks of Janet. . . . Yes, Janet, it is I, although you would scarcely recognize me. Here, on the other hand — let me introduce you to her — is the tramp steamer *Oedipus Tyrannus*, outward bound for hell. When you come to think of it — an ideal match. Both of us born of Viking blood, both robbed of our countries and left to make out as best we can; both, finally, with the same wandering, harbourless, dispossessed characteristics. Her very history is enough to fill me with a narcissistic compassion! (50–51)

Seeking acceptance by the crew at all costs ("he knew that they thought he wasn't one of them" [17] but rather one of those "bloody toffs who come to sea for experience" [21]), Dana is self-absorbed to the extent that — like Hugh, Geoffrey, Yvonne, and Jacques — he virtually shuts out the world around him, is only vaguely aware that a war rages close to his ship. "I forgot to mention," he tells a German he has befriended in a harbor pub, that "there was a war on about half a mashie shot away, it being June 1927, but that has not [*sic*] part in the story" (89). To be sure, the only story Hilliot can tell is his own. Yet here too the novel is ironic: we realize that "ultra"-

marine Hilliot is only playing at marine to satisfy his own adolescent fantasies.

Dana's narcissism, like Hugh's, dons the garb of "the universal experience of sublimated all-embracing love for mankind." "Where are the slaves that must be freed, the children who must have milk?" Dana asks. "I shall find them. I must find them" (170–71). Yet this grandiose garb ("Had he no right . . . to seek 'the star that shines above the lives of men'?" [33]) cannot conceal his fear of "living" (32) and his self-hate ("Hilliot stared for a moment down into the depths of his own contemptibleness, and searched vainly there for a truth" [35]). Likening himself to both a "hero" and a "monster" (76), and likening his literary powers to both Shakespeare's (95) and a failed author's with "diarrhoea scribendi simply" (90), Dana, like mythic Narcissus, paradoxically loves and hates himself.

Finally, like Hugh, Dana uses women and seafaring as self-objects to reflect the positive self-image he craves yet which always eludes him. Reasoning that acceptance by the crew would legitimize him in Janet's eyes (22) — "If Janet could only see [all of] this with him!" (29) — Dana achieves momentary harmony when he believes that this acceptance has been realized: "[A]ll at once he had a perfectly clear vision of himself. . . . Instantly there was no lack of order in his life, no factors wrongly coordinated, no loose tangled ends" (158). Yet we realize just how chimeric Dana's new-found euphoria is when, shortly later, he imagines an admiring letter from Janet (who has probably forgotten all about him): "Dana dear, I love you such a terrific lot, and I want you to be happy always. I loved our talk last Sunday evening . . . because you were so manly. . . . But I must ask you — how do you like being a sailor? Is it very hard work? I just live for the day when you come back. Heaps and heaps of love, Your own Janet" (168–69). Fabricating the "heaps of love" that are not forthcoming, Dana compensates for his feeling of emptiness with a narcissistic response.

To the extent that the major characters of *Ultramarine* and *Under the Volcano* are represented as immersed in and victimized by a "culture of narcissism," then, civilization in these novels — which is conflated into the visions of its self-regarding characters — is represented as narcissistically diseased. For it can only be a narcissistically diseased civilization, these novels suggest, that convinces its subjects "that the way to deal with the stresses associated with this culture is to withdraw into the self" (Alford 18). In *Ultramarine* and *Under the Volcano* Joycean "paralysis" has given way to Lowryan "disease"; in these later fictions there is even less hope for the patient's recovery. This stated, however, it is clear that both Joyce's and Lowry's works share the conception of civilization as a blinding torch — one that obscures more than reveals the troubled condition of the "civilized."

In his biography of Malcolm Lowry, Douglas Day wisely cautions against readings of *Under the Volcano* that fail to investigate it as "*Gestalt*" (321). It is in this spirit that I have advanced the claim that narcissism — as pathology and ethos — plays a major role in the novel, and that the two angles of exploration pursued here not only clarify the depiction of civilization in Lowry's early fiction but suggest that we may place Narcissus beside Faust as a major characterological archetype for *Under the Volcano*. If it is true that the representation of Narcissus, as Lawrence Thornton maintains, has metamorphosed "from the time of the Romantics, who thought he symbolized the virtues of self-observation and the powers inherent in the self, to the Modernist and Post-Modernist concentration on his sterility" (201), then *Under the Volcano*, in its delineation of the Consul, also retains an aspect of the romantic conception of this figure, even if it strongly emphasizes the modern one. As Lowry himself maintains, although the novel is concerned principally "with the forces in man which cause him to be terrified of himself," it is also about the achievement of insight, for "there is even a hint of redemption for the poor old Consul at the end, who realizes that he is after all part of humanity" (*Selected Letters* 66, 85).

What Lowry describes here might be called Geoffrey's "cosmic," as opposed to "egoistic," narcissism: the artist's ability to behold reality as a creative vision of the self. Ovid's Narcissus, according to Gaston Bachelard, "has not given himself over exclusively to contemplation of himself. His own image is the center of a world," which "is a superb creation that requires only inaction, only a dreamer's attitude" (24). In this way too the Consul's "ineluctable personal disaster," as he himself imagines, "might even be found at the end to contain a certain element of triumph" (*Under the Volcano* 139). For through his cosmic narcissism and sense of humor[20] — both of which Kohut deems "transformations of [egoistic] narcissism" that help us to achieve "ultimate mastery over the demands of the narcissistic self" ("Forms" 457) — Geoffrey, however, fleetingly, comes to terms with his predicament and glimpses a rich reality, no matter how horrible, that the others cannot even imagine. In this paradoxical manner, Lowry's leading Narcissus embraces his self-wagered fate — loves and hates, desires and destroys himself.

Notes

 1   Introduction

1   Eloise Knapp Hay, for example, takes *Heart of Darkness* to be depicting "images of European men and women whose history has passed on to them a torch of illusion which they carry into 'backward' territories" (107). The "moral darkness of Africa," Hay argues, "is not the simple darkness of native 'ignorance,' but of white men who have blinded themselves and corrupted the natives by their claim to be light-bearers" (134). And Ian Watt views Conrad's (and Marlow's) attitude in *Heart of Darkness* as one of enjoining us "to defend ourselves in full knowledge of the difficulties to which we have been blinded by the illusions of civilisation" (253). For more on this, see Sexton.

2   "Civilization" was also a cause célèbre in France, Germany, and the United States. Writing in *The Decay and the Restoration of Civilization* (1923), for example, Albert Schweitzer maintains that "at the end of the last century and the beginning of this there appeared a number of works on civilization with the most varied titles" (2). Some of these include *The Conventional Lies of Our Civilization* (1884), *Civilisation: Its Cause and Cure* (1889), *The Law of Civilization and Decay* (1896), *Civilization and Progress* (1898), *Principles of Western Civilisation* (1902), *A Theory of Civilisation* (1914), *The Unity of Western Civilization* (1915), *Civilization and Womanhood* (1916), *Is Civilization a Disease?* (1917), *The Salvaging of Civilization* (1921), *The Evolution of Civilization* (1922), *The Decay and the Restoration of Civilization* (1923), *Civilization and Ethics* (1923), *Saturated Civilization* (1926), *What Is Civilization?* (1926), *Man and Civilization* (1927), *Where Is Civilization Going?* (1927), *Civilisation* (1928), *Imperialism and Civilization* (1928), *Essentials of Civilization* (1929), *What Is European Civilization? And What Is Its Future?* (1929), *The Biology of Civilization* (1930), *The Civilized Man* (1930), *Our Contemporary Civilization* (1935),

Women and a Changing Civilisation (1935), *The Will to Civilization* (1938), *Civilization on Trial* (1948), *A Manual of Civilization* (1949).

3 "The 'saving,'" McDiarmid writes, "works two ways: the poets were, themselves, part of the 'civilization' that needed a community, an audience, to validate it. For postromantic poets such as Yeats, Eliot, and Auden, saving civilization entailed the mutual redemption of art and society. Society needed art to express its common bonds and develop its self-consciousness; but art needed society to redeem it from solipsism" (7–8).

4 My project differs methodologically from McDiarmid's in two substantial respects. First, this study appropriates a historical model of literary scholarship and takes advantage of the possibilities afforded by viewing literary texts as critiques of culture. Second, this project seeks to bridge the gap, however incrementally, between studies concerned with psychological and sociological processes in literature: the "subject" of civilization in this study referring both to the topic of civilization in its totality and to the individual within civilization.

5 Soon after in this essay, Conrad speaks of England's "very strong hold on me as the embodiment of a beneficent and gentle spirit; that it was dear to me not as an inheritance, but as an acquisition, as a conquest in the sense in which a woman is conquered — by love, which is a sort of surrender" ("Poland Revisited" 148). Note here too Conrad's explicit desire to overlook England's "sinister" side.

6 The final paragraph of *Movements*, in a chapter entitled "The Unification of Germany," is eerily prophetic of World War II and particularly the rise of Adolph Hitler. "But we must never forget that mankind lives by a twofold motive: the motive of peace and increase, and the motive of contest and martial triumph. As soon as the appetite for martial adventure and triumph in conflict is satisfied, the appetite for peace and increase manifests itself, and *vice versa*. It seems a law of life. Therefore a great united Europe of productive working-people, all materially equal, will never be able to continue and remain firm unless it unites also round one great chosen figure, some hero who can lead a great war, as well as administer a wide peace. It all depends on the will of the people. But the will of the people must concentrate in one figure, who is also supreme over the will of the people. He must be chosen, but at the same time responsible to God alone. Here is a problem of which a stormy future will have to evolve the situation" (344). For an insightful study of Lawrence's history textbook, see Salgado.

7 This duplicity is also apparent in Lawrence's travel essay, "Europe v. America" (1926), where Lawrence *defends* European civilization against the charge made by some Americans that it has run its course, is all played out. "One may be sick of certain aspects of European civilization," Lawrence insists, "but they're in ourselves, rather than in Europe" (117).

8 See G. J. Watson for an insightful look at Joyce's complex and ambiguous orientation toward the Irish revival and English rule in Ireland.

9 In *A Room of One's Own*, for example, Woolf speaks, pace Coleridge, of the androgynous mind as "fully fertilised" and using "all its faculties." "Perhaps a mind that is purely masculine cannot create," she continues, "any more than a mind that is purely feminine" (102). For more on Woolf and androgyny, see Heilbrun.

10 For more on the Conrad–Lowry connection, see my "'Civilization' under Western Eyes: Lowry's *Under the Volcano* as a Reading of Conrad's *Heart of Darkness*."

11 For brief treatments of the history of the word "civilization," see Bagby 159–62, Bierstedt 264–78, Gunn 8–12, McEachran 41–44, and Williams, *Keywords* 48–50. Bierstedt notes

the "variegated and colorful career" of "civilization," concluding that "we have found no consistency at all in the use of the term 'civilization' and no consensus on the phenomenon it is supposed to symbolize. . . . civilization is tightly bound to sociocultural conditions, and its meaning is a function, therefore, of the culture, age, period, or society in which definitions of it are proposed" (276).

12   "Culture" and "civilization" came of age together in the late eighteenth century, and throughout the nineteenth and twentieth centuries were defined synonymously or in opposition to one another. For more on this, see Williams, *Marxism and Literature* 11–20. Examples of those who refuse to make any distinction between these two terms are E. B. Tylor in *The Origins of Culture* (1873) and T. S. Eliot in *Notes towards the Definition of Culture* (1948). Those who distinguish between them more sharply include Matthew Arnold in *Culture and Anarchy* (1869) and F. R. Leavis in "Mass Civilization and Minority Culture" (1930). For Arnold and Leavis civilization refers to achievements more "mechanical and external," culture to things more cerebral and aesthetic.

13   Along these lines, Bernard Bergonzi reminds us that during the final decades of the last century a number of novels appeared describing "catastrophic future wars" in which England was invaded by outsiders and brought to the brink of defeat. "It is true," Bergonzi writes, "that many of these works were written with a homiletic purpose, to encourage the nation to a greater state of military efficiency, but this does not prevent them being, at the same time, expressions of the prevalent mood, whatever their author's stated intentions" (12).

14   See my "Kindred by Choice: Joyce's *Exiles* and Goethe's *Elective Affinities*" for the suggestion that Joyce was conversant with German literary history.

15   One need only note the titles of some contemporary books to understand the great degree to which organic and teleological metaphors pervaded the discourse of civilization: *Civilisation: Its Cause and Cure* (1889), *Degeneration* (1892), *The Law of Civilization and Decay* (1896), *Civilization and Progress* (1898), *Is Civilization a Disease?* (1917), *The Decline of The West* (1918, 1922), *The Evolution of Civilization* (1922), *The Decay and the Restoration of Civilization* (1923), *Where Is Civilization Going?* (1927), *The Biology of Civilization* (1930), *Progress and Catastrophe* (1937), *The Passing of the European Age* (1948).

16   Who can doubt, for example, that Spencer's sense of civilization's evolution derives from Darwin's notion, expressed in *The Descent of Man* (1871), that "all civilized nations were once barbarous" (509). Nevertheless, even more than Spencer, it is writers like C. C. Walker who take Darwinian thinking to its illogical conclusions by insisting that it explains the "Law of History": "If there is a Law of History, and no historian doubts that it exists," Walker writes in his *Biology of Civilization* (1930), "it must be sought in the science that deals with organic laws" (10–11).

17   See Kershner, "Degeneration," for a discussion of the pervasiveness of this kind of thinking at the turn of the century and beyond.

18   In Chapters 5 and 7 I treat late-Freudian theory, Adorno, and Lasch in detail.

19   Trueblood betrays this hope when he writes that "the emphasis on the sickness [of civilization] is very important because only through accurate diagnosis is there a chance of successful recovery" (12).

20   G. E. Moore's *Principia Ethica* (1903) was influential within the Bloomsbury Group generally. In particular, Bell must have found this philosopher's subsumption of ethics into aesthetics attractive. Arnold's influence on Bell is also apparent in *Civilization*. Sounding like Arnold in *Culture and Anarchy* (1869), Bell here speaks of "Reasonableness" and a "Sense of Values" — his two prerequisites for civilization — as being catalysts for

further good: "a taste for truth and beauty, tolerance, intellectual honesty . . . a desire for complete self-expression and for a liberal education, a contempt for utilitarianism and philistinism, in two words — sweetness and light" (120). However, Walter Pater's *Renaissance* (1893) is the touchstone of Bell's "light essay." Originally entitled *The New Renaissance, Civilization* is rhetorically close to Pater's text at a number of points, such as when it equates being "completely civilized" with experiencing "the most intense and exquisite states of mind" (147).

21   The terms are Leonard Woolf's and E. M. Forster's, respectively.

22   Conspicuously absent in this debate over civilization are the voices of women. To be sure, the scarcity of females in the public debate over civilization is in large measure due to their exclusion from it, and to the prevailing masculinist sense of women, expressed in *Heart of Darkness*, as blindfolded and in the dark, as "out of touch with truth," and as properly belonging in "that beautiful world of their own" (16, 49). As C. G. Jung argues in *Civilization in Transition*, "for women Logos is a deadly boring kind of sophistry if she is not actually repelled and frightened by it" (124). For Jung her natural habitat is the world of emotions, not ideas.

Nevertheless, many women, among them Virginia Woolf (see Chapter 4), would not be consigned to silence on such a "male" concern as civilization. Harriet B. Bradbury, in *Civilization and Womanhood* (1916), for example, offers a caveat on the subject of women in civilization. It is only "when both men and women have . . . set themselves to solve together the problems of our civilization," she writes, that "these problems will be solved, and not before" (207). Similarly, in "Women and Modern Civilization" (1926), Ramsay Traquair warns that "the end of a civilization too much controlled by men is impractical abstraction, that of one too much controlled by women, utilitarian materialism" (192). Moreover, she continues, Europe "owes her greatness to the balance of man and woman. There abstract thought, art, and pure knowledge — those manly virtues — have been balanced by the society-forming, utilitarian instincts of women" (193). And Winifred Holtby, in *Women and a Changing Civilisation* (1935), insists that straitening gender roles detract from rather than enhance civilization.

Not surprisingly, male writing on this subject tended to be even more clichéd as well as milder in resolution. Women were taken, virtually across the board, to be social, erotic, and intuitive complements to male abstraction, purity, and rationality. Hector MacPherson's comment is typical: "Civilization on its highest and noblest side is rooted in motherhood," he writes, and "even in primitive society the strength of affection fostered by the maternal relationship [does] something to counteract the force of the purely selfish feeling, and to increase the fund of sociality" (126). In a similar spirit John H. Wilkins closes his drama *Civilization:*

> To feel that woman and her angel love,
> Are the true rectifiers of the world;
> And that to her, and her alone, we owe
> The charm that makes our ruggedness a garden.
> Yes, hand in hand must Truth and Honor walk,
> With woman for the guide! That's Civilization! (81)

Trite, sentimental, and condescending, such discourse casts women in the eternal roles of erotic guides and spiritual aides to men — the true conductors of the business, and reapers of the profits, of civilization.

23   Consider, for example, Conrad's conception of artistic production as expressed in his essay "Books." Although the "art of the novelist" is "simple," at the same time it is "the most elusive of all creative arts." "After all," Conrad continues, "the creation of a world is not a small undertaking except perhaps to the divinely gifted. In truth every novelist must begin by creating for himself a world, great or little, in which he can honestly believe" (6).

24   Along these lines, Ford Madox Ford writes that he agrees with Conrad on the following axiom: "The first business of [literary] Style is to make work interesting: the second business of Style is to make work interesting: the third business of Style is to make work interesting: the fourth business of Style is to make work interesting" (206).

25   Eagleton himself even lauds Bakhtin for producing "a materialist poetics" ("Wittgenstein's Friends" 118). Elsewhere he praises Bakhtin for his conception of the "Carnivalesque" ("Bakhtin, Schopenhauer, Kundera").

26   For recent essay collections to discuss and debate the new historicism and the sociology of literature, respectively, see Veeser, and Ferguson.

27   See the "Presidential Forum" in *Profession*, "Breaking Up/Out/Down — The Boundaries of Literary Study," for a sense of the recent ascendancy of various interdisciplinary approaches to literary study. Also see the special issues of *Journal of the Midwest Modern Language Association* ("Cultural Studies and New Historicism") and *South Atlantic Quarterly* ("Writing Cultural Criticism").

28   No one explains Bakhtin's anti-Saussurean and undeconstructive theory of language more succinctly than James F. Knapp: "Bakhtin refuses to remove language from its social context, an operation that would permit us to imagine that language is ideal and unitary . . . coherent and unchanging. . . . Bakhtin's position might seem to resemble that of deconstruction, but its premises, as well as its practical consequences for criticism, are very different indeed. While deconstructionists use the notion of difference to construct a metaphysical argument, alleging that difference is universally present because it is of the essence of Language itself, Bakhtin sees linguistic difference as the sign that languages are fundamentally social, that they are the record of historical order, contention and change. Focusing on particular language performances, rather than on the abstraction, Language, Bakhtin insists that any utterance, or written text, must be understood in relation to the historical conditions of its production" (78–79).

29   For four recent volumes that treat and challenge Bakhtin's conclusions in provocative ways, see Hirschkop and Shepherd, *Bakhtin and Cultural Theory*; Holquist, *Dialogism: Bakhtin and His World*; Morson and Emerson, *Mikhail Bakhtin: Creation of a Prosaics*, and *Rethinking Bakhtin: Extensions and Challenges*. Other important discussions of Bakhtin's achievement include Clark and Holquist, Bialostosky, Morson, and Todorov.

30   For more on Marxism's intersections with Bakhtin, see Williams, *Marxism and Literature*, and Tony Bennett, *Formalism and Marxism*.

31   Notably, Geertz, like Bakhtin and Eagleton, views Saussure's structural linguistics — and the kind of thinking about language, literature, and culture that extends from it — with deep suspicion. All three undoubtedly would agree with Fredric Jameson's charge that structuralism is "a pure formalism" for interpreting all works of art as statements "about language" ("Metacommentary" 15). For insightful discussions of the relationship between Geertz's thought and Marxism, see Pecora, "The Limits of Local Knowledge," and La Capra, *Soundings in Critical Theory*, chapter 5, "Culture and Ideology: From Geertz to Marx."

32   Like Dominick La Capra in *History, Politics, and the Novel*, I seek in this study to "depart

from two seemingly opposed but perhaps complimentary and mutually reinforcing tendencies in recent criticism: overcontextualization, historicization, and documentary reductionism, on the one hand, and formalistic hypostatization — including the universalizing fixation . . . of deconstructive techniques — on the other" (209–10).

33   With this in mind, Chapters 3, 5, and 7 stand as a gloss on Freud's determination that "the liberty of the individual is no gift of civilization" but, in fact, "was greatest before there was any civilization" (*Civilization and Its Discontents* 42). For Conrad the connection between psychology and culture is always a close one: "the psychology of individuals, even in the most extreme instances," he writes, "reflects the general effect of the fears and hopes of its time" ("Autocracy and War" 85). In the chapter on Joyce, the ideas of Max Horkheimer and Theodor Adorno are shown to grow out of late-Freudian thinking, just as in the final chapter on Lowry the ideas of Christopher Lasch and Richard Sennett are shown to derive, in large measure, from the clinical observations of Heinz Kohut and Otto Kernberg. This evolution in theories reflects an evolution in thinking during the period under consideration (from the 1910s and 1920s of Joyce's fiction to the 1930s and 1940s of Lowry's), as Kohut develops Freud's thinking on narcissism, just as Lasch may be said to play off of Adorno's sociocultural speculations (note, for example, how similar Lasch's "culture of narcissism" is to Adorno's "culture-industry").

34   It is also notable that Conrad, Joyce, and Lowry are nationally, culturally, and linguistically marginalized émigrés, at the fringe, rather than at the center, of British artistic and intellectual life. Although each defines himself as a non-*engagé* writer (with the former two taking Flaubert's disengagement as a model and the latter physically disengaging himself in rural British Columbia), each of them, paradoxically, produces fiction that reflects a deep concern with the simultaneously captivating and destructive, illuminating and mystifying, powers of civilization. Rather than simply bemoaning "the immense panorama of futility and anarchy which is contemporary history" (Eliot, "*Ulysses*, Order, and Myth" 177), the literature of Conrad, Joyce, and Lowry instead critiques it by revealing its rhetorical biases, by exposing the inadequacy of those theories of civilization that inform it, and by representing it, respectively, as gamelike, paralyzed, and narcissistic. Similarly, Lawrence, who roams far and wide of England, and Woolf, who is de facto marginalized by her gender, are cultural eccentrics whose novels, nevertheless, squarely address their "civilized" English readers. The former figure backward-looking, the latter forward-looking, both Lawrence and Woolf create fictions at one and the same time deeply invested in and deeply suspicious of the discourse of civilization.

For Eagleton this explains why these "experimental" authors — marginal rather than mainstream "English" ones — are provocative, original, and enduring. In his recent "The End of English," Eagleton argues that such writers were "able to carry through [an] audacious feat of inverted imperialism precisely because they lacked those vested emotional interests in an English literary tradition which hamstrung the natives": "James, Conrad, Eliot, Pound, Yeats, Joyce and Beckett could approach indigenous English traditions from the outside, objectify and appropriate them for their own devious ends, estrange and inhabit English culture in a single act, as those reared within its settled pieties could not. Positioned as they were within essentially peripheral histories, such artists could view native English lineages less as a heritage to be protected than as an object to be problematized" (1). And "problematize" it they did. Writing in *Exiles and Emigrés*, Eagleton further points out that these marginalized writers "had immediate access to alternative cultures and traditions: broader frameworks against which, in a highly creative tension, the erosion of contemporary order could be situated and partially understood" (15). And "In no case are these alternatives merely points of refuge," he concludes; "they are themselves deeply implicated in the general undermining of civilised order" (18).

* 2   "Rebarbarizing Civilization"

1   Privately, however, Darwin was less enthusiastic about Spencer's achievement. Darwin's notebooks, for example, record that Spencer's "deductive manner of treating every subject is wholly opposed to my frame of mind" and that his "conclusions never convince me" (quoted in Howard 94).

2   To get an idea of Spencer's significance in these years, see Will Durant, who devotes nearly 10 percent of *The Story of Philosophy* (1926) to Spencer (381–434) — more space than he gives to Plato, Aristotle, Kant, or Nietzsche. And Hector MacPherson, writing in 1900, deems Spencer an "epoch-maker" of the caliber of "Descartes, Locke, Spinoza, Hume, Kant, Hegel" (v). For F. A. P. Barnard, Spencer is "not only the profoundest thinker of our time, but the most capacious and most powerful intellect of all time" (quoted in Hofstadter 31).

3   Allan Hunter, writing about Spencer's *Data of Ethics*, explains that "there was a cheap edition of this highly influential work in 1894, which would seem to indicate that Spencer was not only still well thought of, but also still in the mainstream of ethical discussion at the time" (87). And James G. Kennedy notes that sales of Spencer's books in the last quarter of the nineteenth century extended into the millions (119, 153).

4   See, for example, Hunter; Levine, "The Novel as Scientific Discourse"; Renner; Saveson; Watt; and Cedric Watts.

5   Exceptions include brief mentions by Green; Hawkins, "Psychology of Colonialism"; Levine, *The Realistic Imagination;* O'Hanlon; and Watt. And in his notes to Conrad's *Congo Diary and Other Uncollected Pieces*, Zdzislaw Najder contends that Conrad's "agnosticism seems to have owed something to Spencer" (73).

6   See Saveson 17–36, and Hunter 86–91.

7   In a letter to William Blackwood on the last day of 1898, for example, Conrad writes of *Heart of Darkness*, "the subject is of our time distinctly. . . . It is a story as much as my *Outpost of Progress* was but, so to speak[,] 'takes in' more — is a little wider — is less concentrated upon individuals" (*Letters* III, 140).

8   In a number of letters written between 1899 and 1902, for example, Conrad insists that *Heart of Darkness* and *Lord Jim* be read together. He originally intended, pace Flaubert's *Trois contes*, to publish the short story "Jim: A Sketch" in a volume with "Heart of Darkness" and "Youth" (*Letters* II, 167), maintaining that "the three tales, each being inspired by a similar moral idea," will make "a homogeneous book" (II, 231). Later, he writes that even the full-length *Jim* was "not . . . planned to stand alone. *H of D* was meant in my mind as a foil, and *Youth* was supposed to give the note" (II, 271). Determining precisely what Conrad meant by this has kept scholars busy for years. Eloise Knapp Hay's interpretation, however, is for me the most convincing: "*Heart of Darkness* was a 'foil' for *Lord Jim* in the contrast it offered between the illusion of a man concerned with personal conduct and the illusion of a man obsessed by race superiority" (177). Hay also notes that the Marlows of the two works are "dissimilar." Although both will "lie" for their

respective secret sharers (Kurtz and Jim), "the Marlow of *Lord Jim* believes that even dangerous knowledge is worthy of public examination, whereas the Marlow of *Heart of Darkness* believes the contrary: that dangerous knowledge must be suppressed" (129). Similarly, Ian Watt maintains that, if *Youth* was Conrad's "Song of Innocence" and *Heart of Darkness* his "Song of Experience," then perhaps *Lord Jim* can be seen as "a dialogue between the two Marlows, with Jim as the voice of his earlier innocence, and Marlow confronting him with the disenchanted voice of later experience" (269). For an alternative position on this issue, see Fleishman, *Conrad's Politics* 107.

9   Ford Madox Ford corroborates such an image of Conrad when he writes, in a personal remembrance, that Conrad favored England because of its readiness "to face Russia with fleet or purse when or wherever they should meet. The first English music-hall song that Conrad heard was: 'We don't want to fight but, by jingo if we do, / We've got the ships, we've got the men, we've got the money too. / We've fought the bear before and so we will again, / The Russians shall not have Constantinople . . .' A Pole of last century — and above all things Conrad was a Pole of last century — could ask nothing better" (56–57).

10 Conrad's Polish anti-Russian sentiment clearly has roots in his father's "Poland and Muscovy" (1864). In this tract Apollo Korzeniowski judges Muscovite civilization to be "terrible, depraved, destructive." Calling Muscovy "the plague of humanity," he writes that "her civilization means envy and [the] negation of human progress" (77).

11 Compare Conrad's view of London here with the one in his 1906 memoir *The Mirror of the Sea*, where the city is labeled "the oldest and the greatest of riverports" (96) and its "growth . . . as a well-equipped port" is described as having "been slow, while not unworthy of a great centre of distribution" (102).

12 In *Heart of Darkness*, as in *The Mirror of the Sea*, the Thames conjures industrial associations: "Amongst the *great commercial streams* of these islands, the Thames is the only one I think open to romantic feeling" (91; my emphasis).

13 Marlow at one point recalls that "there was a big concern, a Company for trade on that river. Dash it all, I thought to myself, they can't trade without using some kind of craft on that lot of fresh water — steamboats!" (*Heart of Darkness* 12).

14 The absolutism of Kurtz's command is made clear when the Russian proudly tells Marlow of an encounter with Kurtz over a small quantity of ivory: "He declared he would shoot me unless I gave him the ivory and then cleared out of the country because he could do so, and had a fancy for it, and there was nothing on earth to prevent him killing whom he jolly well pleased" (*Heart of Darkness* 56).

15 Similarly, a passage on Russia in Spencer's *Facts and Comments* (1902) appears uncannily prophetic of events represented in Conrad's novel of nine years later, *Under Western Eyes*: "Along with that unceasing subjugation of minor nationalities by which its imperialism is displayed, what do we see within its own organization? We have its vast army, to service in which everyone is actually or potentially liable; we have an enormous bureaucracy ramifying everywhere and rigidly controlling individual lives. . . . As a result of the pressure felt personally and pecuniarily, we have secret revolutionary societies, perpetual plots, chronic dread of social explosions; and while everyone is in danger of Siberia, we have the all-powerful head of this enslaved nation in constant fear for his life. Even when he goes to review his troops, rigorous precautions have to be taken by a supplementary army of soldiers, policemen, and spies . . . while similar precautions, which from time to time fail, have ever to be taken against assassination by explosion, during drives and railway-journeys" (164–65).

16 Writing years after his employment, Conrad observes that in the Belgian Congo, "created by the act of European powers[,] ruthless, systematic cruelty towards the blacks is the basis of administration, and bad faith towards all the other states the basis of commercial policy" (*Letters* III, 97).

17 See, for example, Hunt Hawkins, "Conrad's Critique of Imperialism in *Heart of Darkness*."

18 Unsurprisingly, both Spencer and Conrad have been taken to task for depicting the "primitive" mind in stereotypical terms (see, for example, Dewey, "Interpretation of the Savage Mind" 173–87, and Street 159–60). Both Spencer, in *Principles of Sociology*, and Marlow, in *Heart of Darkness*, attempt to defuse such criticisms. Spencer, for example, writes that "the words 'civilised' and 'savage' must have given to them meanings differing greatly from those which are current. That broad contrast usually drawn wholly to the advantage of the men who form large nations, and to the disadvantage of the men who form simple groups, a better knowledge obliges us profoundly to qualify" (II, 233). And Marlow suggests that we simply hate and fear that which we do not understand, observing that in our "civilized" view of "the jungle," "the incomprehensible . . . is also detestable" (10).

19 Roger Scruton's 1982 *Dictionary of Political Thought* defines "Military-Industrial Complex" as "a pattern of relations sometimes thought to exist between high-ranking industrialists concerned in the manufacture of military technology, and military advisors, concerned in making themselves useful (perhaps even indispensable) to a government" (298).

20 Writing in 1917 Stanton Coit sees a broader military-industrial alliance: "the facts of history prove that every great war during the last three centuries has been undertaken in the service of foreign traders, who call upon their government to back their claims" (122–23). In *The Decline of the West* Spengler goes so far as to claim that "Imperialism is Civilization unadulterated" (I, 36).

21 The case can be made that *Heart of Darkness* defuses the West's claim to superiority over the non-West by subverting the oppositions on which the West bases its hegemony: godly/godforsaken, complex/simple, mind/body, language/gesture, logic/illogic, rational/irrational, good/evil, efficient/inefficient, order/chaos, sane/insane, day/night, light/dark, historic/prehistoric, culture/nature, and so forth. For more on this idea, see Chapter 3.

22 Avrom Fleishman rightly points out that "Conrad's African tales, even more than his Asian ones, demonstrate that the contact of Europeans and natives encourages the submerged barbarism of the superficially civilized whites to express itself by genocide." "Not only are the natives stirred up by the rapacious policies of the imperialists," he continues, "but the whites become more savage than the 'savages'" (*Conrad's Politics* 90).

23 For two different interpretations of Spencer's role in the phenomenon of Social Darwinism, see Arendt 178–79, and Williams, "Social Darwinism" 86–102.

24 "Outpost," Patrick Brantlinger aptly notes, "clearly implies that between civilization and the savagery that worships fetishes and practices cannibalism there is little to choose" (*Bread and Circuses* 138). In this connection, Benita Parry maintains that "by revealing the disjunctions between high-sounding rhetoric and sordid ambitions and indicating the purposes and goals of a civilisation dedicated to global expansionism and hegemony, Conrad's writings engender a critique more destructive of imperialism's ideological premises than do the polemics of his contemporary opponents of empire" (10). And

Eloise Knapp Hay correctly speaks of Conrad's "maturing effect on English letters," due to his ability to call attention to "the horror in certain political realities that were being overlooked by comfortable, law-abiding English citizens and politicians" (11).

25   This phrase improved on Darwin's appellation "natural selection," as Darwin himself came to see "the advantages of H. Spencer's excellent expression of the 'survival of the fittest' " (quoted in Carneiro xx).

26   Although *Lord Jim* too alludes to the "stream of civilisation" (138) and to the "laws and order of progress" (206), it is clearly more idealistic and less ironic on this score than *Heart of Darkness*, even if a "privileged" member of Marlow's interlocutors doubts that Jim can remain faithful to his code: Jim lacks "a firm conviction in the truth of ideas racially our own, in whose name are established the order, the morality of an ethical progress" (206). Here Jim is shown to differ from Kurtz, who has no qualms about holding such a conviction.

✻ 3   The London Fog

1   In *Heart of Darkness*, for example, although the deconstruction of the rhetoric by which civilization distinguishes itself from savage domains is most prominent, the "civilization as game" trope is also evident. For example, the accountant aboard the *Nellie* — who has an economic stake in his nation's "civilizing mission" — "had brought out already a box of dominoes and was toying architecturally with the bones" (7). Marlow speaks of his cat-and-mouse intrigues with Kurtz as "a boyish game" (64) and refers to looking for a ship on which to explore the world as "that game" (11). Moreover, the line that separates "civilization" and "uncivilization" is blurred in virtually all of Conrad's works, from *Almayer's Folly* (1895) to *Victory* (1915), in which East and West become metaphors for each other and in which the European who ventures into "the jungle" engages in a civilized "will to power" at the expense of his own life. This deconstructive strategy is even apparent in Conrad's memoir *The Mirror of the Sea*, in which the Thames and Congo rivers are depicted in similar terms. Of the former river, for example, Conrad writes that "The houses of Gravesend crowd upon the shore with an effect of confusion as if they had tumbled down haphazard from the top of the hill at the back" (94), and "the narrow lanes coming down to the foreshore resemble the paths of smashed bushes and crumbled earth where big game comes to drink on the banks of tropical streams" (96). Like *Heart of Darkness*, *The Mirror of the Sea* blurs the Thames and Congo rivers together nearly beyond recognition.

2   I do not mean "deconstruct" in the Derridean sense. For more on this, see note 7.

3   This critical orientation toward Conrad's fiction has been largely neglected. Although readers since the turn of the century have noted that "Mr. Conrad tells his tales . . . by the conflict of the East and the West, of savagery and civilisation" (Sherry, *Critical Heritage* 109), few have scrutinized precisely what the relation between "civilization" and "savagery" in Conrad's work suggests. This is in part because readers of *Heart of Darkness* until quite recently remained under the sway of Albert Guerard's staggering critical influence — particularly his claim that Marlow's trek to Africa in search of secret-sharer Kurtz essentially pertains to psychology, to Marlow's "inner journey." This is undoubtedly what Raymond Williams refers to when he complains that "a whole school of criticism has succeeded in emptying *Heart and Darkness* of its social and historical content" (*The*

English Novel 145). Yet many subsequent readers attempting to shift the emphasis of the story from the internal psyche to the external world have ended up committing themselves to the position that Conrad's Congo stands "completely outside the conventions and norms of European civilization" (Meyers 57). To the contrary, I hope to demonstrate that Conrad's Congo is precisely constructed upon such conventions and norms. This same reader goes on to argue that "Conrad believes that civilization can flourish only when it is carefully nourished and guarded by a few select men . . . who remain faithful to their code of honor. It cannot be transplanted and cannot survive in remote places where great temptation and danger exist" (58). I take this conclusion to be equally specious, for in *Heart of Darkness* and *The Secret Agent* it is civilization and not its "opposite" (whether the jungle in the former or anarchy in the latter) wherein physical violence, intellectual duplicity, and moral blindness are fashioned into high arts.

4   Conrad has often been attacked on these grounds, most famously by African novelist Chinua Achebe, who deems him a "racist." For more on this, see the special issue of *Conradiana* (24:3, [1992]) on *Heart of Darkness* that I guest-edit. My own feeling is that, although it is true that "Marlow is solidly and naively Victorian in his moral outlook" (Ruthven 42), Conrad is not. It may well be that Conrad is able to evade many standard Victorian views on race and empire because he is not originally English — because he views England from the marginal perspective of the outsider. As George Orwell aptly puts it of Conrad's appeal, it "springs from the fact that he was a European and not an Englishman" (III, 388). Orwell is also right to attribute to Conrad "a sort of grown-upness and political understanding which would have been almost impossible to a native English writer at that time" (IV, 489).

5   In a letter of 1903 Conrad admits, "J'ai pris grand soin de donner une origine cosmopolite à Kurtz" (*Letters* III, 93). Other readers too have noticed the extent to which Kurtz is represented as the apotheosis of civilization. Eloise Knapp Hay, for example, deems Kurtz "civilization's superman" (149); Jerry Wasserman calls him "the quintessence of civilization" (105); and R. B. Kershner refers to him as "Europe's finest flower" ("Degeneration" 432).

6   The trope of "Africa as body" pervades *Heart of Darkness*. For example, reference is made to "the bowels of the land" (33), "the face of the forest," the "limb of some tree" (45), "a scar in the hillside," and a "shudder of the soil" (20), all of which animate the African landscape, render it as human physis. Additionally, Marlow affirms of the Congo River (when he had seen it on a map as a child), "the snake had charmed me" (12). Are we to understand this to be the serpent that tempts Eve (or for that matter Kurtz) to learn the secret of "dark knowledge" (Africa)? Clearly, the novel invokes but then resolutely undercuts such clichés. For a fascinating discussion of this issue, see Sullivan.

7   In a brilliant essay Donald M. Kartiganer clarifies the extent to which we may view Marlow's reading of the relation between civilization and jungle as "deconstructive." In that *Heart of Darkness* "revers[es] standard hierarchies, unearth[es] hidden agendas, expos[es] the contradictions of assertion and philosophic ground, tracing their progress through the contemplation and eventual rejection of a host of available patterns," we may take it as deconstructive. However, this deconstruction is not of the Derridean variety for Kartiganer, as Marlow's reading of his experience "is not an interpretive stance; it is the indispensable prelude to a stance, a recognition of possibilities." "Deconstruction," he continues, "*becomes* interpretation, an experience of meaning, only when it is invested with the passion of commitment" (173). Similarly, Aaron Fogel argues that, "despite

some apparent resemblances," the "process" of *Heart of Darkness* "is not primarily 'deconstructive.'" "Conrad is not as interested," he writes, "in the tropes and actions we call deconstruction . . . as in outlining the inescapably disproportionate forces at work in any dialogue" (179–80). Patrick Reilly also discusses this subversion of conventional tropes when he writes that "*Heart of Darkness* challenges th[e] axiom of cultural superiority by refuting the conventional division into backward and advanced, savage and civilized, dark and light, insisting instead upon a single world and a unified experience" (53). Eloise Knapp Hay refers to this textual phenomenon as Conrad's "repeated reversals or inversions of normal patterns of imagery" (137); and Benita Parry argues that the novella's "antinomian categories are subjected to a radical rearrangement subverting Europe's customary imagery, so that instead of denoting purity, virtue, clarity and veracity, white and light . . . come to signify corruption, evil, confusion and lies" (22).

8   Hay rightly notes that *Heart of Darkness* may be read in part as a "profound inquiry into" the "criterion of efficiency" (141). Interestingly, as late as 1948 this kind of rhetoric was still used to highlight the differences between "civilized" and "uncivilized" domains: "Australia has taken into her own hands the stupendous task of exploring her vast deserted interior," Eric Fischer writes, "and has fulfilled that task with the same thoroughness and efficiency which European explorers of different origin displayed in Africa" (102). Note here not only the association of "civilization" with "efficiency" but the notion that central Australia, like Africa (think of Marlow's blank map), is "deserted" until the Europeans arrive.

9   This "stretch of the Thames . . . is to other watersides of river ports what a virgin forest would be to a garden," Conrad then writes. "It is a thing grown up, not made. It recalls a Jungle by the confused, varied, and impenetrable aspect of the buildings that line the shore [which] hide the depths of London's infinitely varied, vigorous, seething life" (*Mirror of the Sea* 94–96).

10 For four provocative discussions of the representation of women (or gender) in *Heart of Darkness*, see Hyland, London, Johanna M. Smith, and Stark.

11 For a fascinating look at this historical phenomenon, see "The Genealogy of the Myth of the 'Dark Continent'" in Brantlinger's *Rule of Darkness*.

12 In *Gone Primitive* Marianna Torgovnick puts it this way: "*Heart of Darkness* thematizes the power of words . . . to mask the reality of what is happening in the Congo" (152).

13 For one such example of this overconfidence, see King Leopold II's article on the sacred mission of civilization in which "the desirable spread of civilisation" is taken for granted (Leopold 126).

14 Two final aspects of the text's critique of civilization merit attention. The first is that the "spreading" of civilization — colonization — disrupts the lives of its victims. Perhaps the best example of this disruption is that the African natives are "paid" nine inches of brass wire weekly for their efforts, a currency completely worthless to them. "So, unless they swallowed the wire itself," Marlow reasons, "or made loops of it to snare the fishes with, I don't see what good their extravagant salary could be to them" (*Heart of Darkness* 42). In his Author's Note to *Youth* Conrad himself remarks, "it is well known that curious men go prying into all sorts of places (where they have no business) and come out of them with all kinds of spoil" (4). And Hay aptly argues that "in *Heart of Darkness* one major theme, if not the ruling theme, is that civilization depends for its conquest of the earth on a combination of lies and forgetfulness" (153). Second, *Heart of Darkness* represents "civilized" Europeans (Marlow and Kurtz excluded) as possessing minds "of the stay-at-home

order" for whom "the immutability of their surroundings" and "the changing immensity of life glide past, veiled not by a sense of mystery but by a slightly disdainful ignorance" (9). Indeed, whether it is Marlow's aunt, Kurtz's Intended, the Company bureaucrats, or Marlow's assembled audience aboard the *Nellie* (which Steve Smith ventures "is unlikely, in any material way, ever to be affected by the contents of the narration" [197]), each is "moored with two good addresses like a hulk with two anchors, a butcher round one corner, a policeman round another, excellent appetites, and temperature normal . . . from year's end to year's end" (48).

15   For this reason I must disagree with Sandya Shetty, who has recently argued that a critic of empire like Conrad "who functions from within the dominant culture must find it well nigh impossible to venture far beyond the very ideological barriers which he purports to dissolve" (462). I also disagree with Irish novelist Liam O'Flaherty's well-known resolve that Conrad accepts "the God of the British Empire as something that must not be surpassed, and [that] all his characters [stand] on tiptoe striving to be like that God" (9).

16   In a 1906 letter to J. B. Pinker, Conrad writes that *The Secret Agent* is "the first story of mine dealing with London. And the ironic treatment of the whole matter is not so easy as it looks" (*Letters* III, 364–65).

17   For passing comments on the significance of games in *The Secret Agent*, see Darras 105; Fleishman, *Conrad's Politics* 203; Guerard 223; Hunter 156, 216; Schwarz 158–59; and Winner 76, 85.

18   Huizinga's sharp division between the "archaic" and the "civilized" mind dates *Homo Ludens* (completed in 1938 but first published in Switzerland in 1944), yet this is explainable when we consider the work as an attack on nazism. "Civilization today," the Dutch Huizinga writes, "is no longer played, and even where it still seems to play it is false play. . . . This is particularly true of politics" (206).

19   See Iser, "The Play of the Text," for a sense of how these categories can profitably be used to explore texts as "games."

20   That each individual in this novel engages in a strategy for survival is suggested by the fact that each group appears to be united and monolithic when it is in reality divided and strife-ridden: the Verlocs (Adolf vs. Winnie), the police (Heat vs. the Assistant Commissioner), the embassy (the new regime of Vladimir vs. the old one of Stott-Wartenheim), and the revolutionists (the Professor vs. the others).

21   See Conroy 141–55 for a fascinating discussion of "the wilderness of eyes portrayed in *The Secret Agent*": the ubiquitous spying, surveillance, and "panopticism" to be found there. Interestingly, in *The Origins of Totalitarianism*, Hannah Arendt describes the double agent in terms uncannily reminiscent of *The Secret Agent*: "The double agent . . . served the cause he was supposed to combat almost as much as, and sometimes more than, the authorities. Frequently he harbored a sort of double ambition: he wanted to rise in the ranks of the revolutionary parties as well as in the ranks of the services. In order to win promotion in both fields, he had only to adopt certain methods which in a normal society belong to the secret daydreams of the small employee who depends on seniority for advancement: through his connections with the police, he could certainly eliminate his rivals and superiors in the party, and through his connections with the revolutionaries he had at least a chance to get rid of his chief in the police" (431).

22   Germane to Verloc's case, Lasch's *The Culture of Narcissism* attributes a narcissistic condition to "gamesmen," including bureaucrats and businessmen (46–47). Hence, looking forward to the chapters on Joyce and Lowry, gamesmanship here may be linked

to narcissism. Clearly, Verloc's narcissism, his "single amiable weakness" that he is "loved for himself," hinders rather than enhances his ability to play the game and to survive.

23   Aaron Fogel aptly characterizes the Verloc relationship as "a 'political' marriage: each has entered into it partly out of unstated politic motives" (191).

24   Even Verloc is said to possess "a sort of inert fanaticism, or perhaps rather . . . a fanatical inertness" (*Secret Agent* 16).

25   It is perhaps significant that when Stevie leaves the carriage in the middle of their ride so that the cabby will not have to whip the horses, the cabby tells Stevie, "Don't you go for trying this silly game again, young fellow" (*Secret Agent* 123). It is also significant that they pass St. Stephen's Cathedral at this point (122).

26   Caillois's theory of how games become social institutions is telling for my reading of *The Secret Agent:* "Under certain conditions, even the games intended by their very nature to be played by a limited number of players exceed the limit. They reflect forms which, while doubtless remaining in the domain of play, evolve a bureaucracy, a complex apparatus, and a specialized, mechanical personality. In a word, they sustain permanent and refined structures, institutions of an official, private, marginal, and sometimes clandestine character, whose status seems nonetheless remarkably assured and durable" (40–41).

27   *The Secret Agent* continues the critique of civilization begun in *Heart of Darkness* in other ways as well. It too touches on the encounter between colonizer and colonized. We learn, for example, that the Assistant Commissioner's "career had begun in a tropical colony. He had liked his work there. It was police work. He had been very successful in tracking and breaking up certain nefarious secret societies amongst the natives" (79–80). Also like *Heart of Darkness, The Secret Agent* is "grotesque satire," a scathing attack on turn-of-the-century bourgeois sentimentality, narrated ironically, and deploying, to cite Conrad's own words in the Author's Note, "caricatural presentation" (7). Indeed, as early as 1908 John Galsworthy recognizes that the novel is a "diagnosis of the departmental Briton" (quoted in Sherry, *Critical Heritage* 208); and Thomas Mann, in his preface to the German edition of the novel, sees it as "tragi-comedy": the "genuine anti-bourgeois style" (241). Likewise, Irving Howe views the "English moderation" represented in *The Secret Agent* as "a form of obtuseness as well as a quality of civilization" (94), which comports with Conrad's own sense, expressed in the Author's Note to *The Secret Agent*, that "man may smile and smile, but he is not an investigating animal. He loves the obvious. He shrinks from explanations" (4). This insight is echoed in Winnie's often repeated thought that "things do not stand much looking into" and in the masses' depiction as "thoughtless like a natural force, pushing on blind and orderly and absorbed, impervious to sentiment, [and] to logic" (67).

28   If *The Secret Agent* appears more cynical a work than *Heart of Darkness*, this is because, in Eloise Knapp Hay's words, "the ironic author [of *The Secret Agent*], whose readers know all there is to know, leaves no question hanging as did the author of *Heart of Darkness*" (263).

✳ 4   Civilization in Post–Great War Bloomsbury

1   For a provocative look at Woolf's appropriation and transformation of Conrad's *Heart of Darkness*, see Neuman.

2   Much disagreement remains as to whether an ideologically and aesthetically coherent "Bloomsbury Group" ever existed. Leon Edel, for example, contends that, although "Bloomsbury friends led their different lives" and "followed different careers," they nevertheless "were linked by old ties, old sympathies, old loyalties, old habits of thought, common opinions" (284). Virginia's husband, Leonard Woolf, on the other hand, holds that "what came to be called Bloomsbury by the outside world never existed in the form given to it by the outside world. For 'Bloomsbury' was and is currently used as a term — usually of abuse — applied to a largely imaginary group of persons with largely imaginary objects and characteristics" (*Beginning Again* 21).

3   See, for example, DeSalvo, *Virginia Woolf's First Voyage*, and Quentin Bell, *Virginia Woolf* I, Appendix D.

4   See Dowling, Heinemann, and Wilson 123.

5   Beverly Ann Schlack detects the presence of *Civilization* in Woolf's *Orlando* in that both texts hold up the eighteenth century as a high point in Western civilization (173). And Elizabeth Steele notes that two copies of *Civilization* were found in the Woolf library, one of which was inscribed "Virginia from Clive" (284).

6   For a complete list of works by Clive Bell, see Bywater 215–42.

7   See, for example, Quentin Bell, *Virginia Woolf* I, 143. Apparently, there was also an amatory side to their relationship. Although not always pronounced, it was enough of an issue that Woolf, as late as 1926, would write to Vita Sackville-West, "Clive has just stood me a terrific lunch and was sweet and found us an old ripe, but not quite virginal, apple, and I love him, and always shall, but not in the go-to-bed or sofa way" (*Letters* III, 281). See DeSalvo, *Virginia Woolf* 69–71 and 84, for more speculations on this amatory relationship.

8   Interestingly, *Chambers Etymological English Dictionary* defines "civilise" as "to reclaim from barbarism: to instruct in arts and refinements" (102), a definition similar to that found in Bell's *Civilization*.

9   To be sure, the ideas of Matthew Arnold, Walter Pater, and, particularly, G. E. Moore stand behind much of Bell's thinking, including his determination that "Civilization comes of reflection and education," and that "Civilization is artificial" (*Civilization* 53). Woolf herself observes that Bell "was a Moorite" in 1906 when he commenced to "write his book on Civilisation" (*Diary* II, 101). For a discussion of the great impact of G. E. Moore's *Principia Ethica* (1903) on the Bloomsbury scene, see Rosenbaum 214–38, and Johnstone 20–45.

10   Bell's secret agenda in attacking censorship in England undoubtedly relates to his first-hand experience of it. His 1915 pamphlet *Peace at Once*, for example, which urged an immediate negotiated settlement to the war, was seized upon its publication and publicly burned by order of the lord mayor of London (see Zwerdling 282).

11   This is not to deny that Woolf's own experience with doctors of the body and mind also contributed to her portraits of Holmes and Bradshaw. As Avrom Fleishman aptly puts it, Woolf's disquisitions on Proportion and Conversion may be regarded "as passionate intrusions by the author, based on personal experience" (*Virginia Woolf* 69).

12   It is also worth noting that Bell's ironic statement that the Great War was fought on behalf of English civilization — the civilization of Shakespeare — echoes in Septimus Smith's decision to volunteer for active war duty: "He went to France to save an England which consisted almost entirely of Shakespeare's plays" (*Mrs. Dalloway* 130). And Bell's complaint that "our civil and spiritual masters think Aristophanes and Shakespeare

indecent," that "neither would be permitted to publish his plays unexpurgated in contemporary England" (*On British Freedom* 18), echoes in Conservative member of Parliament Richard Dalloway's attitude toward Shakespeare, as imagined by Peter Walsh: "Richard Dalloway got on his hind legs and said that no decent man ought to read Shakespeare's sonnets because it was like listening at keyholes (besides the relationship was not one he approved)" (113).

13   Leonard Woolf went on to write that both "Bell's method and his assumptions are wrong and are bound to lead to wrong conclusions" (*Diary* III, 184).

14   In *A Room of One's Own*, published a year after *Civilization*, Woolf may be replying to Bell when she writes, "Women have had less intellectual freedom than the sons of Athenian slaves" (112).

15   Hence, it is difficult for me to agree with Carolyn G. Heilbrun, who reads Bell's statements about women in *Civilization* as expressions of his belief that there is a necessary "connection between civilization and androgyny" (118). Nevertheless, I do agree with Heilbrun that much of "Bloomsbury consciously rejected the Victorian stereotypes of 'masculine' and 'feminine' in favor of an angrogynous ideal" (126), that, in general, "their perception of the androgynous nature necessary to civilization was embodied in their work as well as in their lives" (135).

16   I am aware that for many readers of this novel, Carolyn G. Heilbrun included, *To the Lighthouse* is Woolf's "best novel of androgyny" (156), though Mrs. Ramsay herself, "far from androgynous or complete," is "as one-sided and as life-denying as her husband." "Readers," Heilbrun continues, "have seldom been clear as to whether her son and daughter reach the lighthouse because her spirit survived her death, or because her death liberated her children" (155). Deeming Mrs. Ramsay an earth mother who perpetuates rather than challenges "undiluted male power" (156), Heilbrun convincingly maintains that Lily Briscoe, "the nonmaternal artist" (158), is the real heroine of the novel for achieving genuine stature other than through the feminine beauty and maternal charm for which Mrs. Ramsay is known and remembered. Along these lines, Woolf may be thinking of Bell when she writes, in *A Room of One's Own*, of a poetry critic, "Mr. B," who denies the feminine side of his mind: "Very able [his criticisms] were, acute and full of learning; but the trouble was, that his feelings no longer communicated; his mind seemed separated into different chambers; not a sound carried from one to the other. Thus, when one takes a sentence of Mr. B into the mind it falls plump to the ground — dead" (105). This comment may be linked to Woolf's argument for an androgynous understanding: "It is fatal to be a man or woman pure and simple; one must be woman-manly or man-womanly" (108). Unsurprisingly, Bell's own perception of Woolf's feminism is far from flattering: "Virginia was, in her peculiar way, an ardent feminist," he writes in *Old Friends*. "What is more, some of her injustices and wanton denigrations can be traced, I think, to female indignation. In political feminism — the Suffrage Movement — she was not much interested. . . . [I]t was not in political action that her feminism expressed itself. . . . Virginia's feminism was genuine and ardent, yet I do not think it played a great part in her life. Certainly the tantrums to which it gave rise were rare and transitory" (101–102). The precise contours of Virginia Woolf's feminism remain controversial. As Alex Zwerdling puts it, "No other element in Woolf's work has created so much confusion and disagreement among her serious readers as her relation to the women's movement" (210). Pamela Transue helps explain why this is so: "Woolf was persistently skeptical of organized political movements in any form and shied away from feminist groups, yet she was

intensely critical of the patriarchal social and political system of values in the western world, particularly as it related to women, and her fiction became a vehicle for her criticisms" (2). For more on this issue, see Black.

17   Interestingly, these two endeavors are associated with Woolf's sister Vanessa (or Lily Briscoe) and Woolf herself, respectively.

18   However, Mrs. Ramsay's daughters exhibit the potential to challenge male authority more than their mother, such as when they insist upon "a wilder life; not always taking care of some man or other; for there was in all their minds a mute questioning of deference and chivalry, of the Bank of England and the Indian Empire, of ringed fingers and lace" (*To the Lighthouse* 14).

19   In the chapter "Conspicuous Leisure," Veblen writes: "It is felt by all persons of refined taste that a spiritual contamination is inseperable from certain offices that are conventionally required of servants. Vulgar surroundings . . . and vulgarly productive occupations are unhesitatingly condemned and avoided. They are incompatible with life on a satisfactory spiritual plane — with 'high thinking.' From the days of the Greek philosophers to the present, a degree of leisure and of exemption from contact with such industrial processes as serve the immediate every day purposes of human life has ever been recognised by thoughtful men as a prerequisite to a worthy or beautiful, or even a blameless, human life. In itself and in its consequences the life of leisure is beautiful and ennobling in all civilised men's eyes" (37–38). It would appear that Bell, in *Civilization*, vigorously seeks to denounce Veblen's claims.

20   For an outline of Virginia Woolf's class background, see Leonard Woolf, *Beginning Again* 74–75.

21   At one point, for example, she writes that "Clive of course changes into an upper class man[,] very loud, familiar, and dashing at once" (*Diary* II, 322).

22   Like Marlow's "excellent Aunt" in Conrad's *Heart of Darkness*, Lady Bruton is associated with England's imperialist mission and with the self-deceiving discourse that surrounds this mission: "if ever a woman could have worn the helmet and shot the arrow, could have led the troops to attack, ruled with indomitable justice barbarian hordes and lain under a shield . . . or made a green grass mound on some primeval hillside, that woman was Millicent Bruton" (*Mrs. Dalloway* 274–75).

23   For more on this, see Bicknell.

24   By the same token, A. D. Moody deems Bloomsbury to be concerned most with advancing a "civilization in the mind" (quoted in Quentin Bell, *Bloomsbury* 11).

✳ 5   Discontent and Its Civilization

1   Bernard Benstock writes that paralysis reverberates "through every aspect of *Dubliners*" (38). And Craig Werner notes that "competing approaches to [*Dubliners*] generally center on disagreements concerning the implications of what nearly all critics have recognized as Joyce's central theme: the paralysis permeating Irish life" (33). This paralysis is no less evident in *Ulysses*, a novel that can be viewed as an elaborate and lengthy *Dubliners* story.

2   *Dialectic of Enlightenment* in many ways grows out of the critique of civilization posed in Freud's two late works.

3   For insightful Freudian interpretations of Joyce's works, see Anderson, Brivic, Gose, Kimball, and Shechner.

4   See Herr, *Anatomy*, for the most sustained and sophisticated argument that Joyce's subjects are the products not of their own autonomy but of the competing discourses of their culture.

5   Joyce also disparagingly refers to Jung, with whom he eventually corresponds over Lucia and *Ulysses*, as "the Swiss Tweedledum" (*Letters* I, 166).

6   Unlike Nietzsche (and Spengler), Freud "scorns to distinguish between culture and civilization" (*FI* 6). Nevertheless, in these texts Freud clearly means "civilization" rather than "culture," if we take seriously his delineation of "barbarian," "which is the opposite of civilized" (*CD* 40).

7   Freud's "narcissism of minor differences" idea dates from his *Group Psychology and the Analysis of the Ego* (1921), in which he writes: "In the undisguised antipathies and aversions which people feel towards strangers with whom they have to do we may recognize the expression of self-love — of narcissism" (34).

8   For more on Freud's critique of civilization, see Brantlinger, *Bread and Circuses* 154–83; Levi 173–83; Levin 124–45; and Wolheim 219–35.

9   Gerty and Eveline share a number of salient characteristics. Each is an aging female adolescent (Gerty is twenty-one; Eveline, nineteen), religious, impoverished, and ill educated, who fears the passing of time (Eveline's "time was running out" [*Dubliners* 39]; "Gerty would never see seventeen again" [*Ulysses* 288]). Moreover, each comes from a home in which the mother is absent and the father (who refuses to give his daughter her freedom) is frequently violent and intoxicated. He is unemployed and manipulative and has his daughter do the household chores. In each case there is little chance of escaping from this state of affairs, yet each conjures an escape fantasy — centered around males — to mask the paralyzing hopelessness of her situation: for Eveline it is Frank who will save her ("Escape! She must escape! Frank would save her" [40]); for Gerty it is "the dark stranger" (Bloom) who will alleviate her discontent. Finally, both Gerty's and Eveline's predicaments are glimpsed by twilight. In each case the seated Dubliner witnesses the arrival of evening and the dimming of hopes.

10 For more on the relation between Gerty's discourse and her predicament, see Richards, and Norris, "Modernism." These two culturally oriented approaches nicely complement Joyce's familiar description of the style of "Nausicaa" — that it is "written in a namby-pamby jammy marmalady drawersy (alto-là!) style" (*Letters*, I, 135) — as well as Hugh Kenner's ingenious formulation of "The Uncle Charles Principle" (15–38) at work in Joyce's texts.

11 In "Clay" Maria too stands "before the mirror" and looks "with quaint affection at the diminutive body which she had so often adorned.... [S]he found it a nice tidy little body" (*Dubliners* 101). Craig Werner aptly notes of this story that, "implicitly commenting on the absence of real communication in spoken language, Joyce transforms conversation into internal monologue, emphasizing his characters' self-absorption" (44). For a masterful reading of "Clay," see Norris, "Narration under a Blindfold."

12 Gerty's boundless conventionality has led Suzette Henke to note correctly that Gerty is "a pawn of social self-definition," the "pathetic victim of social and religious enculturation," and, hence, that "Nausicaa" is in fact directed "less against Gerty than against the manipulative society of which she is a product" (147, 132, 134).

13 For Hélène Cixous, Little Chandler "suffers, as do all Joyce's Dubliners, from a sickness which acts as the unifying theme of the fifteen stories, paralysis" (89).

14 For more on this, see Herring, *Uncertainty Principle* 55, and Ghiselin 327.

15   In his essay, "Ireland, Island of Saints and Sages," Joyce seems to agree with Chandler: "No one who has any self-respect stays in Ireland," he writes, "but flees afar as though from a country that has undergone the visitation of an angered Jove" (171).

16   This idea is also reflected in Joyce's "After the Race," in which the Dublin "sightseers," who gather "in clumps to watch the cars" race homeward, are described as raising "the cheers of the gratefully oppressed": "through this channel of poverty and inaction the Continent sped its wealth and industry" (*Dubliners* 42).

17   Many other male subjects in *Dubliners* suffer from the narcissism of minor differences. Consider the unnamed protagonist of "Araby" ("I imagined that I bore my chalice safely through a throng of foes" [31]), the protagonist of "A Painful Case" ("Mr. James Duffy lived in Chapelizod because he wished to live as far as possible from the city of which he was a citizen and because he found all the other suburbs of Dublin mean, modern and pretentious" [107]), and the most discussed character in *Dubliners*, Gabriel Conroy from "The Dead." He more than anyone is depicted as completely absorbed in the little differences — of language, gesture, education, gender, and class — that separate him from the flock: "The indelicate clacking of the men's heels and the shuffling of their soles reminded [Gabriel] that their grade of culture differed from his" (179).

18   I am indebted to R. B. Kershner for encouraging me to think of *Dialectic of Enlightenment* in connection with *Ulysses*. In his masterful *Joyce, Bakhtin, and Popular Literature*, Kershner points out that the work of Adorno and Horkheimer, "in analyzing the paradigms of bourgeois culture[,] has sensitized the modern reader to the varieties of social rationalization that permeate" so many strata of literature (11). For more on the *Ulysses–Dialectic of Enlightenment* connection, see Knapp 141–43.

19   See Jay 86–112, for a discussion of the influence of psychoanalysis on Frankfurt School thinking.

20   For more on the Freud–Adorno/Horkheimer connection, see Adorno, "Freudian Theory," and Lunn 234–36. In "Sociology and Psychology," Adorno goes as far as to number Freud's "introduction of the concept of narcissism" into psychoanalysis among his "most magnificent discoveries" (88).

21   Phillip Herring convincingly links these two episodes by arguing that "structurally and thematically, Lotuseaters points unwaveringly towards the Nausicaa episode" ("Lotus-eaters" 83).

22   See, for example, Henke; Herr, *Anatomy;* Richards; and Wicke. Wicke most recently and thoroughly argues for the significance of viewing *Ulysses* as a "narrative in a culture being expressed, furthered, and masked by a new literature with no discernible author and no particular reader — advertising" (121).

23   For Richard Ellmann, *Ulysses* suggests that "narcissism and cruelty over sentimentality equal religion," and that "self-mutilation, like religious self-denial and penance, is a perverse pleasure, a form of narcissism" (44–45). And for Frank Budgen, advertisement in *Ulysses* is a "drug" because "it flattens and numbs till the victim walks meekly to the sales counter" (82).

24   In this essay Joyce also mocks "the much-trumpeted progress of this century," complaining that it "consists largely of a heap of machines the very purpose of which is to gather in haste and fury the scattered elements of utility and knowledge and to redistribute them to each member of the collectivity who is in a position to pay a slight tax" ("Universal Literary Influence" 19).

25   See, for example, Devlin; Henke; Herr, *Anatomy;* and Norris, "Modernism."

26   In this connection, the "technic" of Bloom's "Lotuseaters" episode is "narcissism," and in "Ithaca" Bloom is said to possess a plaster "statue of Narcissus, sound without echo, desired desire" (*Ulysses* 599), an "image of Narcissus purchased by auction" (583). Freud's 1908 paper, "'Civilized' Sexual Morality and Modern Nervousness," sheds additional light on Bloom's relation to Gerty and Martha. As Richard Wolheim puts it succinctly of Freud's ideas in this paper, "Contemporary sexual morality . . . rested upon a combination of repression and frustration, and, in so far as repression failed or frustration proved excessive, it gave rise to two characteristic practices — both of which Freud thought baneful — by which it was at once maintained and evaded: prostitution and masturbation" (223).

27   For an insightful discussion of Joyce's politics in "Cyclops," see Cixous 241–63.

28   See Arendt 3–120 for a sense of the centrality of anti-Semitism in modern European political culture.

29   In *Barbarians Within and Without*, Leonard Woolf ingeniously touches on this phenomenon: "The barbarian is . . . not only at our gates; he is always within the walls of our civilization, inside our minds and our hearts. In times of storm and stress within any society, his appeal is very strong. He offers immediate satisfaction of the simple instincts, love, hatred, and anger. He offers to help us to forget our own unhappiness by making other people still more unhappy. He shows us how we may forget our sense of frustration and the intolerable burden of responsibility in blind obedience. . . . He gives us the simple satisfaction of violence and destruction, the destruction of society, of the complicated network of rules and regulations, standards and morality which constitute civilization and which all of us feel entangling, frustrating, choking our animal instincts and desires" (65–66).

30   As Cheryl Herr puts the relationship between style and subjectivity in Joyce's fiction, "One of the things that Joyce's insistent alluding makes clear is that thinking, the streaming of consciousness, the content of interior monologue, the very shape of the self are woven from the materials of one's culture ("Art and Life" 25).

✳ 6   The Sense of an Ending

1   In 1929, for example, Wyndham Lewis would refer to "the Europe of spenglerism" (123); and in 1940 F. Scott Fitzgerald would deem Spengler's ideas the "dominant supercessive" ones of the coming age (quoted in George Watson 108). It is reported that 90,000 copies of Spengler's *Decline of the West* were in print by 1926, and that by 1955 this number had soared to 140,000 (translator's preface ix; Werner xxi). Spengler's magnum opus, social theorist Pitirim Sorokin writes, "has proved to be one of the most influential, controversial, and durable masterpieces of the first half of the twentieth century in the fields of social science, philosophy of history, and German philosophy. It catapulted an unknown high-school teacher into the ranks of the century's most influential social thinkers" (72).

2   As early as 1927, for example, philosopher/historian R. G. Collingwood attacked *The Decline of the West* as "lacking in orientation," "unsound on fundamentals," "ill-thought-out," and "committed to the methodical falsification of facts" ("Oswald Spengler" 322). For accounts of Spengler's reception in Germany, see the translator's preface to *The Decline* ix–xi, and Hughes 89–97. Spengler responds to critics of *The Decline of the West* in his "Pessimism?" essay.

3   See, for example, Northrop Frye's 1974 reconsideration of *The Decline of the West*, in which he demonstrates the impact of Spengler on such major figures of literary modernism as Eliot, Yeats, Pound, Lewis, and Auden. Also see McDiarmid xii and 3, for a brief discussion of the Spenglerian aspects of Yeats, Eliot, and Auden between the wars. And George Watson (99–100 and 104) notes Spengler's influence on such disparate figures as D. H. Lawrence, F. Scott Fitzgerald, and Arnold Toynbee.

4   See, for example, White, *The Content of Form: Narrative Discourse and Historical Representation*.

5   In *Selected Essays* Spengler comments scathingly on progressivist theories like Spencer's: "I see no progress, no goal, no avenue for humanity," he writes, "except in the heads of the Western progress-Philistines" (quoted in Sunic 60).

6   Douglas Day, for example, speaks of *Under the Volcano* as "the greatest religious novel of this century (350); and Scott Sanders calls *The Plumed Serpent* a "religious romance" (138). Along these lines, an original reviewer of Lawrence's novel identified it as "an intensely religious book" (Draper 263).

7   We read there, "by the time the *Untergang des Abendlands* [*sic*] appeared, Clifford was a smashed man" (quoted in Martz 118). In the final version of *Lady Chatterley's Lover* Spengler is not directly invoked but is everywhere felt. At one point in the novel, for example, Tommy Dukes insists that "our civilization is going to fall. It's going down the bottomless pit, down the chasm," to which Aunt Eva responds, "I believe our civilization is going to collapse" (116).

8   In *Paleface*, Wyndham Lewis devotes part of a chapter to his thesis that Lawrence is "a follower of the Bergson–Spengler school." For other brief references to the Lawrence–Spengler connection, see Delavenay 453–55; George H. Ford 174; Hochman 218; Leavis, "D. H. Lawrence" 138–41; Sanders 94; and George Watson 99–100. Mitzi M. Brunsdale notes Lawrence's "demonstrable interest in German literature and philosophy" (5), and Emile Delavenay maintains that as early as 1917 Lawrence's philosophy "was evolving in close sympathy with the Germans of the day" (454). In *D. H. Lawrence and German Literature* Armin Arnold notes that Lawrence studied German in high school and at the University of Nottingham, and that by 1912 his German "was quite good although far from correct grammatically." "He had not much difficulty in reading or speaking the language," Arnold continues; "[H]e had a rich vocabulary, if little formal background" (33–34). And for Ford Madox Ford in *Return to Yesterday*, according to Arnold, "Lawrence was a well-read German scholar who had absorbed Nietzsche, Marx, and Wagner as his daily breakfast" (33).

9   For other brief references to the Lowry–Spengler connection, see Ackerley and Clipper, notes 104.5, 105.9, and 311.4; Cripps 98; Kilgallin, *Lowry* 207 and Appendix B; Kilgallin, "Faust" 31–34; and Markson 150.

10 In German, *Kultur* and *Zivilisation*. Interestingly, Spengler's distinction here derives from Nietzsche in *The Will To Power*: "*Culture contra Civilization* . . . one should not be deceived about the abysmal antagonism of culture and civilization." The "means of civilization," Nietzsche then writes, "which lead to disintegration and necessarily to decadence, should not be confused with culture" (75). Spengler claimed that Nietzsche (because of his "questioning faculty") and Goethe (because of his "method") were his two mentors.

11 For helpful contextualizations of *The Decline of the West*, see Brantlinger, *Bread and Circuses* 222–27 (the Frankfurt School); Iggers 229–68 (German historiography); Levi 102–48 (Toynbee and the philosophy of history); MacMaster (Danilevsky and cyclical

theories of civilization); Mazlish 307–50 (Western European historiography); Sorokin 72–112 (modern social theory); and Sunic (Spengler today).

12 Interestingly, L. D. Clark also discusses the cyclical symbolism of Joyce's *Finnegans Wake*, Yeats's later poetry, and Eliot's *Four Quartets* (129), each of which clearly incorporates *The Decline* in some way.

13 I have used the Modern Library translation of this sentence. In Atkinson's original translation the word "exhaustion" reads "taking-down," which is far less clear.

14 J. Barry has noticed that both Spengler and Lawrence pit "the over-intellectualized self . . . against the instinctive self" (158). Interestingly, David Daiches describes Lawrence's outlook in terms uncannily Spenglerian: "[A]s he confronted modern civilization," Daiches writes, Lawrence "was driven desperate; he saw too clearly its deficiencies, its terrible mechanizing of personality, its denial of the deeper reaches of emotional experience in favor of brittle intellectualism" (151).

15 It is probably no coincidence that Maximilian, the unpopular Austrian emperor of Mexico from 1864 to 1867, also had a wife named Carlota who, before Maximilian's execution by Juarez's forces, returned to Europe (and eventually died insane).

16 Strangely, the marriage of Kate and Cipriano would seem to contradict this thesis.

17 Also worth noting are the numerous allusions to *The Plumed Serpent* in *Under the Volcano*. For example, both novels make frequent references to scorpions, bougainvillea, the Rivera frescoes, volcanoes, and to the Mexican law forbidding anyone from aiding an injured person under penalty of being accused of causing the injury itself. Both novels speak of Mexico as "hopeless," "doomed," and "deadly." And Kate's perceptions of Mexico clearly presage Geoffrey's: "The country gave [Kate] a strange feeling of hopelessness and of dauntlessness. Unbroken, eternally resistant, it was a people that lived without hope, and without care. Gay even, and laughing with indifferent carelessness" (*Plumed Serpent* 76). Also foreshadowing Geoffrey, Kate is depicted as one who "could not escape from Mexico" (204). David Markson argues that Lowry's novel works "in the inescapable shadow of *The Plumed Serpent*" (162); Tony Kilgallin reports that Lowry read *The Plumed Serpent* and found it "pretty dreadful" (*Lowry* 160); and one Mexican historian likens the fascist Sinarchistas in *Under the Volcano* to "a page torn from Lawrence's *Plumed Serpent*" (quoted in Ackerley and Clipper 257). Ackerley and Clipper argue that Lowry's "overblown, transparently jaunty prose" during the bullfight scene of *Under the Volcano* "seems to be in direct imitation" of D. H. Lawrence's bullfight scenes in *The Plumed Serpent* (323). For more on the Lawrence–Lowry Mexican connection, see Veitch, and Ronald G. Walker.

18 The novel's most dramatic adumbration of the Second World War and the Holocaust of European Jewry comes on its last page: "[T]he world itself was bursting, bursting into black spouts of villages catapulted into space, with himself [Geoffrey] falling through it all, through the inconceivable pandemonium of a million tanks, through the blazing of ten million burning bodies, falling" (*Under the Volcano* 375).

19 Lowry apparently found Spengler's theory more convincing than Yeats's, for he complains in a letter about "*The Vision*" (*sic*): "I got so that I could make just one cone work" (250).

20 In Chapter 7 I explore Geoffrey's narcissism and the novel's representation of a narcissistically diseased civilization.

21 Of course, this is also one of the central problems posed by *The Plumed Serpent*.

22 For more on Lawrence and primitivism, see Ruthven, and Torgovnick, *Gone Primitive* 159–74.

23 This has been done most thoroughly by L. D. Clark in *Dark Night of the Body*.

24 Think, for example, of works by Thomas Mann, Oscar Wilde, and W. B. Yeats, not to mention G. E. Moore's philosophic attempts in *Principia Ethica* to reconcile these opposed categories. Yeats's "Choice," for example — which begins: "The intellect of man is forced to choose / Perfection of the life, or of the work, / And if it take the second must refuse / A heavenly mansion, raging in the dark" (*Collected Poems* 242) — makes this tension explicit. Here, as in Lowry's high modernist tragedy, the Flaubertian allure of a perfectible *objet d'art* is opposed to a world hopelessly in disrepair.

25 Although Jonathan Arac fruitfully explores the "carnivalesque" aspects of *Under the Volcano*, employing "Bakhtin's help to describe the 'nuts and bolts' that fit together to make the book, for all its copious variety, go around in one smooth circle in a carnival path of loss and return" (488), it remains to explore the nature and function of dialogism and polyphony as a means of grasping Lowry's transformation of *The Decline of the West*, by which this totalizing "encyclopedia" is rendered a narrow polemic.

26 Bakhtin would not find Lawrence's novel to be polyphonic, as Lawrence's authorial voice overpowers all others. We are not "supposed" to question Quetzalcoatl once Kate has accepted it as her creed, for example. On the other hand, Bakhtin would regard the *Volcano* to be a novel in that it appropriates and transforms other texts, *The Decline of the West* among them.

27 Indeed, Spengler views socialism to be no less than the West's "*own mode of spiritual extinction*," an "end-phenomenon" that is "completely misunderstood even by its exponents, who present it as a sum of rights instead of as one of duties" (*The Decline* I, 356, 351). "Socialist Nirvana," Spengler continues, "has its justification insofar that European weariness covers its flight from the struggle for existence under catchwords of world-peace, Humanity and brotherhood of Man" (I, 357).

28 Michael Cripps argues that this exchange "brings into clear focus their apparently antithetical attitudes to the political struggles of the 1930s, and to the question of political action in general" (85). But whereas Cripps concludes that Geoffrey and Hugh "enact different strategies by which the 'imperial self' pursues its manifest destiny" (86), I believe that *Under the Volcano* deflates *The Decline* by placing it within a larger dialogue about the course of civilization.

29 In *The Modes of Modern Writing* David Lodge aptly notes that Lawrence's "narrative voice, however much it varies in tone . . . and whatever character's consciousness it is rendering, is always basically the same, unmistakably Lawrentian." "Not for him," Lodge continues, "the mimicry, the pastiche, the rapid shifts of voice and linguistic register, that we encounter in Joyce or Eliot" (quoted in Lodge, "Lawrence, Dostoevsky, Bakhtin" 20).

✳ 7 The Subject of Civilization

1 See Kilgallin, "Faust," for a superior general overview of the relationship of *Under the Volcano* to various Faust narratives.

2 See Chapter 1 for an analysis of this tradition in conceptualizing civilization.

3 Lowry himself admits that he did "everything short of giving" Geoffrey two heads "to make him non-autobiographical in the usual sense" ("Work in Progress" 77).

4 The only other references to narcissism in Lowry criticism are passing ones: Daniel B. Dodson relates the Consul's "psychic arrestment resulting in narcissistic containment" to

his guilt and self-destruction (26); and Ronald Binns writes that "Yvonne's indifference to political reality is symptomatic of her narcissism" (49). Another aspect of the novel's narcissism is what might be called its "structural narrative narcissism": the work's formal self-referentiality or metafictionality. Binns, for example, writes that self-absorption "is the very condition of the text itself. *Under the Volcano* is curiously self-regarding, both physically, as a book, and as a fiction" (52). Indeed, in everything from the text's narrative circularity (with chapter 1, as Richard K. Cross writes, serving as the book's "overture and coda" [27]) and internal monologue narration (in which we are for the most part restricted to the consciousness of one or another of the novel's quartet of main characters) to the text's "spatial form" and dense literary and self-allusiveness, *Under the Volcano* continually calls attention to its quality as a structurally narcissistic narrative. Victor Sage also takes this tack, arguing that "Lowry's book is a pre-eminently narcissistic text, implying, in its very texture, a running description of its own nature as 'epic' and 'tragic,'" and that its "language is a farrago of narcissism" (38, 35). For two general discussions of this issue, see Hutcheon 17–35, and Zweig 265–68.

5   James Hillman identifies the chthonic elements of the Narcissus myth as moisture, narcotic drowsiness, death, and "the signal importance given to the *image*, which takes one into the depths" (222). The chthonic aspects of Lowry's Cuernavaca are easy to discern. Transpiring on two consecutive "Days of the Dead" (2 November 1938 and 2 November 1939), *Under the Volcano* is pervaded with images of the infernal in which death and life intermingle. For more on this, see Day's discussion of the "chthonic level" of the novel (327–32).

6   Lowry's novel mirrors Ovid's story in yet two other ways. Just as there were "others," "young men also," "on whom Narcissus / Had visited frustration" (Ovid 69), so too Hugh and Dr. Arturo Díaz Vigil exhibit a captivation with the Consul. Even Jacques feels the pull of this man, remembering how in youth he "had felt oddly attracted to him" (*Under the Volcano* 16). Geoffrey himself views his influence on Laruelle as having been "enormous" and "all-permeating" (210). Additionally, both works are "viewed" from the perspective of foreknowledge: the myth from the standpoint of Tiresias's prophecy, and the novel from the standpoint of Vigil and Laruelle a year later. In many literary appropriations of this myth subsequent to Ovid's, Narcissus drowns by falling into the pool that reflects his image. These later versions also resonate with Lowry's story of one who literally drinks himself into oblivion.

7   For discussions of this tradition's successes and failures, see Alexander, and Fromm.

8   Binns 45, Cripps 93, and Cross 51 discuss the means by which *Under the Volcano* intentionally prefigures the genesis, significance, and outcome of World War II. It is certainly intentional that the Consul's murder-suicide coincides with World War II and its widespread destruction.

9   Jeffrey Berman writes of the connection between Ovid's and Freud's versions of Narcissus: "A love story fraught with disturbing ironies and paradoxes, Ovid's myth of Echo and Narcissus contains the psychological complexity of a Freudian case study" and "contains ideas that are as old as the ancient Greeks and as modern as the latest clinical research" (5, 8).

10 This is one reason why I consider Joyce with Freud, and Lowry with Kohut and Kernberg.

11 In *The Analysis of the Self* (1971) and *The Restoration of the Self* (1977), Kohut posits his "Psychology of the Self" (rejecting both Freud's structural theory and object relations

psychology), which argues that pathological narcissism and normal narcissism exist together on a continuum. For Kohut, it is necessary to maintain viable "selfobjects" and channels of empathy in infancy and throughout life. In *Borderline Conditions and Pathological Narcissism* (1975), Kernberg posits his "ego psychological object relations theory," which holds that narcissism constitutes its own distinct pathology and unique organization. Kernberg employs the terminology of Freud's structural theory and hence is closer in spirit to traditional psychoanalysis. See Alford 43–50 and Berman 20–35 for superior short discussions of Kohut's and Kernberg's points of intersection and divergence. Also see Bouson 11–29 for a discussion of Kohut and the process of reading.

12   Among the most prevalent of these explanations is that the Consul's alcoholism, like most of his traits, is autobiographical, mirroring the author's own addiction and guilt. In one place, for example, Lowry refers to *Under the Volcano* as "a satire upon myself" (*Selected Letters* 144) and, in another, as "an authentic drunkard's story" ("Preface to a Novel" 15). Nevertheless, the reasons behind Geoffrey's (and Lowry's) dipsomania are not completely addressed by such claims and demand further investigation.

13   Along these lines, Sue Vice has recently noted Geoffrey's "oscillation between being (narcissistically) hyper-aware of [himself] and turning to self-obliteration" (100).

14   For a fascinating discussion of Yvonne's role in Geoffrey's alcohol addiction, see MacGregor.

15   Regardless of its controversiality, Edward Engelberg views the popularity itself of *The Culture of Narcissism* to be telling. "What this suggests," he writes, is that "in this century narcissism has generated a great deal of interest, has become a perspective from which modern cultural behavior is being evaluated, and even when presented on a more popular, less clinical level as in Lasch's book has attracted millions of readers whether they see self-love as a palliative to our modern anxieties or as a destructive element to an ever-increasing cultural worship-ritual of the self" (27).

16   Jeffrey Berman perceives a strong link between Lasch's work and Kohut's, Kernberg's, and Freud's and argues that *The Culture of Narcissism* "generalizes Ovid's myth into a social and cultural phenomenon" (3).

17   I will not rehearse the debate that has raged around Lasch's study except to mention that it generally has been praised for its critique of twentieth-century capitalist culture while being criticized for upholding the nineteenth-century nuclear family as an ideal against which today's family should be judged. For more on this debate, see Diggins and Kann, and the symposium devoted to Lasch's study in *Salmagundi*.

18   Notice how close Lasch at times comes to Spengler. In a recent essay Tomislav Sunic discusses Spengler in terms reminiscent of Lasch: "Indeed," he writes, "who could have predicted that a society capable of launching rockets to the moon or curing diseases that once ravaged the world could also become a civilization plagued by social atomization, crime, and addiction to escapism?" (55).

19   There is some critical precedent for viewing Dana as an early version of Hugh. Tony Bareham, for example, argues that Hugh "resembles Hilliot more than Geoffrey himself" (34). And Margerie Lowry notes that Malcolm "changed the name of [Dana's] ship from *Nawab* to *Oedipus Tyrannus*, to conform with Hugh's ship in *Under the Volcano*" (9).

20   Stephen Tifft is correct to point out that "at times the Consul is so critically aware of his fictions that he will puncture his own tragic rhetoric with a comic self-irony that is quite charming and humanizing" (68).

Works Cited

Achebe, Chinua. "An Image of Africa." *Chant of Saints: A Gathering of Afro-American Literature, Art, and Scholarship* 313–25. Ed. Michael S. Harper and Robert B. Stepto. Urbana: U of Illinois P, 1979.

Ackerley, Chris, and Lawrence J. Clipper. *A Companion to "Under the Volcano."* Vancouver: U of British Columbia P, 1984.

Adams, Brooks. *The Law of Civilization and Decay: An Essay on History.* New York: Macmillan, 1896.

Adorno, Theodor W. *Aesthetic Theory.* Ed. Gretel Adorno and Rolf Tiedemann. London: Routledge & Kegan Paul, 1984.

Adorno, Theodor W. "Culture Industry Reconsidered." *New German Critique* 6 (1975): 12–19.

Adorno, Theodor W. "Freudian Theory and the Pattern of Fascist Propaganda." *The Essential Frankfurt School Reader* 118–37. Ed. Andrew Arato and Eike Gebhardt. New York: Continuum, 1982.

Adorno, Theodor. "Sociology and Psychology." *New Left Review* 46 (1967): 67–80, and 47 (1968): 79–91.

Adorno, Theodor. "Spengler after the Decline." *Prisms* 53–72. Cambridge: MIT Press, 1981.

Alexander, Jeffrey C., et al., eds. *The Micro-Macro Link.* Berkeley: U of California P, 1987.

Alford, C. Fred. *Narcissism: Socrates, the Frankfurt School, and Psychoanalytic Theory.* New Haven: Yale UP, 1988.

Allier, Raoul. *The Mind of the Savage.* London: G. Bell and Sons, 1929.

Anderson, Chester. "Leopold Bloom as Dr. Sigmund Freud." *Mosaic* 6 (1972): 23–43.

Arac, Jonathan. "The Form of Carnival in *Under the Volcano.*" *PMLA* 92 (1977): 481–89.

Arendt, Hannah. *The Origins of Totalitarianism.* New York: Harcourt Brace Jovanovich, 1973.

Arnold, Armin. *D. H. Lawrence and German Literature.* Montreal: H. Heinemann, 1963.

Arnold, Matthew. *Culture and Anarchy.* 1869. Cambridge: Cambridge UP, 1960.

Ashley, Roscoe Lewis. *Our Contemporary Civilization: A Study of the Twentieth Century Renaissance.* New York: Henry Holt, 1935.

Bachelard, Gaston. *Water and Dreams: An Essay on the Imagination of Matter.* Dallas: Pegasus Foundation, 1983.

Bagby, Philip. *Culture and History: Prolegomena to the Comparative Study of Civilizations.* London: Longmans Green, 1958.

Bakhtin, M. M. *The Dialogic Imagination: Four Essays.* Austin: U of Texas P, 1981.

Bakhtin, M. M. "Discourse in the Novel." *The Dialogic Imagination* 259–422.

Bakhtin, M. M. "Epic and Novel." *The Dialogic Imagination* 3–40.

Bakhtin, M. M. "From Notes Made in 1970–71." *Speech Genres* 132–58.

Bakhtin, M. M. "The Problem of Speech Genres." *Speech Genres* 60–102.

Bakhtin, M. M. "The Problem of the Text." *Speech Genres* 103–31.

Bakhtin, Mikhail. *Problems of Dostoyevsky's Poetics.* Minneapolis: U of Minnesota P, 1984.

Bakhtin, M. M. "Response to a Question from the *Novy Mir* Editorial Staff." *Speech Genres* 1–9.

Bakhtin, M. M. *Speech Genres and Other Late Essays.* Ed. Caryl Emerson and Michael Holquist. Austin: U of Texas P, 1986.

Bakhtin, M. M. "Toward a Methodology for the Human Sciences." *Speech Genres* 159–72.

Bareham, Tony. *Malcolm Lowry.* New York: St. Martin's Press, 1989.

Barry, J. "Oswald Spengler and D. H. Lawrence." *English Studies in Africa* 12 (1969): 151–61.

Beckerath, Herbert von. *In Defense of the West: A Political and Economic Study.* Durham: Duke UP, 1942.

Bell, Clive. *Art.* New York: Capricorn, 1958.

Bell, Clive. *On British Freedom.* New York: Harcourt Brace, 1923.

Bell, Clive. *Civilization and Old Friends.* Two vols. in one. Chicago: U of Chicago P, 1973.

Bell, Clive. *Pot-Boilers.* London: Chatto & Windus, 1918.

Bell, Quentin. *Bloomsbury.* New York: Basic Books, 1968.

Bell, Quentin. *Virginia Woolf: A Biography.* Two vols. in one. New York: Harcourt Brace, 1972.

Bender, Todd K. *A Concordance to Conrad's "Heart of Darkness."* New York: Garland, 1979.

Bennett, Arnold. *The Journal of Arnold Bennett.* New York: Viking, 1933.

Bennett, Tony. *Formalism and Marxism.* London: Methuen, 1979.

Benstock, Bernard. *James Joyce.* New York: Frederick Ungar, 1985.

Bergonzi, Bernard. *The Early H. G. Wells: A Study of the Scientific Romances.* Toronto: U of Toronto P, 1961.

Berman, Jeffrey. *Narcissism and the Novel.* New York: New York UP, 1990.

Bialostosky, Don H. "Dialogics as an Art of Discourse in Literary Criticism." *PMLA* 101 (1986): 788–97.

Bicknell, John W. "Mr. Ramsay Was Young Once." *Virginia Woolf and Bloomsbury: A Centenary Celebration* 52–67. Ed. Jane Marcus. Bloomington: Indiana UP, 1987.

Bierstedt, Robert. *Power and Progress: Essays on Sociological Theory.* New York: McGraw-Hill, 1974.

Binns, Ronald. *Malcolm Lowry.* London: Methuen, 1984.

Black, Naomi. "Virginia Woolf and the Women's Movement." *Virginia Woolf: A Feminist Slant* 180–97. Ed. Jane Marcus. Lincoln: U of Nebraska P, 1983.

Bonheim, Helmut. *Joyce's Benefictions.* Berkeley: U of California P, 1964.

Bouson, J. Brooks. *The Empathic Reader: A Study of the Narcissistic Character and the Drama of the Self.* Amherst: U of Massachusetts P, 1989.

Boyle, Robert. "A Little Cloud." *James Joyce's "Dubliners": Critical Essays* 84–92. Ed. Clive Hart. New York: Viking, 1969.

Bradbury, Harriet B. *Civilization and Womanhood.* Boston: Richard G. Badger, 1916.

Brantlinger, Patrick. *Bread and Circuses: Theories of Mass Culture as Social Decay.* Ithaca: Cornell UP, 1983.

Brantlinger, Patrick. *Rule of Darkness: British Literature and Imperialism, 1830–1914.* Ithaca: Cornell UP, 1988.

Brivic, Sheldon. *Joyce between Freud and Jung.* Port Washington, NY: Kennikat Press, 1980.

Bruns, Gerald. *Modern Poetry and the Idea of Language: A Critical and Historical Study.* New Haven: Yale UP, 1974.

Brunsdale, Mitzi M. *The German Effect on D. H. Lawrence and His Works, 1885–1912.* Bern: Peter Lang, 1978.

Budgen, Frank. *James Joyce and the Making of "Ulysses."* Bloomington: Indiana UP, 1960.

Buitenhuis, Peter. *The Great War of Words: British, American, and Canadian Propaganda and Fiction, 1914–1933.* Vancouver: U of British Columbia P, 1987.

Bywater, William G. *Clive Bell's Eye.* Detroit: Wayne State UP, 1975.

Caillois, Roger. *Man, Play, and Games.* Glencoe, IL: Free Press, 1961.

Carneiro, Robert L. Introduction. *The Evolution of Society: Selections from Herbert Spencer's "Principles of Sociology"* ix–lvii. Chicago: U of Chicago P, 1967.

Carpenter, Edward. *Civilisation: Its Cause and Cure, and Other Essays.* 1889. London: Allen & Unwin, 1916.

Casson, Stanley. *Progress and Catastrophe: An Anatomy of Human Adventure.* New York: Harper and Brothers, 1937.

Chambers Etymological English Dictionary. 1912. New York: Pyramid Books, 1968.

Chessick, Richard D. *Psychology of the Self and the Treatment of Narcissism.* Northvale, NJ: Jason Aronson, 1985.

Cixous, Hélène. *The Exile of James Joyce.* New York: David Lewis, 1972.

Clark, Katerina, and Michael Holquist. *Mikhail Bakhtin.* Cambridge: Harvard UP, 1984.

Clark, L. D. *Dark Night of the Body: D. H. Lawrence's "The Plumed Serpent."* Austin: U of Texas P, 1964.

Coit, Stanton. *Is Civilization a Disease?* Boston: Houghton Mifflin, 1917.

Collingwood, R. G. *The New Leviathan; or, Man, Society, Civilization, and Barbarism.* Oxford: Oxford UP, 1942.

Collingwood, R. G. "Oswald Spengler and the Theory of Historical Cycles." *Antiquity* 1 (1927): 311–25.

Conrad, Joseph. "Author's Note to *Almayer's Folly.*" Wright 159–60.

Conrad, Joseph. "Author's Note to *The Nigger of the 'Narcissus.'*" Wright 160–64.

Conrad, Joseph. "Author's Note to *The Secret Agent.*" *The Secret Agent* 3–8.

Conrad, Joseph. "Author's Note to *Youth.*" *Heart of Darkness* 3–5.

Conrad, Joseph. "Autocracy and War." *Notes on Life and Letters* 83–114.

Conrad, Joseph. "Books." *Notes on Life and Letters* 3–10.

Conrad, Joseph. *The Collected Letters.* 4 vols. (to date). Ed. Frederick R. Karl and Laurence Davies. Cambridge: Cambridge UP, 1983, 1986, 1988, 1990.

Conrad, Joseph. *Congo Diary and Other Uncollected Pieces.* Ed. Zdzislaw Najder. Garden City, NY: Doubleday, 1978.

Conrad, Joseph. "The Crime of Partition." *Notes on Life and Letters* 115–33.

Conrad, Joseph. *Heart of Darkness*. Ed. Robert Kimbrough. 3rd ed. New York: Norton, 1988.

Conrad, Joseph. *Lord Jim*. Ed. Thomas C. Moser. New York: Norton, 1968.

Conrad, Joseph. *The Mirror of the Sea*. 1906. Marlboro, VT: Marlboro Press, 1988.

Conrad, Joseph. *Notes on Life and Letters*. Garden City, NY: Doubleday, 1921.

Conrad, Joseph. "An Outpost of Progress." *Tales of Unrest* 86–117. Garden City, NY: Doubleday, 1925.

Conrad, Joseph. *A Personal Record*. 1912. Marlboro, VT: Marlboro Press, 1982.

Conrad, Joseph. "Poland Revisited." *Notes on Life and Letters* 141–73.

Conrad, Joseph. *The Secret Agent: A Simple Tale*. Ed. Bruce Harkness and S. W. Reid. Cambridge: Cambridge UP, 1990.

Conrad, Joseph. "Travel." *Last Essays* 84–92. Garden City, NY: Doubleday, 1926.

Conrad, Joseph. *Victory*. 1915. Garden City, NY: Doubleday, 1957.

Conroy, Mark. *Modernism and Authority: Strategies of Legitimation in Flaubert and Conrad*. Baltimore: Johns Hopkins UP, 1985.

Costa, Richard Hauer. *Malcolm Lowry*. New York: Twayne, 1972.

Cripps, Michael. "*Under the Volcano:* The Politics of the Imperial Self." *Canadian Literature* 95 (1982): 85–101.

Cross, Richard K. *Malcolm Lowry: A Preface to His Fiction*. Chicago: U of Chicago P, 1980.

Crozier, John Beattie. *Civilization and Progress*. 4th ed. London: Longmans Green, 1898.

Daiches, David. *The Novel and the Modern World*. Chicago: U of Chicago P, 1960.

Darras, Jacques. *Joseph Conrad and the West: Signs of Empire*. London: Macmillan, 1982.

Darwin, Charles. *The Origin of Species and The Descent of Man*. New York: Modern Library, 1936.

Day, Douglas. *Malcolm Lowry: A Biography*. 1973. New York: Oxford UP, 1984.

Delavenay, Emile. *D. H. Lawrence, the Man and His Work: The Formative Years, 1885–1919*. Carbondale: Southern Illinois UP, 1972.

DeSalvo, Louise A. *Virginia Woolf's First Voyage: A Novel in the Making*. Totowa, NJ: Rowman & Littlefield, 1980.

DeSalvo, Louise A. *Virginia Woolf: The Impact of Childhood Sexual Abuse on Her Life and Work*. Boston: Beacon Press, 1989.

Devlin, Kimberly J. "The Female Eye: Joyce's Voyeuristic Narcissists." *New Alliances in Joyce Studies* 135–43. Ed. Bonnie Kime Scott. Newark: U of Delaware P, 1988.

Dewey, John. *Art as Experience*. New York: Perigee, 1934.

Dewey, John. "Interpretation of the Savage Mind." *Philosophy and Civilization* 173–87. Gloucester, MA: Peter Smith, 1968.

Diamond, Stanley. *In Search of the Primitive: A Critique of Civilization*. New Brunswick, NJ: Transaction Books, 1974.

Diggins, John P., and Mark E. Kann, eds., *The Problem of Authority in America*. Philadelphia: Temple UP, 1981.

Dodson, Daniel B. *Malcolm Lowry*. New York: Columbia UP, 1970.

Douglas, Sholto. *A Theory of Civilisation*. New York: Macmillan, 1914.

Dowling, David. *Bloomsbury Aesthetics and the Novels of Forster and Woolf*. New York: St. Martin's Press, 1985.

Draper, R. P., ed. *D. H. Lawrence: The Critical Heritage*. New York: Barnes & Noble, 1970.

Durant, Will. *The Story of Philosophy*. 1926. New York: Simon & Schuster, 1933.

Eagleton, Terry. "Bakhtin, Schopenhauer, Kundera." Hirschkop and Shepherd 178–88.

Eagleton, Terry. *Criticism and Ideology: A Study in Marxist Literary Theory*. London: Verso, 1978.

Eagleton, Terry. "The End of English." *Textual Practice* 1 (1987): 1–9.

Eagleton, Terry. *Exiles and Emigrés: Studies in Modern Literature*. New York: Schocken Books, 1970.

Eagleton, Terry. "Form, Ideology, and *The Secret Agent*." *Against the Grain: Selected Essays* 23–32. London: Verso, 1986.

Eagleton, Terry. "Ideology and Scholarship." *Historical Studies and Literary Criticism* 114–25. Ed. Jerome J. McGann. Madison: U of Wisconsin P, 1985.

Eagleton, Terry. *Literary Theory: An Introduction*. Minneapolis: U of Minnesota P, 1983.

Eagleton, Terry. "Wittgenstein's Friends." *Against the Grain: Selected Essays* 99–130. London: Verso, 1986.

Edel, Leon. *Bloomsbury: A House of Lions*. New York: Avon Books, 1980.

Edmonds, Dale. "Mescallusions; or, The Drinking Man's *Under the Volcano*." *Journal of Modern Literature* 6 (1977): 277–88.

Edmonds, Dale. "*Under the Volcano*: A Reading of the 'Immediate Level.'" *Tulane Studies in English* 16 (1968): 63–105.

Eliot, T. S. *Notes towards the Definition of Culture*. New York: Harcourt Brace, 1948.

Eliot, T. S. "*Ulysses*, Order, and Myth." *Selected Prose of T. S. Eliot* 175–78. Ed. Frank Kermode. New York: Harcourt Brace Jovanovich, 1975.

Ellmann, Richard. *Ulysses on the Liffey*. New York: Oxford UP, 1972.

Engelberg, Edward. *Elegiac Fictions: The Motif of the Unlived Life*. University Park: Pennsylvania State UP, 1989.

Epstein, Perle. "Malcolm Lowry: In Search of Equilibrium." *A Malcolm Lowry Catalogue* 15–25. New York: Woolmer, 1968.

Falk, David. "Self and Shadow: The Brothers Firmin in *Under The Volcano*." *Texas Studies in Literature and Language* 27 (1985): 209–23.

Ferguson, Susan, et al., eds. *Critical Inquiry* 14 (1988). Special issue, "The Sociology of Literature."

Fine, Reuben. *Narcissism, the Self, and Society*. New York: Columbia UP, 1986.

Fischer, Eric. *The Passing of the European Age: A Study of the Transfer of Western Civilization and Its Renewal in Other Continents*. New York: Russell & Russell, 1948.

Fleishman, Avrom. *Conrad's Politics: Community and Anarchy in the Fiction of Joseph Conrad*. Baltimore: Johns Hopkins UP, 1967.

Fleishman, Avrom. "The Landscape of Hysteria in *The Secret Agent*." *Conrad Revisited: Essays for the Eighties* 89–105. Ed. Ross C. Murfin. University: U of Alabama P, 1985.

Fleishman, Avrom. *Virginia Woolf: A Critical Reading*. Baltimore: Johns Hopkins UP, 1975.

Fogel, Aaron. "Coerced Speech and the Oedipus Dialogue Complex." Morson and Emerson, *Rethinking Bakhtin* 173–96.

Ford, Ford Madox. *Joseph Conrad: A Personal Remembrance*. Boston: Little, Brown, 1924.

Ford, George H. *Double Measure: A Study of the Novels and Stories of D. H. Lawrence*. New York: Holt, Rinehart & Winston, 1965.

Forrest, Gary G. *Alcoholism, Narcissism, and Psychopathology*. Springfield, IL: Charles C. Thomas, 1983.

Forster, E. M. *Abinger Harvest*. New York: Harcourt Brace, 1936.

Forster, E. M. *Two Cheers for Democracy*. New York: Harcourt Brace, 1951.

Foulke, Robert. "The Elegiac Structure of Conrad's *The Mirror of the Sea*." *Literature and Lore of the Sea* 154–60. Ed. Patricia Ann Carlson. Amsterdam: Rodopi, 1986.

Fowler, Albert V. Preface. *War and Civilization*, by Arnold Toynbee. Ed. Albert V. Fowler. New York: Oxford UP, 1950.

Freud, Sigmund. *Civilization and Its Discontents*. New York: Norton, 1961.

Freud, Sigmund. "'Civilized' Sexual Morality and Modern Nervousness." Riviere II, 76–99.

Freud, Sigmund. *The Future of an Illusion*. New York: Norton, 1961.

Freud, Sigmund. *Group Psychology and the Analysis of the Ego*. New York: Norton, 1959.

Freud, Sigmund. "On Narcissism: An Introduction." Riviere IV, 30–59.

Fromm, Erich. *The Sane Society*. New York: Rinehart, 1955.

Frye, Northrop. *Anatomy of Criticism*. Princeton: Princeton UP, 1957.

Frye, Northrop. "*The Decline of the West* by Oswald Spengler." *Daedalus* 103 (1974): 1–13.

Geertz, Clifford. "Art as a Cultural System." *Local Knowledge* 94–120.

Geertz, Clifford. "Blurred Genres: The Refiguration of Social Thought." *Local Knowledge* 19–35.

Geertz, Clifford. Introduction. *Local Knowledge* 3–16.

Geertz, Clifford. *Local Knowledge: Further Essays in Interpretive Anthropology*. New York: Basic Books, 1983.

Geertz, Clifford. "Thick Description: Toward an Interpretive Theory of Culture." *The Interpretation of Cultures* 3–30. New York: Basic Books, 1973.

Ghiselin, Brewster. "The Unity of Joyce's *Dubliners*." *James Joyce, "Dubliners": Text, Criticism, and Notes* 316–32. Ed. Robert Scholes and A. Walton Litz. New York: Viking, 1969.

Gombrich, E. H. *Art and Illusion: A Study in the Psychology of Pictorial Representation*. 2nd ed. Princeton: Princeton UP, 1961.

Gose, Elliott B. *The Transformation Process in Joyce's "Ulysses."* Toronto: U of Toronto P, 1980.

Grace, Sherrill E. "Malcolm Lowry and the Expressionist Vision." *The Art of Malcolm Lowry* 93–111. Ed. Anne Smith. New York: Barnes & Noble, 1978.

Grace, Sherrill E. *The Voyage that Never Ends: Malcolm Lowry's Fiction*. Vancouver: U of British Columbia P, 1982.

Graff, Gerald. *Professing Literature: An Institutional History*. Chicago: U of Chicago P, 1987.

Green, Martin. *Dreams of Adventure, Deeds of Empire*. New York: Basic Books, 1979.

Guerard, Albert J. *Conrad the Novelist*. Cambridge: Harvard UP, 1958.

Gunn, Giles. *The Culture of Criticism and the Criticism of Culture*. New York: Oxford UP, 1987.

Haas, Wilhelm. *What Is European Civilization? And What Is Its Future?* London: Oxford UP, 1929.

Hale, William Harlan. *Challenge to Defeat: Modern Man in Goethe's World and Spengler's Century*. New York: Harcourt Brace, 1932.

Harrison, John R. *The Reactionaries*. London: Victor Gollancz, 1967.

Hawkins, Hunt. "Conrad and the Psychology of Colonialism." *Conrad Revisited: Essays for the Eighties* 71–87. Ed. Ross C. Murfin. University: U of Alabama P, 1985.

Hawkins, Hunt. "Conrad's Critique of Imperialism in *Heart of Darkness*." *PMLA* 94 (1979): 286–99.

Hawthorn, Jeremy. "*Ulysses*, Modernism, and Marxist Criticism." *James Joyce and Modern Literature* 112–25. Ed. W. J. McCormack and Alistair Stead. London: Routledge & Kegan Paul, 1982.

Hay, Eloise Knapp. 1963. *The Political Novels of Joseph Conrad*. Chicago: U of Chicago P, 1981.

Heilbrun, Carolyn G. *Toward a Recognition of Androgyny*. New York: Norton, 1982.

Heilman, Robert B. "The Possessed Artist and the Ailing Soul." *Malcolm Lowry: The Man and His Work* 16–25. Ed. George Woodcock. Vancouver: U of British Columbia P, 1971.

Heinemann, Jan. "The Revolt against Language: A Critical Note on Twentieth-Century Irrationalism with Special Reference to the Aesthetico-Philosophical Views of Virginia Woolf and Clive Bell." *Orbis Litterarum* 32 (1977): 212–28.

Heller, Erich. "Oswald Spengler and the Predicament of the Historical Imagination." *The Disinherited Mind* 159–72. Middlesex: Penguin Books, 1961.

Henderson, Philip. *The Novel Today: Studies in Contemporary Attitudes.* London: Bodley Head, 1936.

Henke, Suzette. "Gerty MacDowell: Joyce's Sentimental Heroine." *Women in Joyce* 132–49. Ed. Suzette Henke and Elaine Unkeless. Urbana: U of Illinois P, 1982.

Henkin, Leo J. *Darwinism in the English Novel, 1860–1910: The Impact of Evolution on Victorian Fiction.* New York: Corporate Press, 1940.

Herr, Cheryl. "Art and Life, Nature and Culture, *Ulysses.*" *Joyce's "Ulysses": The Larger Perspective* 19–38. Ed. Robert D. Newman and Weldon Thornton. Newark: U of Delaware P, 1987.

Herr, Cheryl. *Joyce's Anatomy of Culture.* Urbana: U of Illinois P, 1986.

Herring, Phillip. "Joyce's Politics." *New Light on Joyce from the Dublin Symposium* 3–14. Ed. Fritz Senn. Bloomington: U of Indiana P, 1972.

Herring, Phillip. *Joyce's Uncertainty Principle.* Princeton: Princeton UP, 1987.

Herring, Phillip. "Lotuseaters." *James Joyce's "Ulysses": Critical Essays* 71–89. Ed. Clive Hart and David Hayman. Berkeley: U of California P, 1974.

Hillman, James. *The Dream and the Underworld.* New York: Harper, 1979.

Hinckley, Lyman. *A Manual of Civilization: A Digest of Human Experience.* New York: William-Frederick Press, 1949.

Hirschkop, Ken, and David Shepherd, eds. *Bakhtin and Cultural Theory.* Manchester: Manchester UP, 1989.

Hochman, Baruch. *Another Ego: The Changing View of Self and Society in the Work of D. H. Lawrence.* Columbia: U of South Carolina P, 1970.

Hofstadter, Richard. "The Vogue of Spencer." *Social Darwinism in American Thought* 31–50. 1944. New York: George Braziller, 1965.

Holquist, Michael. *Dialogism: Bakhtin and His World.* London: Routledge, 1990.

Holtby, Winifred. *Women and a Changing Civilisation.* New York: Longmans Green, 1935.

Horkheimer, Max, and Theodor W. Adorno. *Dialectic of Enlightenment.* New York: Continuum, 1987.

Howard, Jonathan. *Darwin.* Oxford: Oxford UP, 1982.

Howe, Irving. "Conrad: Order and Anarchy." *Politics and the Novel* 76–113. New York: Meridian, 1957.

Hughes, H. Stuart. *Oswald Spengler: A Critical Estimate.* New York: Scribner's, 1952.

Huizinga, J. *Homo Ludens: A Study of the Play-Element in Culture.* London: Routledge & Kegan Paul, 1949.

Hunter, Allan. *Joseph Conrad and the Ethics of Darwinism: The Challenges of Science.* London: Croom Helm, 1983.

Hutcheon, Linda. *Narcissistic Narrative: The Metafictional Paradox.* New York: Methuen, 1984.

Hyland, Peter. "The Little Woman of the *Heart of Darkness.*" *Conradiana* 20 (1988): 3–11.

Iggers, Georg G. *The German Conception of History: The National Tradition of Historical Thought from Herder to the Present.* Middletown, CT: Wesleyan UP, 1968.

Iser, Wolfgang. "The Play of the Text." *Prospecting* 249–61.

Iser, Wolfgang. *Prospecting: From Reader Response to Literary Anthropology.* Baltimore: Johns Hopkins UP, 1989.

Iser, Wolfgang. "Toward a Literary Anthropology." *Prospecting* 262–84.

Jameson, Fredric. "Imaginary and Symbolic in Lacan." *The Ideologies of Theory: Essays, 1971–1986.* Vol. I, 75–115. Minneapolis: U of Minnesota P, 1988.

Jameson, Fredric. "Metacommentary." *PMLA* 86 (1971): 9–18.

Jameson, Fredric. *The Political Unconscious: Narrative as a Socially Symbolic Act.* Ithaca: Cornell UP, 1981.

Jay, Martin. *The Dialectical Imagination: A History of the Frankfurt School and the Institute of Social Research, 1923–1950.* Boston: Little, Brown, 1973.

Johnston, Judith L. "The Remediable Flaw: Revisioning Cultural History in *Between the Acts.*" *Virginia Woolf and Bloomsbury: A Centenary Celebration* 253–77. Ed. Jane Marcus. Bloomington: Indiana UP, 1987.

Johnstone, J. K. *The Bloomsbury Group.* New York: Noonday Press, 1954.

Jones, Thomas Jesse. *Essentials of Civilization: A Study in Social Values.* New York: Henry Holt, 1929.

Journal of the Midwest Modern Language Association 24 (1991): 1–99. Special issue, "Cultural Studies and New Historicism." Ed. Rudolf E. Kuenzli.

Joyce, James. *Dubliners: Text, Criticism, and Notes.* Ed. Robert Scholes and A. Walton Litz. New York: Viking, 1969.

Joyce, James. "Ireland, Island of Saints and Sages." *The Critical Writings of James Joyce* 153–74. Ed. Ellsworth Mason and Richard Ellmann. New York: Viking, 1959.

Joyce, James. *Letters of James Joyce.* Vol. I, ed. Stuart Gilbert. Vols. II and III, ed. Richard Ellmann. New York: Viking, 1957, 1966.

Joyce, James. "A Portrait of the Artist." *A Portrait of the Artist as a Young Man* 257–66.

Joyce, James. *A Portrait of the Artist as a Young Man: Text, Criticism, and Notes.* Ed. Chester Anderson. New York: Viking, 1968.

Joyce, James. *Ulysses: The Corrected Text.* New York: Vintage Books, 1986.

Joyce, James. "The Universal Literary Influence of the Renaissance." *James Joyce in Padua* 19–23. Ed. Louis Berrone. New York: Random House, 1977.

Jung, C. G. *Civilization in Transition.* New York: Pantheon, 1964.

Kartiganer, Donald M. "The Divided Protagonist: Reading as Repetition and Discovery." *Texas Studies in Literature and Language* 30 (1988): 151–78.

Katz, John. *The Will to Civilization: An Inquiry into the Principles of Historic Change.* 1938. New York: Arno Press, 1975.

Kennedy, James G. *Herbert Spencer.* Boston: Twayne, 1978.

Kenner, Hugh. *Joyce's Voices.* Berkeley: U of California P, 1978.

Kermode, Frank. "Lawrence and the Apocalyptic Types." *Word in the Desert* 14–38. Ed. C. B. Cox and A. E. Dyson. Oxford: Oxford UP, 1968.

Kermode, Frank. *The Sense of an Ending: Studies in the Theory of Fiction.* Oxford: Oxford UP, 1967.

Kernberg, Otto F. *Borderline Conditions and Pathological Narcissism.* New York: Jason Aronson, 1975.

Kernberg, Otto F. "Narcissism." *Introducing Psychoanalytic Theory* 126–36. Ed. Sander L. Gilman. New York: Brunner/Mazel, 1982.

Kershner, R. B. "Degeneration: The Explanatory Nightmare." *Georgia Review* 40 (1986): 416–44.

Kershner, R. B. *Joyce, Bakhtin, and Popular Literature: Chronicles of Disorder*. Chapel Hill: U of North Carolina P, 1989.

Kidd, Benjamin. *Principles of Western Civilisation*. London: Macmillan, 1902.

Kilgallin, Anthony R. "Faust and *Under the Volcano*." *Malcolm Lowry: The Man and His Work* 26–37. Ed. George Woodcock. Vancouver: U of British Columbia P, 1971.

Kilgallin, Tony. *Lowry*. Erin, Ont.: Press Porcepic, 1973.

Kimball, Jean. "Freud, Leonardo, and Joyce: The Dimensions of a Childhood Memory." *The Seventh of Joyce* 57–73. Ed. Bernard Benstock. Bloomington: Indiana UP, 1982.

Kimbrough, Robert. "Conrad's *Youth* (1902): An Introduction." *The Norton Critical Edition of Conrad's "Heart of Darkness"* 406–18. Ed. Robert Kimbrough. 3rd ed. New York: Norton, 1988.

Knapp, James F. *Literary Modernism and the Transformation of Work*. Evanston, IL: Northwestern UP, 1988.

Kohut, Heinz. *The Analysis of the Self: A Systematic Approach to the Psychoanalytic Treatment of Narcissistic Personality Disorders*. New York: International UP, 1971.

Kohut, Heinz. "Forms and Transformations of Narcissism." Ornstein I, 427–60.

Kohut, Heinz. *The Restoration of the Self*. New York: International UP, 1977.

Kohut, Heinz. "The Self in History." Ornstein II, 771–82.

Kohut, Heinz. "Thoughts on Narcissism and Narcissistic Rage." Ornstein II, 625–58.

Korzeniowski, Apollo. "Poland and Muscovy." *Conrad under Familial Eyes* 75–88. Ed. Zdzislaw Najder. Cambridge: Cambridge UP, 1983.

La Capra, Dominick. *History, Politics, and the Novel*. Ithaca: Cornell UP, 1987.

La Capra, Dominick. *Soundings in Critical Theory*. Ithaca: Cornell UP, 1989.

Lasch Christopher. *The Culture of Narcissism: American Life in an Age of Diminishing Expectations*. New York: Norton, 1979.

Lasch, Christopher. "Politics and Social Theory: A Reply to the Critics." *Salmagundi* 46 (1979): 194–202.

Lawrence, D. H. "Education of the People." *Reflections on the Death of a Porcupine and Other Essays* 85–166. Ed. Michael Herbert. Cambridge: Cambridge UP, 1988.

Lawrence, D. H. "Enslaved by Civilization." *Assorted Articles* 137–46. New York: Knopf, 1930.

Lawrence, D. H. "Europe v. America." *Phoenix: The Posthumous Papers of D. H. Lawrence* 117–18. London: William Heinemann, 1936.

Lawrence, D. H. "On Human Destiny." *Assorted Articles* 242–58. New York: Knopf, 1930.

Lawrence, D. H. *Lady Chatterley's Lover*. New York: Grove Press, 1957.

Lawrence, D. H. *Letters of D. H. Lawrence: Volume II, June 1913–October 1916*. Ed. George J. Zytaruk and James T. Boulton. Cambridge: Cambridge UP, 1981.

Lawrence, D. H. [Lawrence H. Davison]. *Movements in European History*. 1921. Oxford: Oxford UP, 1925.

Lawrence, D. H. *The Plumed Serpent*. 1926. Ed. L. D. Clark. Cambridge: Cambridge UP, 1987.

Leavis, F. R. "D. H. Lawrence." *For Continuity* 111–48. 1933. Freeport, NY: Books for Libraries Press, 1968.

Leavis, F. R. *The Great Tradition*. New York: New York UP, 1967.

Leavis, F. R. "Mass Civilization and Minority Culture." *Education and the University: A Sketch for an "English School"* 141–71. 2nd ed. Cambridge: Cambridge UP, 1948.

Lee, Hermione. *The Novels of Virginia Woolf*. New York: Holmes & Meier, 1977.

Leopold II. ["The Sacred Mission of Civilization"]. *The Norton Critical Edition of "Heart of Darkness"* 126–30. Ed. Robert Kimbrough. 3rd ed. New York: Norton, 1988.

Levi, Albert William. *Philosophy and the Modern World.* 1959. Chicago: U of Chicago P, 1977.

Levin, Gerald. *Sigmund Freud.* Boston: Twayne, 1975.

Levine, George. "The Novel as Scientific Discourse: The Example of Conrad." *Novel* 21 (1988): 220–27.

Levine, George. *The Realistic Imagination: English Fiction from Frankenstein to Lady Chatterley.* Chicago: U of Chicago P, 1981.

Lewis, Wyndham. *Paleface: The Philosophy of the "Melting-Pot."* London: Chatto & Windus, 1929.

Lodge, David. "Lawrence, Dostoevsky, Bakhtin: D. H. Lawrence and Dialogic Fiction." *Renaissance and Modern Studies* 29 (1985): 16–32.

London, Bette. "Reading Race and Gender in Conrad's Dark Continent." *Criticism* 31 (1989): 235–52.

Lowry, Malcolm. "Preface to a Novel." *Malcolm Lowry: The Man and His Work* 9–15. Ed. George Woodcock. Vancouver: U of British Columbia P, 1971.

Lowry, Malcolm. *Selected Letters.* 1965. Ed. Harvey Breit and Margerie Bonner Lowry. New York: Capricorn, 1969.

Lowry, Malcolm. *Selected Poems.* Ed. Earle Birney and Margerie Lowry. San Francisco: City Lights, 1962.

Lowry, Malcolm. *Ultramarine.* 1933. Harmondsworth: Penguin Books, 1974.

Lowry, Malcolm. *Under the Volcano.* 1947. New York: Lippincott, 1965.

Lowry, Malcolm. "Work in Progress: The Voyage that Never Ends." *Malcolm Lowry Review* 21/22 (1987/88): 72–99.

Lowry, Margerie. "Introductory Note." Malcolm Lowry, *Ultramarine* 7–10.

Lunn, Eugene. *Marxism and Modernism: An Historical Study of Lukács, Brecht, Benjamin, and Adorno.* Berkeley: U of California P, 1982.

McCabe, Joseph. *The Evolution of Civilization.* New York: G. P. Putnam's Sons, 1922.

McCormack, W. J. "Nightmares of History: James Joyce and the Phenomenon of Anglo-Irish Literature." *James Joyce and Modern Literature* 77–107. Ed. W. J. McCormack and Alistair Stead. London: Routledge & Kegan Paul, 1982.

McDiarmid, Lucy. *Saving Civilization: Yeats, Eliot, and Auden between the Wars.* Cambridge: Cambridge UP, 1984.

McEachran, F. *The Civilized Man.* London: Faber & Faber, 1930.

MacGregor, Catherine. "Conspiring with the Addict: Yvonne's Co-dependency in *Under the Volcano.*" *Mosaic* 24 (1991): 145–62.

MacMaster, Robert E. "Danilevsky and Spengler: A New Interpretation." *Journal of Modern History* 26 (1954): 154–61.

MacPherson, Hector. *Spencer and Spencerism.* New York: Doubleday, 1900.

Maddox, James H., Jr. *Joyce's "Ulysses" and the Assault upon Character.* New Brunswick, NJ: Rutgers UP, 1978.

Mann, Thomas. "Conrad's 'The Secret Agent.'" *Past Masters* 231–47.

Mann, Thomas. "On the Theory of Spengler." *Past Masters* 217–27.

Mann, Thomas. *Past Masters and Other Papers.* New York: Knopf, 1933.

Marcus, Jane. *Virginia Woolf and the Languages of Patriarchy.* Bloomington: Indiana UP, 1987.

Markson, David. *Malcolm Lowry's "Volcano": Myth, Symbol, Meaning.* New York: Times Books, 1978.

Martz, Louis L. "The Second Lady Chatterley." *The Spirit of D. H. Lawrence: Centenary Essays* 106–24. Ed. Gamini Salgado and G. K. Das. Totowa, NJ: Barnes & Noble, 1988.

Marvin, F. S. "Britain's Place in Western Civilisation." *The New Past and Other Essays on the Development of Civilisation* 171–83. Ed. E. H. Carter. Oxford: Basil Blackwell, 1925.

Marvin, F. S. *The Unity of Western Civilisation.* London: Oxford UP, 1915.

Mazlish, Bruce. *The Riddle of History: The Great Speculators from Vico to Freud.* New York: Harper & Row, 1966.

Mendelsohn, Sigmund. *Saturated Civilization.* New York: Macmillan, 1926.

Mendelson, Edward. Introduction. *Pynchon: A Collection of Critical Essays* 1–15. Ed. Edward Mendelson. Englewood Cliffs, NJ: Prentice-Hall, 1978.

Meyers, Jeffrey. "Joseph Conrad: The Meaning of Civilization." *Fiction and the Colonial Experience* 55–78. Totowa, NJ: Rowman & Littlefield, 1973.

Milbury-Steen, Sarah L. *European and African Stereotypes in Twentieth-Century Fiction.* New York: New York UP, 1981.

Mill, John Stuart. "Civilisation." 1836. *The Victorian Prophets: A Reader from Carlyle to Wells* 70–103. Ed. Peter Keating. London: Fontana, 1981.

Miller, Christopher. *Blank Darkness: Africanist Discourse in French.* Chicago: U of Chicago P, 1985.

Moore, G. E. *Principia Ethica.* Cambridge: Cambridge UP, 1903.

Morson, Gary Saul. "Bakhtin and the Present Moment." *American Scholar* 60 (1991): 201–22.

Morson, Gary Saul, and Caryl Emerson. *Mikhail Bakhtin: Creation of a Prosaics.* Stanford: Stanford UP, 1990.

Morson, Gary Saul, and Caryl Emerson, eds. *Rethinking Bakhtin: Extensions and Challenges.* Evanston, IL: Northwestern UP, 1989.

Nearing, Scott. *Where Is Civilization Going?* New York: Vanguard Press, 1927.

Neuman, Shirley. "*Heart of Darkness,* Virginia Woolf, and the Spectre of Domination." *Virginia Woolf: New Critical Essays* 57–76. Ed. Patricia Clements and Isobel Grundy. Totowa, NJ: Barnes & Noble, 1983.

New, William H. *Malcolm Lowry.* Toronto: McClelland & Stewart, 1971.

Nietzsche, Friedrich. *The Will To Power.* Ed. Walter Kaufmann. New York: Vintage Books, 1968.

Nisbet, Robert. *History of the Idea of Progress.* New York: Basic Books, 1980.

Nordau, Max. *The Conventional Lies of Our Civilization.* 1884. 2nd ed. Chicago: L. Schick, 1887.

Nordau, Max. *Degeneration.* 1892. New York: Howard Fertig, 1968.

Norris, Margot. "Modernism, Myth, and Desire in 'Nausicaa.'" *James Joyce Quarterly* 26 (1988): 37–50.

Norris, Margot. "Narration under a Blindfold: Reading Joyce's 'Clay.'" *PMLA* 102 (1987): 206–15.

O'Flaherty, Liam. *Joseph Conrad: An Appreciation.* 1925. New York: Haskell House, 1973.

O'Hanlon, Redmond. *Joseph Conrad and Charles Darwin: The Influence of Scientific Thought on Conrad's Fiction.* Edinburgh: Salamander Press, 1984.

Ornstein, Paul H., ed. *The Search for the Self: Selected Writings of Heinz Kohut, 1950–1978.* 2 vols. New York: International UP, 1978.

Ortega y Gasset, José. *The Revolt of the Masses.* 1929. Notre Dame, IN: U of Notre Dame P, 1985.

Orwell, George. *The Collected Essays, Journalism, and Letters of George Orwell.* 4 vols. Ed. Sonia Orwell and Ian Angus. New York: Harcourt Brace and World, 1968.

Ovid. *Metamorphoses.* Trans. Rolfe Humphries. Bloomington: Indiana UP, 1955.

Oxford English Dictionary. Oxford: Oxford UP, 1933.

Parry, Benita. *Conrad and Imperialism: Ideological Boundaries and Visionary Frontiers.* London: Macmillan 1983.

Patai, Daphne. "Gamesmanship and Androcentrism in Orwell's *1984.*" *PMLA* 97 (1982): 856–70.

Pater, Walter. *The Renaissance: Studies in Art and Poetry.* 1893. Berkeley: U of California P, 1980.

Pecora, Vincent P. "The Limits of Local Knowledge." Veeser 243–76.

Peel, J. D. Y. *Herbert Spencer: The Evolution of a Sociologist.* London: William Heinemann, 1971.

Pound, Ezra. *Selected Poetry.* New York: New Directions, 1957.

Profession 89. "Presidential Forum: Breaking Up/Out/Down — The Boundaries of Literary Study" 2–22.

Rapoport, David C. "Military and Civil Societies: The Contemporary Significance of a Traditional Subject in Political Thought." *Political Studies* 12 (1964): 178–201.

Reilly, Patrick. *The Literature of Guilt: From Gulliver to Golding.* Iowa City: U of Iowa P, 1988.

Renner, Stanley. "The Garden of Civilization: Conrad, Huxley, and the Ethics of Evolution." *Conradiana* 7 (1975): 109–20.

Richards, Thomas Karr. "Gerty MacDowell and the Irish Common Reader." *ELH* 52 (1985): 755–76.

Richardson, Miles, and Malcolm C. Webb, eds. *The Burden of Being Civilized: An Anthropological Perspective on the Discontents of Civilization.* Athens: U of Georgia P, 1986.

Riviere, Joan, ed. *Collected Papers of Freud.* 5 vols. London: Hogarth, 1950.

Rosenbaum, S. P. *Victorian Bloomsbury: The Early History of the Bloomsbury Group.* New York: St. Martin's Press, 1987.

Ruotolo, Lucio P. *The Interrupted Moment: A View of Virginia Woolf's Novels.* Stanford: Stanford UP, 1986.

Ruthven, K. K. "The Savage God: Conrad and Lawrence." *Word in the Desert* 39–54. Ed. C. B. Cox and A. E. Dyson. Oxford: Oxford UP, 1968.

Sage, Victor. "The Art of Sinking in Prose: Charles Jackson, Joyce, and *Under the Volcano.*" *Malcolm Lowry: Eighty Years On* 35–50. Ed. Sue Vice. New York: St. Martin's Press, 1989.

Salgado, Gamini. "Lawrence as Historian." *The Spirit of D. H. Lawrence: Centenary Essays* 234–47. Ed. Gamini Salgado and G. K. Das. Totowa, NJ: Barnes & Noble, 1988.

Salmagundi 46 (1979): 166–202. Symposium, "Christopher Lasch and the Culture of Narcissism."

Sanders, Scott. *D. H. Lawrence: The World of the Five Major Novels.* New York: Viking, 1973.

San Juan, Epifano, Jr. *James Joyce and the Craft of Fiction: An Interpretation of "Dubliners."* Rutherford, NJ: Fairleigh Dickinson UP, 1972.

Sarvan, C. P. "Racism and the *Heart of Darkness.*" *The Norton Critical Edition of Conrad's "Heart of Darkness"* 280–85. Ed. Robert Kimbrough. 3rd ed. New York: Norton, 1988.

Satinover, Jeffrey. "Science and the Fragile Self: The Rise of Narcissism, the Decline of God." *Pathologies of the Modern Self: Postmodern Studies on Narcissism, Schizophrenia, and Depression* 84–113. Ed. David Michael Levin. New York: New York UP, 1987.

Saveson, John E. *Joseph Conrad: The Making of a Moralist.* Amsterdam: Rodopi, 1972.

Schlack, Beverly Ann. *Continuing Presences: Virginia Woolf's Use of Literary Allusion*. University Park: Pennsylvania State UP, 1979.

Schwarz, Daniel R. *Conrad: "Almayer's Folly" to "Under Western Eyes."* Ithaca: Cornell UP, 1980.

Schweitzer, Albert. *Civilization and Ethics*. London: Adam and Charles Black, 1949.

Schweitzer, Albert. *The Decay and the Restoration of Civilization*. London: Adam and Charles Black, 1923.

Scruton, Roger. *A Dictionary of Political Thought*. London: Macmillan, 1982.

Senn, Fritz. "Nausicaa." *James Joyce's "Ulysses": Critical Essays* 277–311. Ed. Clive Hart and David Hayman. Berkeley: U of California P, 1974.

Sennett, Richard. *The Fall of Public Man: On the Social Psychology of Capitalism*. 1977. New York: Vintage Books, 1978.

Sexton, Mark S. "Kurtz's Sketch in Oils: Its Significance to *Heart of Darkness*." *Studies in Short Fiction* 24 (1987): 387–92.

Shaffer, Brian W. " 'Civilization' under Western Eyes: Lowry's *Under the Volcano* as a Reading of Conrad's *Heart of Darkness*." *Conradiana* 22 (1990): 143–56.

Shaffer, Brian W. "Kindred by Choice: Joyce's *Exiles* and Goethe's *Elective Affinities*." *James Joyce Quarterly* 26 (1989): 199–212.

Shaffer, Brian W., ed. *Conradiana* 24:3 (1992). Special issue on teaching *Heart of Darkness*.

Shechner, Mark. *Joyce in Nighttown: A Psychoanalytic Inquiry*. Berkeley: U of California P, 1974.

Sherry, Norman. *Conrad*. New York: Thames & Hudson, 1988.

Sherry, Norman, ed. *Conrad: The Critical Heritage*. London: Routledge & Kegan Paul, 1973.

Sherry, Norman. *Conrad's Western World*. Cambridge: Cambridge UP, 1971.

Shetty, Sandya. "*Heart of Darkness:* Out of Africa Some New Thing Never Comes." *Journal of Modern Literature* 15 (1989): 461–74.

Smith, Johanna M. " 'Too Beautiful Altogether': Patriarchal Ideology in *Heart of Darkness*." *Joseph Conrad, "Heart of Darkness": A Case Study in Contemporary Criticism* 179–95. Ed. Ross C. Murfin. New York: St. Martin's Press, 1989.

Smith, Steve. "Marxism and Ideology: Joseph Conrad, *Heart of Darkness*." *Literary Theory at Work: Three Texts* 181–200. Ed. Douglas Tallack. London: B. T. Batsford, 1987.

Sorokin, Pitirim A. *Social Philosophies of an Age of Crisis*. Boston: Beacon Press, 1951.

South Atlantic Quarterly 91/1 (1992). Special issue, "Writing Cultural Criticism."

Spencer, Herbert. *Facts and Comments*. New York: D. Appleton, 1902.

Spencer, Herbert. *First Principles*. New York: D. Appleton, 1890.

Spencer, Herbert. "The Morals of Trade." *Essays: Scientific, Political, and Speculative*. Vol. III, 113–51. New York: D. Appleton, 1896.

Spencer, Herbert. *Principles of Sociology*. 1904. 3 vols. Osnabrück: Otto Zeller, 1966.

Spencer, Herbert. "Progress: Its Law and Cause." *Essays: Scientific, Political, and Speculative*. Vol. I, 8–62. New York: D. Appleton, 1896.

Spencer, Herbert. *Social Statics, Together with Man Versus the State*. 1892. New York: D. Appleton, 1913.

Spender, Stephen. Introduction. *Under the Volcano*, by Malcolm Lowry. New York: Lippincott, 1965.

Spengler, Oswald. *Aphorisms*. Chicago: Regnery, 1967.

Spengler, Oswald. *The Decline of the West*. Two vols. in one. New York: Knopf, 1939.

Spengler, Oswald. "Pessimism?" *Selected Essays* 133–54. Chicago: Regnery, 1967.

Stark, Bruce R. "Kurtz's Intended: The Heart of *Heart of Darkness*." *Texas Studies in Literature and Language* 16 (1974): 535–55.

Steele, Elizabeth. *Virginia Woolf's Literary Sources and Allusions: A Guide to the Essays*. New York: Garland, 1983.

Storck, John. *Man and Civilization: An Inquiry into the Bases of Contemporary Life*. New York: Harcourt Brace, 1927.

Street, Brian V. *The Savage in Literature: Representations of "Primitive" Society in English Fiction, 1858–1920*. London: Routledge & Kegan Paul, 1975.

Sullivan, Zoreh T. "Enclosure, Darkness, and the Body: Conrad's Landscape." *Centennial Review* 25 (1981): 59–79.

Sunic, Tomislav. "History and Decadence: Spengler's Cultural Pessimism Today." *CLIO* 19 (1989): 51–62.

Symons, Arthur. *Notes on Joseph Conrad, with Some Unpublished Letters*. London: Meyers, 1925.

Tawney, R. H. *Equality*. 1931. New York: Barnes & Noble, 1965.

Tessitore, John. "Freud, Conrad, and *Heart of Darkness*." *College Literature* 7 (1980): 30–40.

Thornton, Lawrence. *Unbodied Hope: Narcissism and the Modern Novel*. Lewisburg, PA: Bucknell UP, 1984.

Tifft, Stephen. "Tragedy as a Meditation on Itself: Reflexiveness in *Under the Volcano*." *The Art of Malcolm Lowry* 46–71. Ed. Anne Smith. New York: Barnes & Noble, 1978.

Todorov, Tzvetan. *Mikhail Bakhtin: The Dialogical Principle*. Minneapolis: U of Minnesota P, 1984.

Torchiana, Donald T. *Backgrounds for Joyce's "Dubliners."* Boston: Allen & Unwin, 1986.

Torgovnick, Marianna. *Gone Primitive: Savage Intellects, Modern Lives*. Chicago: U of Chicago P, 1990.

Toynbee, Arnold. *Civilization on Trial*. London: Oxford UP, 1948.

Toynbee, Arnold. *War and Civilization*. Ed. Albert V. Fowler. New York: Oxford UP, 1950.

Transue, Pamela J. *Virginia Woolf and the Politics of Style*. Albany: State U of New York P, 1986.

Traquair, Ramsay. "Women and Modern Civilization." *What Is Civilization?* 175–98. Ed. Hendrik Van Loon. New York: Duffield, 1926.

Trueblood, D. Elton. "The Sickness of Civilization." *The Predicament of Modern Man* 1–26. New York: Harper & Row, 1944.

Tylor, E. B. *The Origins of Culture*. 1873. New York: Harper & Row, 1958.

Van Loon, Hendrik. Introduction. *What Is Civilization?* Ed. Hendrik Van Loon. New York: Duffield, 1926.

Veblen, Thorstein. *The Theory of the Leisure Class: An Economic Study of Institutions*. 1899. New York: Modern Library, 1934.

Veeser, H. Aram. *The New Historicism*. New York: Routledge, 1989.

Veitch, Douglas W. *Lawrence, Greene, and Lowry: The Fictional Landscape of Mexico*. Waterloo, Ont.: Wilfrid Laurier UP, 1978.

Vice, Sue. "Fear of Perfection, Love of Death and the Bottle." *Malcolm Lowry: Eighty Years On* 92–107. Ed. Sue Vice. New York: St. Martin's Press, 1989.

Vinge, Louise. *The Narcissus Theme in Western European Literature up to the Early 19th Century*. Lund: Gleerups, 1967.

Walker, C. C. *The Biology of Civilization*. Toronto: Macmillan, 1930.

Walker, Ronald G. *Infernal Paradise: Mexico and the Modern English Novel*. Berkeley: U of California P, 1978.

Walzl, Florence. "*Dubliners:* Women in Irish Society." *Women in Joyce* 31–56. Ed. Suzette Henke and Elaine Unkeless. Urbana: U of Illinois P, 1982.

Walzl, Florence. "Pattern of Paralysis in Joyce's *Dubliners.*" *College English* 22 (1961): 221–28.

Wasserman, Jerry. "Narrative Presence: The Illusion of Language in *Heart of Darkness.*" *Critical Essays on Joseph Conrad* 102–13. Ed. Ted Billy. Boston: G. K. Hall, 1987.

Watson, G. J. "The Politics of *Ulysses.*" *Joyce's "Ulysses": The Larger Perspective* 39–58. Ed. Robert D. Newman and Weldon Thornton. Newark: U of Delaware P, 1987.

Watson, George. *Politics and Literature in Modern Britain.* Totowa, NJ: Rowman & Littlefield, 1977.

Watt, Ian. *Conrad in the Nineteenth Century.* Berkeley: U of California P, 1979.

Watts, Cedric. *Conrad's "Heart of Darkness": A Critical and Contextual Discussion.* Milan: Mursia International, 1978.

Watts, Mary S. *Civilization. Three Short Plays* 85–137. New York: Macmillan, 1917.

Wellek, René, and Austin Warren. *Theory of Literature.* New York: Harcourt Brace, 1956.

Wells, H. G. *The Salvaging of Civilization: The Probable Future of Mankind.* New York: Macmillan, 1921.

Werner, Craig Hansen. *Dubliners: A Pluralistic World.* Boston: Twayne, 1988.

Werner, Helmut. "Editor's Preface to the German-Language Abridged Edition." *The Decline of the West,* by Oswald Spengler. New York: Modern Library, 1962.

White, Hayden. *The Content of Form: Narrative Discourse and Historical Representation.* Baltimore: Johns Hopkins UP, 1987.

Wicke, Jennifer. *Advertising Fictions: Literature, Advertisement, and Social Reading.* New York: Columbia UP, 1988.

Wiley, Paul L. "*Lord Jim* and the Loss of Eden." *Twentieth Century Interpretations of "Lord Jim"* 46–52. Ed. Robert E. Kuehn. Englewood Cliffs, NJ: Prentice-Hall, 1969.

Wilkins, John H. *Civilization. The Modern Standard Drama: A Collection of the Most Popular Acting Plays.* Vol. XIII. Ed. F. C. Wemyss. New York: Samuel French, n.d.

Williams, Raymond. "The Bloomsbury Fraction." *Problems* 148–69.

Williams, Raymond. *The English Novel from Dickens to Lawrence.* London: Chatto & Windus, 1970.

Williams, Raymond. *Keywords: A Vocabulary of Culture and Society.* New York: Oxford UP, 1976.

Williams, Raymond. *Marxism and Literature.* Oxford: Oxford UP, 1977.

Williams, Raymond. *Problems in Materialism and Culture: Selected Essays.* London: Verso, 1980.

Williams, Raymond. "Social Darwinism." *Problems* 86–102.

Wilson, Edmund. *Axel's Castle: A Study in the Imaginative Literature of 1870–1930.* 1931. New York: Norton, 1984.

Wiltshire, David. *The Social and Political Thought of Herbert Spencer.* Oxford: Oxford UP, 1978.

Winner, Anthony. *Culture and Irony: Studies in Joseph Conrad's Major Novels.* Charlottesville: UP of Virginia, 1988.

Wolheim, Richard. *Freud.* London: Fontana, 1971.

Woolf, Leonard. *Barbarians Within and Without.* New York: Harcourt Brace, 1939.

Woolf, Leonard. *Beginning Again.* New York: Harcourt Brace, 1964.

Woolf, Leonard. *Imperialism and Civilization.* London: Hogarth, 1928.

Woolf, Virginia. *The Diary of Virginia Woolf.* Vols. II (1920–24) and III (1925–30). Ed. Ann Olivier Bell. New York: Harcourt Brace Jovanovich, 1978, 1980.

Woolf, Virginia. *Jacob's Room.* New York: Harcourt Brace, 1922.

Woolf, Virginia. *The Letters of Virginia Woolf: Volume III, 1923–1928.* Ed. Nigel Nicolson and Joanne Trautmann. New York: Harcourt Brace Jovanovich, 1978.

Woolf, Virginia. *Mrs. Dalloway.* New York: Harcourt Brace, 1925.

Woolf, Virginia. *A Room of One's Own.* New York: Harcourt Brace, 1929.

Woolf, Virginia. *To the Lighthouse.* New York: Harcourt Brace, 1927.

Woolf, Virginia. *A Writer's Diary.* Ed. Leonard Woolf. New York: Harcourt Brace, 1954.

Wright, Walter F., *Joseph Conrad on Fiction.* Lincoln: U of Nebraska P, 1964.

Yeats, William Butler. *The Collected Poems.* New York: Macmillan, 1956.

Yeats, William Butler. *A Vision.* New York: Macmillan, 1966.

Zabel, Morton Dauwen. Introduction. *The Mirror of the Sea and a Personal Record,* by Joseph Conrad. New York: Anchor Books, 1960.

Zweig, Paul. *The Heresy of Self-Love: A Study of Subversive Individualism.* 1968. Princeton: Princeton UP, 1980.

Zwerdling, Alex. *Virginia Woolf and the Real World.* Berkeley: U of California P, 1986.

Index

Achebe, Chinua, 173 n
Adams, Brooks, 125
Adorno, Theodor W., 1–2, 24, 102, 111, 112, 113–20, 121, 138, 154, 168 n
Alford, C. Fred, 113
Allier, Raoul, 20, 31, 34
Anti-Semitism, 43, 113, 117–20, 184 n. *See also* Adorno, Theodor W.; Joyce, James: Bloom; Horkheimer, Max
Arac, Jonathan, 185 n
Arendt, Hannah, 53, 175 n
Aristotle, 64
Arnold, Armin, 183 n
Arnold, Matthew, 17, 27, 165 n, 165–66 n, 177 n

Bachelard, Gaston, 161
Bakhtin, Mikhail, 11, 36, 45, 61, 79, 80, 99, 122, 133, 139, 185 n; cultural hermeneutics, 37–39
Barbarism, 26–27, 29–30, 31, 33, 34, 50–51, 53–55, 66–67, 94, 113, 117, 171 n, 182 n; and trope of darkness, 56–57, 65, 68, 70, 78, 173 n. *See also* Blinding torch: trope of blindness; Uncivilization
Barry, J., 124, 134, 184 n

Barzun, Jacques, 125
Beckerath, Herbert von, 25, 27, 29
Bell, Clive, vii, 13, 20, 27–28, 28–29, 30, 32, 41, 42, 79, 80–99, 117, 177 n
Bell, Quentin, 90, 177 n
Benjamin, Walter, 112, 113
Bennett, Arnold, 61
Benstock, Bernard, 179 n
Berman, Jeffrey, 148, 186 n, 187 n
Binns, Ronald, 130, 132, 137, 186 n
Blinding torch, 2, 5, 7, 11, 14, 15, 31, 50, 64, 67, 78, 142, 143, 160, 163 n; doubleness of, 2–3, 6, 7, 14, 64, 66; and trope of blindness, 2, 7, 12, 59, 60, 66, 117–18, 119. *See also* Civilization: representations of
Bonheim, Helmut, 120
Boyle, Robert, 111
Bradbury, Harriet B., 166 n
Brantlinger, Patrick, 171 n
Bruns, Gerald, 36
Budgen, Frank, 181 n
Buitenhuis, Peter, 42
Burke, Edmund, 15

Caillois, Roger, 71, 72, 74, 77, 176 n
Carpenter, Edward, 14, 22, 23

Casson, Stanley, 21
Civilization, 3, 4, 5, 8–9, 10, 11, 12, 14–35,
    80, 103–5, 108, 125, 168 n; and Caesar-
    ism, 48, 50, 95, 126, 130; and class struc-
    ture, 23–24, 31–34, 48, 74, 79, 81, 84,
    93–97, 107; definitions of, 5, 14–18, 19,
    22–23, 26, 27, 28–29, 32, 164–65 n, 172–
    73 n; discourse of, 3–4, 5, 8, 11, 12, 13,
    14, 17–19, 28, 33, 35, 37–39, 66, 69,
    165 n; as game, 43, 64, 70–78, 172 n, 175–
    76 n; as paradox, 3, 5, 6–8, 9, 10, 12, 13–
    14, 16, 30–31, 42, 53–54, 55, 56, 60, 64,
    66–69, 73, 97, 111, 113, 114, 119, 164 n;
    representations of, 2–3, 5, 6–7, 8, 11, 13–
    14, 42, 43, 44, 56, 64, 80, 103, 143, 145,
    147, 153, 160, 168 n; theory of, 4, 15–16,
    18–28, 31–35, 41, 47–48, 80–81, 83–84,
    94, 104–5, 112, 122, 125–26; trope of
    nation-state/state of mind, 25–28, 30–31,
    83, 99, 103–4; trope of progress/retro-
    gression, 18–25, 42, 46, 47–49, 52–53,
    53–55, 58–59, 60, 113, 119, 170 n; trope
    of sacred domain/propaganda tool, 28–
    35, 42, 114, 171 n; and women, 2, 9, 12–
    13, 42, 67, 81, 88–89, 90–91, 166 n,
    178 n. See also Uncivilization
Cixous, Hélène, 110, 180 n
Clark, L. D., 127, 184 n
Coit, Stanton, 20, 23, 24, 29
Collingwood, R. G., 27, 29, 32–33, 182 n
Conrad, Joseph, vii, 2, 5, 6–8, 13, 41, 43,
    48–49, 52–53, 63, 64, 69, 157, 159, 167 n,
    168 n, 169 n, 172–73 n; Almayer's Folly, 5;
    "Books," 2; Heart of Darkness, 2, 11, 41,
    42, 43, 45, 47–57, 64–70, 73, 78, 80,
    169 n, 172 n, 176 n; Kurtz, 2, 14, 48, 50–
    51, 54, 55, 57, 65, 68, 69, 170 n, 172 n;
    Lord Jim, 5, 42, 47, 51, 55, 172 n; Marlow,
    2, 12, 14, 34, 45, 49, 50, 52, 54, 57, 68, 80,
    169–70 n, 172 n; The Mirror of the Sea, 6–
    7, 172 n; Nostromo, 5; "An Outpost of
    Progress," 3, 6, 41, 47, 57–60, 64; "Po-
    land Revisited," 8, 164 n; The Secret Agent,
    2, 42, 43, 70–78, 175 n, 178 n; Under West-
    ern Eyes, 5, 170 n; Victory, 5, 63; Youth, 5,
    70
Costa, Richard Hauer, 156
Cripps, Michael, 124, 155, 185 n, 186 n
Cross, Richard K., 150, 155, 186 n
Crozier, John Beattie, 18, 27, 53
Culture, 6–17, 23–24, 37, 38–39, 40, 72,
    126, 134, 165 n, 180 n

Culture-industry, 43, 113–14, 115, 116, 154.
    See also Adorno, Theodor W.;
    Horkheimer, Max; Joyce, James: Gerty
    MacDowell; Ulysses

Daiches, David, 4, 184 n
Danilevsky, Nikolai, 125
Darras, Jacques, 59, 64
Darwin, Charles, 19, 46, 51, 165 n, 169 n
Day, Douglas, 158, 161, 183 n
Devlin, Kimberly J., 105
Dewey, John, 3, 29, 171 n
Diamond, Stanley, 24, 31
Dodson, Daniel B., 185 n
Douglas, Sholto, 21, 27, 41
Durant, Will, 169 n

Eagleton, Terry, 36, 70–71, 77, 167 n, 168 n;
    ideology as discourse, 39–40
Edel, Leon, 94, 177 n
Edmonds, Dale, 149
Eliot, T. S., 23, 32, 165 n, 183 n
Ellmann, Richard, 181 n
Engelberg, Edward, 187 n

Fine, Reuben, 152–53
Fischer, Eric, 31
Fitzgerald, F. Scott, 182 n
Fleishman, Avrom, 80, 171 n, 177 n
Fogel, Aaron, 173–74 n
Ford, Ford Madox, 4, 61, 69, 167 n, 170 n
Forster, E. M., 4, 5, 23, 27, 80
Forrest, Gary G., 149, 152
Foulke, Robert, 6
Fowler, Albert V., 29
Frankfurt School, 43, 102, 112, 181 n
Freud, Sigmund, 9, 24, 31, 43, 102–6, 108–
    11, 115, 119, 120, 146–47, 147–48, 152–
    53, 168 n, 181 n
Fromm, Erich, 112
Frye, Northrop, 3, 123, 183 n

Garnett, Edward, 5
Geertz, Clifford, 36–37, 71, 72–73, 167 n;
    thick description, 40–41
Ghiselin, Brewster, 102
Gombrich, E. H., 38
Grace, Sherrill E., 147
Graff, Gerald, 41
Guerard, Albert J., 70, 172 n

Harrison, John R., 136
Hawthorn, Jeremy, 103

Hay, Eloise Knapp, 56, 67, 75, 163 n, 169–70 n, 172 n, 173 n, 174 n

Heilbrun, Carolyn G., 178 n

Heilman, Robert B., 150–51

Heller, Erich, 122, 137

Henderson, Philip, 81

Henke, Suzette, 180 n

Henkin, Leo J., 46

Herr, Cheryl, 112, 180 n, 181 n, 182 n

Hillman, James, 186 n

Hochman, Baruch, 124, 127, 128

Holtby, Winifred, 166 n

Horkheimer, Max, 102, 112, 113–20, 154, 168 n

Huizinga, J., 71–74, 77, 175 n

Hunter, Allan, 46, 169 n

Iser, Wolfgang, 1, 175 n

Jameson, Fredric, 112, 122, 167 n

Joyce, James, 2, 10–12, 43, 101, 168 n; Bloom, 114–20, 182 n; Dubliners, 2, 10, 11, 42, 101, 102, 109–12, 181 n; Exiles, 103; Finnegans Wake, 103; Gerty Mac-Dowell, 105–9, 114, 120, 156; "Ireland, Island of Saints and Sages," 11–12, 107, 181 n; Little Chandler, 109–12; A Portrait of the Artist as a Young Man, 103, 104, 159; Ulysses, 2, 10, 12, 42, 101, 113, 114; "The Universal Literary Influence of the Renaissance," 115

Jung, C. G., 67–68, 166 n

Kartiganer, Donald M., 173 n

Katz, John, 3, 17, 25

Kennedy, James G., 169 n

Kernberg, Otto F., 148, 149, 150, 153, 168 n, 187 n

Kershner, R. B., 22, 109, 173 n, 181 n

Kibera, Leonard, 65

Kilgallin, Anthony R., 124, 184 n

Kimbrough, Robert, 49, 67

Knapp, James F., 167 n

Kohut, Heinz, 148–52, 153, 158, 161, 168 n, 186–87 n

Korzeniowski, Apollo, 170 n

La Capra, Dominick, 167–68 n

Lasch, Christopher, 24, 153–58, 168 n, 187 n

Lawrence, D. H., 2, 8–10, 42, 123, 133, 138, 185 n; "Education of the People," 9; "En-slaved by Civilization," 9, 10; "Europe v. America," 164 n; Fantasia of the Unconscious, 127, 133; Lady Chatterly's Lover, 8, 124, 134, 136; Movements in European History, 10, 164 n; "On Human Destiny," 134; The Plumed Serpent, 2, 42, 121, 123–25, 127–29, 133–36, 141, 184 n; The Rainbow, 8, 124; Sons and Lovers, 8; Women in Love, 8, 9, 124, 135, 136

Leavis, F. R., 4, 134, 137, 165 n

Levin, Gerald, 103

Lewis, Wyndham, 4, 124, 136, 182 n, 183 n

Lodge, David, 185 n

Lowry, Malcolm, 2, 13–14, 42, 123, 138, 140–41, 147, 153, 161, 168 n, 185 n; Geoffrey Firmin, 121, 123, 124, 130, 131, 133, 137–38, 141, 144–53, 155, 161; Ultramarine, 43, 145, 153, 155, 159–60; Under the Volcano, 2, 13, 42, 43, 121, 123–25, 130–33, 136–41, 143–47, 149–59, 161, 184 n, 186 n

McCabe, Joseph, 15, 21, 25

McCormack, W. J., 120

McDiarmid, Lucy, 3, 4

MacPherson, Hector, 19, 19–20, 30–31, 58–59, 166 n, 169 n

Mann, Thomas, 140, 185 n

Marcus, Jane, 91, 95

Marcuse, Herbert, 112

Markson, David, 124, 145, 184 n

Marvin, F. S., 20–21, 35

Mendelsohn, Sigmund, 20, 23

Mendelson, Edward, 123

Milbury-Steen, Sarah L., 52

Mill, John Stuart, 15

Moore, G. E., 27, 165–66 n, 177 n, 185 n

Narcissism, 24, 42, 43, 76, 85, 105–12, 115, 118, 119, 143–61, 168 n, 175 n, 182 n, 185–86 n, 186–87 n. See also Freud, Sigmund; Kernberg, Otto F.; Kohut, Heinz; Ovid

New, William H., 149

Nisbet, Robert, 46

Nordau, Max, 5, 23, 125

Norris, Margot, 180 n

O'Flaherty, Liam, 175 n

Ortega y Gasset, José, vii, 28

Ovid, 145–46, 161, 186 n

Parry, Benita, 65, 171 n
Patai, Daphne, 71
Pater, Walter, 27, 166 n, 177 n
Porter, Katherine Ann, 136
Pound, Ezra, 22

Reilly, Patrick, 78, 174 n
Ruthven, K. K., 8, 125

Sackville-West, Vita, 82, 177 n
Sage, Victor, 186 n
Sanders, Scott, 183 n
Satinover, Jeffrey, 138
Saveson, John E., 46
Schlack, Beverly Ann, 177 n
Schwarz, Daniel R., 175 n
Schweitzer, Albert, 20, 23, 24, 26, 30, 163 n
Scruton, Roger, 171 n
Senn, Fritz, 106
Sennett, Richard, 153, 154, 156, 158, 168 n
Shechner, Mark, 105
Sherry, Norman, 57, 172 n
Shetty, Sandya, 175 n
Sorokin, Pitirim, 182 n
Spencer, Herbert, 19–20, 21–22, 25, 41–42, 45, 46–61, 63–64, 122, 123, 169 n, 171 n. *See also* Civilization, esp. theory of, and trope of progress/retrogression
Spender, Stephen, 130, 153
Spengler, Oswald, 3, 8, 13, 19, 22, 23, 24, 25, 41, 42, 121–24, 125–33, 133–42, 187 n. *See also* Civilization, esp. theory of
Steele, Elizabeth, 177 n
Storck, John, 15
Sunic, Tomislav, 122, 187 n
Symons, Arthur, 59

Tawney, R. H., 96–97
Thornton, Lawrence, 145, 161
Tifft, Stephen, 131, 187 n
Todorov, Tzvetan, 37
Transue, Pamela, 91, 178 n
Traquair, Ramsay, 166 n
Trueblood, D. Elton, 22, 24, 30
Tylor, E. B., 165 n

Uncivilization, 21–22, 23–24, 29, 31–34, 66–67, 135, 172 n; and jungle trope, 13–14, 65, 66–73, 173 n. *See also* Civilization: paradox of

Van Loon, Hendrik, 27
Veblen, Thorstein, 94, 179 n
Vice, Sue, 187 n
Vico, Giambattista, 125

Wallace, Alfred Russel, 46
Walzl, Florence, 102
Wasserman, Jerry, 70, 173 n
Watson, G. J., 164 n
Watson, George, 122
Watt, Ian, 47, 55, 57, 163 n, 170 n
Watts, Cedric, 47, 55, 59, 64
Waugh, Evelyn, 4
Wells, H. G., 22, 26, 29–30
Werner, Helmut, 122
White, Hayden, 123
Wilde, Oscar, 185 n
Wiley, Paul L., 51
Wilkins, John H., 16, 18, 34, 166 n
Williams, Raymond, 15–16, 17, 99, 165 n, 172 n
Wiltshire, David, 51, 57
Winner, Anthony, 64, 175 n
Wolheim, Richard, 182 n
Woolf, Leonard, 25–26, 28, 30, 31, 33, 89, 182 n
Woolf, Virginia, 2, 12–13, 42, 80–99; *Jacob's Room*, 80, 82, 97; *Mrs. Dalloway*, 2, 42, 80–81, 84–89, 90, 93–98, 177 n; *Orlando*, 177 n; *A Room of One's Own*, 13, 89, 92, 178 n; *To the Lighthouse*, 2, 12, 42, 79, 80–81, 89–94, 98; *The Voyage Out*, 81

Yeats, William Butler, vii, 4, 130, 164 n, 168 n, 183 n, 185 n

Zabel, Morton Dauwen, 6
Zwerdling, Alex, 81, 86, 94, 95, 178 n

DATE DUE

DEMCO, INC. 38-2931